Brief Contents

W9-BUE-948

Real
Essays
ESSENTIALS

Real
Essays
ESSENTIALS

From Drafting to Revising

Miriam Moore
Lord Fairfax Community College

Susan Anker

bedford/st.martin's
Macmillan Learning

Boston | New York

For Bedford/St. Martin's

Vice President, Editorial, Macmillan Learning Humanities: Edwin Hill
Senior Program Director for English: Leasa Burton
Program Manager: Karita France dos Santos
Executive Marketing Manager: Joy Fisher Williams
Director of Content Development: Jane Knetzger
Senior Development Editor: Gillian Cook
Assistant Editor: Suzanne H. Chouljian
Content Project Manager: Andrea Cava
Senior Workflow Project Manager: Jennifer Wetzel
Production Supervisor: Brianna Lester
Senior Media Project Manager: Rand Thomas
Project Management: Lumina Datamatics, Inc.
Composition: Lumina Datamatics, Inc.
Permissions Editor: Angela Boehler
Permissions Assistant: Allison Ziebka
Permissions Associate: Claire Paschal
Permissions Manager: Kalina Ingham
Photo Researcher: Donna Ranieri, Lumina Datamatics, Inc.
Text Researcher: Mark Schaefer, Lumina Datamatics, Inc.
Text Design: Claire Seng-Niemoeller
Cover Design: John Callahan
Cover Image: VIDOK/Getty Images
Printing and Binding: LSC Communications

Manufactured in the United States of America.

3   2   1   0   9   8
f   e   d   c   b   a

For information, write: Bedford/St. Martin's, 75 Arlington Street, Boston, MA 02116

ISBN 978-1-319-15345-8

Acknowledgments

Text acknowledgments and copyrights appear at the back of the book on pages 289–90, which constitute an extension of the copyright page. Art acknowledgments and copyrights appear on the same page as the art selections they cover.

Contents

PART TWO
Writing Different Kinds of Essays   74

PART FOUR
Grammar, Punctuation, and Mechanics   224

15. Basic Grammar: An Overview   224

A Note to Students from Miriam Moore

A Note to Students from Susan Anker

Preface

Curriculum redesign has transformed developmental English courses in recent years. For many instructors, this has led to classes with greater diversity in student preparedness than ever before. *Writing Essentials Online: A Macmillan LaunchPad* has been developed to enable instructors to meet the diverse needs of their students by providing flexible, modular writing instruction from sentence to essay level. It is supported by a series of three brief books, each of which focuses on a particular set of writing skills that build on each other, guiding students as they grow as writers.

- *Real Skills Essentials: From Sentence to Paragraph*
- *Real Writing Essentials: From Paragraph to Essay*
- *Real Essays Essentials: From Drafting to Revising*

Real Essay Essentials: From Drafting to Revising

Real Essays Essentials (like *Real Skills Essentials* and *Real Writing Essentials*) reframes writing for students who view it as irrelevant and impossible—presenting writing instead as eminently learnable, fundamentally useful, potentially life-changing, and, therefore, worthy of students' best efforts. *Real Essays Essentials* is written in a brief format that highlights essential concepts in print while offering extensive resources for expansion, practice, and review online.

Core Features

Brief, Affordable Format.   The text offers what's essential for the essay level course—process-oriented writing instruction and focused grammar lessons—in a concise and affordable format.

Real-World Examples.   Samples of real students' writing demonstrate the concepts covered and give students confidence that good writing skills are achievable. These models address such real-world issues and concerns as parenting, peer pressure, and the importance of getting involved on campus and in the community.

Four Basics Boxes.   Presenting essay writing in manageable increments, these boxes break down the essentials of topics such as revision, good paragraphs, and argument. For traditional rhetorical modes, the Four Basics highlight essential features of all academic essays: a clear thesis, strong supporting points, substantially developed details, and a coherent organization.

Support for Reading, Critical Thinking, and Text-based Writing.   An emphasis on reading strategies and responding to texts through summary and paraphrase highlights the importance of careful reading to effective writing. Marginal questions encourage students to pause and think critically during the reading process, and questions following readings invite students to summarize, make connections, and integrate readings in their own writing.

Writing Critically

Summarize

- What is important about the text?
- What is the purpose, the big picture?
- Who is the intended audience?
- What are the main points and key support?

Analyze

- What elements have been used to convey the main point?
- Do any elements raise questions? Do any key points seem missing or undeveloped?

Synthesize

- What do other sources say about the topic of the text?
- How does your own (or others') experience affect how you see the topic?
- What new point(s) might you make by bringing together all the different sources and experiences?

Evaluate

- Based on your application of summary, analysis, and synthesis, what do you think about the material you have read?
- Is the work successful? Does it achieve its purpose?
- Does the author show any biases? Are there any hidden assumptions? If so, do they make the piece more or less effective?

Questions for Reflection and Transfer. At the end of each of the rhetorical modes chapters, students are asked to reflect on what works and what does not work in their writing process, building metacognitive habits to promote transfer from one writing situation to the next. Students are also prompted to investigate how rhetorical modes are used in their intended majors and careers.

Focus on the Four Most Serious Errors. *Real Essays Essentials* concentrates first on the four types of grammatical errors that matter most: fragments, run-ons, errors in subject-verb agreement, and errors of verb tense and form, and helps students avoid making them. Once students master these four topics and start building their editing skills, they are better prepared to tackle the grammar errors treated in later chapters.

Writing Essentials Online: A Macmillan LaunchPad

An all-in-one resource, *Writing Essentials Online* combines a proven approach to developmental writing instruction with sentence-to-essay-level support in a single, flexible digital product.

- **Comprehensive instruction** from all three *Essentials* texts (*Real Skills Essentials, Real Writing Essentials,* and *Real Essays Essentials*) provides easy-to-customize modular content that addresses sentence-to-essay-level writing skills and includes additional readings, downloadable information sheets (common transitions, word parts, editing and proofreading marks, a guide to grammar terminology, and graphic organizers), and detailed information on MLA and APA documentation styles for quick reference.
- **Diagnostics** provide opportunities to assess areas for improvement and assign additional exercises based on students' needs. Visual reports show performance by topic, class, and student as well as improvement over time.
- **LearningCurve**, adaptive quizzing for targeted learning, focuses on the areas in which each student needs the most help.
- **Integrate *Writing Essentials Online*** with your school's learning management system so that your class is always on the same page.

As with any of the *Essentials* texts, *Real Essays Essentials* can be packaged with *Writing Essentials Online* at a significant discount. For more information, contact your Macmillan Learning sales representative.

We're all in. As always.

Bedford/St. Martin's is as passionately committed to the discipline of English as ever, working hard to provide support and services that make it easier for you to teach your course your way.

Find **community support** at the Bedford/St. Martin's English Community (community.macmillan.com), where you can follow our *Bits* blog for new teaching ideas, download titles from our professional resource series, and review projects in the pipeline.

Choose **curriculum solutions** that offer flexible custom options, combining our carefully developed print and digital resources, acclaimed works from Macmillan's trade imprints, and your own course or program materials to provide the exact resources your students need.

Rely on **outstanding service** from your Bedford/St. Martin's sales representative and editorial team. Contact us or visit **macmillanlearning .com** to learn more about any of the options below.

Choose from Alternative Formats of *Real Essays Essentials*

Bedford/St. Martin's offers a range of formats. Choose what works best for you and your students:

- *Paperback.* To order the print edition, use ISBN 978-1-319-15345-8.
- *Popular e-Book formats.* For details of our e-Book partners, visit **macmillanlearning.com/ebooks**.

Instructor Resources

You have a lot to do in your course. We want to make it easy for you to find the support you need—and to get it quickly.

The *Instructor's Manual for Real Essays Essentials* is available as a PDF that can be downloaded from **macmillanlearning.com**. Visit the instructor resources tab for *Real Essays Essentials*. In addition to chapter overviews and teaching tips, the instructor's manual includes sample syllabi and detailed information on working with developmental writers integrating critical thinking into the course, facilitating cooperative learning, teaching ESL students, assessing student writing, and much more.

Acknowledgments

Real Essays Essentials grew out of a collaboration with teachers and students across the country and with the talented staff of Bedford/St. Martin's. I am grateful for the thoughtful contributions of all who shepherded this project from concept to completion, especially the support of Karita France dos Santos and the tireless effort and creativity of my editor on this project, Gillian Cook. I would like to acknowledge as well my colleagues at Lord Fairfax Community College and across the Virginia Community College System. Finally, thanks to my husband, Michael, for unwavering patience, and to Mandy, Mallory, and Murray.

Reviewers

I would like to thank the following instructors for their many good ideas and suggestions for this edition. Their insights were invaluable.

Jose Amaya, Marshalltown Community College; Nikki Aitken, Illinois Central College; Valerie Badgett, Lon Morris College; Michael Briggs, East Tennessee State University; Tara Broeckel, Oakland Community College; Andrew Cavanaugh, University of Maryland University College; Kim Davis, Oakland Community College; Dawna DeMartini, Sacramento City College; Debra Justice, Ashland Community College; Russell Keevy, Technical College of the Lowcountry; Jeff Kosse, Iowa Western Community College; Mimi Leonard, Wytheville Community College; Lynn Lewis, Oklahoma State University; Trina Litteral, Ashland Community College; Katie Lohinski, Harford Community College; Leanne Maunu, Palomar College; Shannon McCann, Suffolk Community College; Loren Mitchell, Hawaii Community College; Jim McKeown, McLennan Community College; Virginia Nugent, Miami Dade College; Lisa Oldaker Palmer, Quinsigamond Community College; Anne Marie Prendergast, Bergen Community College; Robert Rietveld, William Penn University; Patricia Roller, Pellissippi State Community College; Gina Schochenmaier, Iowa Western Community College; Marcea Seible, Hawkeye Community College; Karen Taylor, Belmont College; Heather Weiss, Technical College of the Lowcountry; Elizabeth Wurz, College of Coastal Georgia; Svetlana Zhuravlova, Lakeland Community College

Students

Many current and former students have helped shape *Real Essays Essentials*, and I am grateful for all of their contributions.

Among the students who provided paragraphs and essays for the book are Josef Ameur, John Around Him, Florence Bagley, Deshon Briggs, Jordan Brown, Daniel Flanagan, Dylan Marcos, Michael McQuiston, Luz Medina, Benjamin Mills, Donnie Ney, Jennifer Orlando, and Jeanine Pepper. Thanks to these students and the many others who submitted their work.

I would also like to thank the nine former students who provided inspirational words of advice and examples of workplace writing which are central to the book. They are Monique Rizer, Juan Gonzalez, Alex Espinoza, Patty Maloney, Rebeka Mazzone, Gary Knoblock, Garth Vaz, and Shawn Brown.

1

Critical Thinking, Reading, and Writing

Making Connections

In order to become a better writer, you need to use critical thinking and reading skills. This chapter explains critical thinking and reading strategies and explores the important connections among critical thinking, reading, and writing.

Critical Thinking

Critical thinking is a process of actively questioning what you see, hear, and read to come to thoughtful conclusions about the information presented. Critical thinking also involves making connections between existing impressions and new ones, and among various beliefs, claims, and bits of information.

We all think critically in our lives when we assess situations. For example, consider the following situation.

PRACTICE 1-1   Analyze a Situation

You walk into a party and see two men yelling and swearing at each other with a group of others crowded around them. The men are in each other's faces, and they are angry.

1. What is going on?

2. What elements of the situation do you notice to assess how bad the situation is?

3. What do you think will happen?

Critical thinking requires that you practice three important skills:

- Identifying and questioning assumptions
- Making inferences
- Recognizing bias

Identifying and Questioning Assumptions

Assumptions—ideas or opinions that we do not question and that we automatically accept as true—can get in the way of clear, critical thinking. In college, work, and everyday life, we often make judgments based on assumptions that we are not even aware of. By identifying these assumptions and questioning them, we stand a better chance of seeing things as they really are and responding to them more effectively.

When questioning assumptions, try to get a bit of distance from them. Imagine what people with entirely different points of view might say. You might even try disagreeing with your own assumptions. Take a look at the following examples.

Questioning Assumptions

SITUATION	ASSUMPTION	QUESTIONS
College: I want to transfer to a four-year school. The tuition is $24,000 a year.	There's no way I can pay that much, so I probably can't go there to get a degree.	• What resources do I have now? • Are there other resources available through financial aid? • What have others done in this situation?
Workplace: The boss moved me from second shift to first shift.	The other people who work on second shift must have complained about me.	• Have other workers been moved? • Have new employees been hired? • How long have I been working at the company? • Could the move have been a reward for good work?

SITUATION	ASSUMPTION	QUESTIONS
Everyday life: The lab report said my cholesterol was too high.	I am going to have start taking expensive prescription drugs.	• Could the report have been related to eating hamburgers and fast food for several weeks before? • Has the level been rising over time? • Do I have other risk factors for heart disease? • Could I try diet and exercise first?

You need to be aware not only of your own hidden assumptions but also of any assumptions hidden in what you read, see, and hear. However confidently a claim is made, never assume that it cannot be questioned.

Making Inferences

Sometimes, speakers and writers do not communicate their intended meaning directly. Instead, they give hints. When listeners or readers use these hints to reach a logical conclusion, they **infer**, or **make an inference**. We use inference on a daily basis, even though we don't think about it consciously. Consider this conversation:

MOTHER:	Are you wearing that to school?
KARINNE:	OK, Mom, I will change.

Karinne's mother asked a yes/no question, but Karinne inferred from the question that her mother thought her clothing was not appropriate. How did she make this inference? First, she considered what her mother stated ("Are you wearing that?") and the specific details of the situation (she was wearing a T-shirt full of holes, and her mother raised her eyebrows when she spoke). When she put the words and the details together, she concluded that her mother was not asking for a yes/no answer. When her mother answered, "Well, get a move on," Karinne's inference was confirmed.

Recognizing Biases

In addition to questioning assumptions and making inferences, it is important for you to recognize **biases**, one-sided and sometimes prejudiced views that may blind you to the truth of any situation. Here is an example:

All politicians are dishonest.

This is an extreme statement that could be contradicted with specific examples of politicians who have no history of fraud or unethical behavior.

Be on the lookout for bias in your own views and in whatever you read, see, and hear. When a statement seems one sided or extreme, ask yourself what facts or points of view might have been omitted.

Assumptions and biases are not necessarily negative. For example, we can assume the best in people and be disappointed as easily as we can assume the worst in people and be pleasantly surprised. The important point is that we are aware of our biases and bring them to light. Being a critical thinker means cultivating self-awareness as well as awareness of others' views. Above all, it means being curious and asking many questions.

Critical Reading

When you practice **critical reading**, you apply your critical thinking skills. To do this, you need to read actively, paying close attention to the text and asking yourself questions about the author's purpose, his or her main point, the support he or she gives, and how good that support is. It is important to think critically as you read, looking out for assumptions and biases (both the author's and your own) as well as information that suggests ideas or points the author is not stating explicitly. You should also consider whether you agree or disagree with the points being made.

Here are four steps of a critical reading process:

2PR   The Critical Reading Process

Preview the reading.

Read the piece actively. Identify the main idea (stated or implied), and consider the quality of the support. Then paraphrase the main idea and major supporting details.

Pause to think during reading. Identify the author's tone, and be alert for logical fallacies.

Review the reading, your marginal notes, and your questions.

CRITICAL
READING
■ **P**review
■ Read
■ Pause
■ Review

2PR   Preview the Reading

Before reading any piece of writing, skim the whole thing, using the following steps.

■   **Read the title, headnote, and introductory paragraphs** to determine the topic and main point of the reading.

- **Read headings, key words, and definitions** to help follow the author's main ideas and important concepts.

- **Look for summaries, checklists, and chapter reviews** to make sure you understand the main points.

- **Read the conclusion** to confirm the reading's main idea.

- **Ask a guiding question**—a question you think the reading might answer—to help keep you focused as you read or turn the text headings and subtitles into questions for which you can find the answers.

2PR   Read the Piece: Find and Paraphrase the Main Point and the Support

CRITICAL
READING
■ **P**review
■ **R**ead
■ Pause
■ Review

After previewing, begin reading carefully for meaning, trying especially to identify the writer's main point and the support for that point.

Read Actively

Taking notes and asking questions as you read will help you understand the author's points and develop a thoughtful response. As you read:

- Double-underline the <u>main idea</u> or write it in the margin.

- Note the <u>major support points</u> by underlining them.

- Note ideas that you agree with by placing a check mark next to them (✓).

- Note ideas that you do not agree with or that surprise you with an ! or X.

- Note ideas you do not understand with a question mark (?).

- Note any examples of an author's or expert's assumptions or biases.

- Jot any additional notes or questions in the margin.

- Consider how parts of the reading relate to the main point.

Main Point, Purpose, and Audience

The **main point** of a reading is the central idea the author wants to communicate. The main point is related to the writer's **purpose**, which can be to explain, to demonstrate, to persuade, to entertain, and/or to inform his or her intended **audience**, which can range from specific (say a particular person) to general (any reader of a periodical). Writers often introduce their main point early, so read the first few paragraphs with special care. If the writer has stated the main point in a single sentence, <u>double-underline</u> it. However, writers do not always state their main idea explicitly. In other words, there might be an **implied main idea** in the writing, in which case you will have to use details and clues from the text to infer the author's point.

Support

Support is the evidence that shows, explains, or proves the main point. The author might use statistics, facts, definitions, or scientific results for support. Or he or she might use memories, stories, comparisons, quotations from experts, and personal observations.

Not all support is good support. When you are reading, ask yourself: What information is the author including to help me understand or agree with the main point? Is the support (evidence) valid and convincing? If not, why not?

In the paragraph below, the main point has been double-underlined and the support has been underlined.

Neighbors who are too friendly can be seen just about anywhere. I mean that both ways. They exist in every neighborhood I have ever lived in and seem to appear everywhere I go. For some strange reason these people become extremely attached to my family and stop in as many as eight to ten times a day. No matter how tired I appear to be, nothing short of opening the door and suggesting they leave will make them go home at night. (I once told an unusually friendly neighbor that his house was on fire, in an attempt to make him leave, and he still took ten minutes to say goodbye.) What is truly interesting about these people is their strong desire to cook for us even though they have developed no culinary skill whatsoever. (This has always proved particularly disconcerting since they stay to watch us eat every bite as they continually ask if the food "tastes good.")

— From Jonathan R. Gould Jr., "The People Next Door"

PRACTICE 1-2 Find the Main Point and Support

Read each of the following paragraphs. Double underline the main point and underline the support.

1.   When we see people chewing gum, we might think it gives an impression of immaturity or unprofessionalism. We all remember teachers in elementary school forbidding gum-chewing, though we never knew why. But new research indicates that chewing gum can actually improve certain kinds of thinking and memory. Subjects in a study conducted by Andrew Scholey in England showed that people who chewed gum during challenging mental tasks performed significantly better than subjects who did not chew gum doing the same tasks. Scholey speculated that the chewing increased heart rate, and therefore increased oxygen flowing to the brain while lowering stress and anxiety. Still, it is not a good idea to chew gum during a job interview as the negative impression of chewing is widespread.

2.   In communities around the United States, people are "time banking," giving their individual skills in return for another's, and building a sense of community in the process. For example, one person might not have a driver's license or a car but needs transportation to a regular appointment. That same person is a good baker, and so offers to make cakes, pies, or cookies in return for transportation to her appointment. Individuals offer up their skills and get what they need in return, when they need it. Time banking in some large cities is funded by AmeriCorps because the groups are large and need a central administration. People involved in time banking are highly satisfied with the practice because it is local, it saves money, and it connects people who might not otherwise meet, strengthening community ties. It also reminds individuals that they have something to contribute as they offer up their skills to their neighbors.

Paraphrasing

Once you have identified the main idea, whether stated or implied, and the author's major support, it is a good idea to paraphrase the key points from a reading for your notes. **Paraphrasing** means restating an idea using your own words and sentence structure, and a paraphrase can help you clarify and remember the most important points of a text. Here are three tips to help you effectively paraphrase key points from your reading.

TIPS FOR EFFECTIVE PARAPHRASING

TIP 1: Do not look at the text when you are taking notes; if you do, it will be very easy to copy instead of paraphrase.

TIP 2: Think about what the writer says for each point, cover the source, and imagine you are explaining that point to one of your friends. Here is one way to begin your paraphrase: "In other words, the writer is saying that. . . ." Write your explanation without looking back at the original.

TIP 3: Avoid cut-and-paste paraphrases. A **cut-and-paste paraphrase** copies the original and then just changes one or two words. For example, here is a major supporting point from Jonathan Gould's paragraph on page 6:

ORIGINAL

> "What is truly interesting about these people is their strong desire to cook for us even though they have developed no culinary skill whatsoever."

CUT-AND-PASTE PARAPHRASE

> Gould says that it's truly interesting that these people have a strong desire to cook for us even though they have developed no cooking skill at all.

Do you see how close the sentence structure and language are to the original? As a result, the cut-and-paste paraphrase is not acceptable. Now compare this to an appropriate paraphrase:

> In his essay, "The People Next Door," Jonathan Gould describes the way good neighbors seem to enjoy preparing food for others, despite their lack of training in the kitchen.

While some of the individual words are the same in this paraphrase, the writer has not borrowed Gould's structure or longer strings of words.

CRITICAL
READING
▪ Preview
▪ Read
▪ Pause
▪ Review

2PR   Pause to Think

In the process of active reading, critical readers identify the writer's tone and they watch for logical fallacies.

Identify the Writer's Tone

Tone is the writer's attitude towards the topic, which might be angry, frustrated, joyful, serious, objective, sarcastic, or worried. In conversations, we determine tone by considering context, body language, word choice, and the features of a speaker's voice, such as raised or lowered pitch. In reading, however, we cannot "hear" a writer's tone, so we rely on context and word choice. To determine the writer's tone, ask yourself the following questions:

- What kind of writing is it? What is its purpose?
- What words has the writer chosen? Are they formal or informal? Positive or negative?

Consider the following comments concerning Congress's failure to pass an immigration-reform bill.

1. The Congress did not pass new legislation. (From a newspaper summary)
2. Heroic senators refused to be bullied into signing that un-American bill. (From a blog post shared on social media)
3. The proposal, which was fair to all parties, failed because a small group of extremist congressmen gave in to the lobbyists and special interest groups. (From an online editorial)
4. Both sides in the debate have strong convictions, but there is still a chance for a compromise. (From a press release from a nonprofit organization)

What is the writer's tone in each sentence? Which words help you understand the writer's tone?

Watch for Logical Fallacies

As you read, look for examples of faulty reasoning. Certain kinds of errors in reasoning are so common that they have their own name—**logical fallacies**. Here are some of the most common examples of faulty reasoning:

Either/Or Extremes.   Assuming that there are only two extreme choices with nothing in between.

> **EXAMPLE:**   My country, love it or leave it.
>
> [**Faulty reasoning:** Should people really either applaud everything a government does or move to a different country?]

Bad Analogy.   Comparing items or circumstances that are not enough alike to make a meaningful comparison.

> **EXAMPLE:**   A human fetus should have the same rights as a human adult.
>
> [**Faulty reasoning:** While some specific rights may be shared by a fetus and an adult, saying they should have all the same rights does not make sense because they are different in many ways. Should a fetus be able to vote, for example?]

Circular Reasoning.   Supporting a position by restating part of it.

> **EXAMPLE:**   I deserve a raise because I need to make more money.
>
> [**Faulty reasoning:** While this may be true, it will not persuade your boss. You need to offer reasons why you are worth more than you are being paid.]

"Everyone Knows."   Appealing to people's general desire to be like the majority by supporting a statement with a claim that all or most other people believe something. A common occurrence of this is when a child says to a parent, "Everybody else's parents are letting them do *X*." This kind of faulty reasoning is also called "the bandwagon effect."

> **EXAMPLE:**   Everyone knows that Apple makes the best computers.
>
> [**Faulty reasoning:** While a certain brand of computer may be popular, it is not likely that all people would agree on a single brand being the best.]

Mistaken Causes or Effects.   Assuming that one thing caused another simply because it occurred beforehand.

> **EXAMPLE:**   The opening of the new liquor superwarehouse caused old Mr. Jones to close up his shop.
>
> [**Faulty reasoning:** Mr. Jones might have closed for a variety of reasons. Your assumption is not evidence of his real reason for closing.]

Overgeneralization.   Making a broad statement that is not supported by enough evidence.

> **EXAMPLE:**   Having grown up with three brothers, I know first-hand that boys are more violent than girls.
>
> [**Faulty reasoning:** A sample of one family is not enough to assume that all boys act in a particular way.]

Oversimplification. Making something seem simple when it is not simple.

> **EXAMPLE:**   If more parking spaces were available on campus, most students would come to class.
>
> [**Faulty reasoning:** Students miss class for many reasons, so saying parking is the problem is too simple.]

2PR   Review and Respond

CRITICAL
READING
- Preview
- Read
- Pause
- Review

After reading, take a few minutes to look back and review. Go over your guiding question, your marginal notes, and your other questions—and connect with what you have read. Consider, "What interested me? What did I learn? How does it fit with what I know from other sources?" When you have reviewed your reading in this way and fixed it well in your mind and memory, it is much easier to respond in class discussion and writing. To write about a reading, you need to generate and organize your ideas, draft and revise your response, and above all, use your critical thinking skills.

A Critical Reader at Work

Read the following piece. The notes in the margin show how one student applied the process of critical reading to an assigned reading.

Deborah Tannen

It Begins at the Beginning

Deborah Tannen is a professor of linguistics at Georgetown University in Washington, D.C. Linguistics — the study of human language — reveals much about people and their culture. Part of Tannen's research in linguistics has focused on differences in how women and men use language and how those differences affect communication. The following excerpt, adapted from her book *You Just Don't Understand* (1990), describes how girls' and boys' language and communication patterns differ from an early age.

GUIDING QUESTION
How do boys and girls differ in their play and the language they use in their play?

1   Even if they grow up in the same neighborhood, on the same block, or in the same house, girls and boys grow up in different worlds of words. Others talk to them differently and expect and accept different ways of talking from them. Most important, children

Main point

She will have to prove this point.

Signals important purpose

learn how to talk, how to have conversations, not only from their parents, but from their peers. . . . Although they often play together, boys and girls spend most of their time playing in same-sex groups. And, although some of the activities they play at are similar, <u>their favorite games are different, and their ways of using language in their games are separated by a world of difference.</u>

What about computers?

2   <u>Boys tend to play outside, in large groups that are hierarchically structured. Their groups have a leader who tells others what to do and how to do it, and resists doing what other boys propose.</u> It is by giving orders and making them stick that high status is negotiated. <u>Another way boys achieve status is to take center stage</u> by telling jokes, and by sidetracking or challenging the stories and jokes of others. <u>Boys' games have winners and losers</u> and elaborate systems of rules, and the players frequently boast of their skill and argue about who is best at what.

Examples (boys' play)

! But don't boys & girls play together — at least sometimes?

3   <u>Girls, on the other hand, play in small groups or in pairs;</u> the center of a girl's social life is a best friend. . . . In their most frequent games, such as jump rope and hopscotch, everyone gets a turn. <u>Many of their activities (such as playing house) do not have winners or losers.</u> Though some girls are certainly more skilled than others, <u>girls are expected not to boast</u> about it, or show that they think they are better than the others. <u>Girls don't give orders;</u> they express their preferences as suggestions, and suggestions are likely to be accepted. Anything else is put down as bossy. <u>They don't grab center stage</u> — they don't want it — so they don't challenge each other directly. And much of the time, they simply sit together and talk. Girls are not accustomed to jockeying for status in an obvious way; they are more concerned that they be liked.

More examples (girls' play)

Does Tannen think these differences affect how adult men and women work together?

Writing Critically about Readings

WRITING CRITICALLY
■ Summarize
■ Analyze
■ Synthesize
■ Evaluate

There are different types of writing in college. In Chapters 2 through 4, we examine the writing process in general and learn how to draft and revise paragraphs and essays. In Chapters 5 through 13, we explore the different techniques for developing an essay, such as narration and illustration, and in Chapter 14, we cover the research essay.

In this section, we discuss the key college skill of writing critically about what you read. In any college course, your instructor may ask you to summarize, analyze, synthesize, or evaluate one or more readings to demonstrate your deep understanding of the material. When you do so, you answer the following questions.

Writing Critically

▪ Summarize

- What is important about the text?
- What is the purpose, the big picture?
- Who is the intended audience?
- What are the main points and key support?

▪ Analyze

- What elements have been used to convey the main point?
- Do any elements raise questions? Do any key points seem missing or undeveloped?

▪ Synthesize

- What do other sources say about the topic of the text?
- How does your own (or others') experience affect how you see the topic?
- What new point(s) might you make by bringing together all the different sources and experiences?

▪ Evaluate

- Based on your application of summary, analysis, and synthesis, what do you think about the material you have read?
- Is the work successful? Does it achieve its purpose?
- Does the author show any biases? Are there any hidden assumptions? If so, do they make the piece more or less effective?

The pages that follow will explain when and how to use summary, analysis, synthesis, and evaluation. The passage below, "Daily Hassles," from *Discovering Psychology*, fifth edition, by Don H. Hockenbury and Sandra E. Hockenbury, is used as the basis for each type of writing that follows.

[handwritten margin notes: "stress caused by a bunch of lil things" and "woman is more stressed"]

Daily Hassles
That's Not What I Ordered!

What made you feel "stressed out" in the last week? Chances are it was not a major life event. Instead, it was probably some unexpected but minor annoyance, such as splotching ketchup on your new white T-shirt, misplacing your keys, or discovering that you've been standing in the wrong line.

Stress researcher **Richard Lazarus** and his colleagues suspected that such ordinary irritations in daily life might be an important source of stress. To explore this idea, they developed a scale measuring **daily hassles**—everyday occurrences that annoy and upset people (DeLongis & others, 1982; Kanner & others, 1981). The *Daily Hassles Scale* measures the occurrence of everyday annoyances, such as losing something, getting stuck in traffic, and even being inconvenienced by lousy weather.

Are there gender differences in the frequency of daily hassles? One study measured the daily hassles experienced by married couples (Almeida & Kessler, 1998). The women experienced both more daily hassles and higher levels of psychological stress than their husbands did. For men, the most common sources of daily stress were financial and job-related problems. For women, family demands and interpersonal conflict were the most frequent causes of stress. However, when women *do* experience a stressful day in the workplace, the stress is more likely to spill over into their interactions with their husbands and other family members (Schulz & others, 2004). Men, on the other hand, are more likely to simply withdraw.

How important are daily hassles in producing stress? The frequency of daily hassles is linked to both psychological distress and physical symptoms, such as headaches and backaches (Bottos & Dewey, 2004; DeLongis & others, 1988). In fact, the number of daily hassles people experience is a better predictor of physical illness and symptoms than is the number of major life events experienced (Burks & Martin, 1985).

Why do daily hassles take such a toll? One explanation is that such minor stressors are *cumulative* (Repetti, 1993). Each hassle may be relatively unimportant in itself, but after a day filled with minor hassles, the effects add up. People feel drained, grumpy, and stressed out. Daily hassles also contribute to the stress produced by major life events. Any major life change, whether positive or negative, can create a ripple effect, generating a host of new daily hassles (Maybery & others, 2007; Pillow & others, 1996).

WRITING CRITICALLY
- **Summarize**
- Analyze
- Synthesize
- Evaluate

Summary

A **summary** is a condensed, or shortened, version of something—often, a longer piece of writing, a movie or television show, a situation, or an event. In writing a summary, you give the main points and key support in your own words.

A formal summary has a topic sentence that states the title of the selection, the author, and the main idea. It includes the major supporting details, but not the minor details, and it refers to the author (or authors) by full name or last name only. The summary relies on strong descriptive verbs, and it concludes with the author's final observations or recommendations. It should be written in your own words, relying on paraphrase for key points, and present information without opinion or comments.

Here is a summary of the textbook excerpt "Daily Hassles." The main point is double-underlined, and the support points are underlined.

> Hockenbury and Hockenbury tell us that <u>daily hassles often</u>
> <u>cause more stress than major problems do</u>. According to studies,
> <u>men and women report different kinds of daily stress and react to</u>
> <u>stress differently</u>, though both experience psychological and phys-
> <u>ical symptoms</u>. Some research shows that <u>daily hassles produce</u>
> <u>stress because their effects are cumulative</u>—that is, they add up
> over time to create major stress.

A summary is a useful way to record information from a reading in
a course notebook. You can put the main points of an article into your
own words for later review. You may also be asked to provide summaries in homework assignments or on tests in order to show that you read
and understood a reading. In addition, summary is an important tool for
keeping track of information for a research project.

Analysis

An **analysis** breaks down the points or parts of something and considers
how they work together to make an impression or convey a main point.
When writing an analysis, you might also consider points or parts that
seem to be missing or that raise questions in your mind. Your analysis of
a reading provides the main points as well as your own reaction to the
piece.

WRITING
CRITICALLY
■ **Summarize**
■ **Analyze**
■ Synthesize
■ Evaluate

Here is an analysis of "Daily Hassles." The main point is double-
underlined, and the support points are underlined.

> We have all read about stress, but Hockenbury and Hock-
> enbury have something new and interesting to say about it: <u>it is</u>
> <u>not the big life crises but the million petty hassles we face every</u>
> <u>day that get to us</u>. They mention a number of different studies on
> hassles and their effects on us. <u>Two of these studies explore gender</u>
> <u>differences, and they conclude that men and women report differ-</u>
> <u>ent kinds of daily hassles and respond to them differently</u>.
>
> These studies seem to involve only married men and women,
> however, which raises areas for further exploration. Do *all* men and
> ⟶

women really experience and respond to hassles differently? For example, would unmarried male and female students be affected in the same ways that married men and women are? In a future paper, I would like to examine the kinds of daily hassles my college friends—both male and female—react to and what symptoms those hassles produce. The subject of hassles and how we react to them seems particularly relevant to students, whose lives are full of stress.

In any college course, your instructor may ask you to write an analysis to show your critical thinking skills and your ability to respond to a reading.

WRITING
CRITICALLY
■ Summarize
■ Analyze
■ Synthesize
■ Evaluate

Synthesis

A **synthesis** pulls together information from additional sources or experiences to make a new point. Here is a synthesis of "Daily Hassles." Because the writer wanted to address some of the questions she raised in her analysis, she incorporated additional details from published sources and from people she interviewed. The various sources the writer pulls together are underlined. Her synthesis of this information helped her arrive at a fresh conclusion.

Stress Reactions: Are Men and Women So Different?

In *Discovering Psychology*, Hockenbury and Hockenbury present evidence that males and females react to different sources of stress and respond differently to them. The studies they use as evidence discuss only married couples, however, and they provide few details about the actual kinds and symptoms of stress. Several other studies, as well as original research done among unmarried college students, provide some additional insights into these questions.

The Mayo Clinic's website, produced by the staff at the Mayo Clinic, suggests that there are two main types of stress: acute stress, which is a response to specific and isolated situations (such as a car accident, a performance, or an exam) and chronic stress, which is longer term and cumulative. Acute, short-term stress can be good for people, prompting them to act. Chronic stress, however, tends to have negative effects, both physical and psychological. Daily hassles

→

can produce either or both types of stress. Physical symptoms include headaches, back pain, stomach upset, and sleep problems. Psychological symptoms include anxiety, anger, depression, and burnout. The site offers numerous articles on stress and stress management, including a stress assessment test.

The website *Healthfinder.gov* lists some of the major causes of stress, among them a heavy workload, chronic illness, daily hassles like traffic, and financial worries. It includes many of the same symptoms of stress that the Mayo Clinic site does, such as headache, digestion problems, trouble with concentration or focus, and irritability (United States Department of Health and Human Services). Neither the *Healthfinder.gov* nor the May Clinic site distinguishes between male and female stress sources or symptoms.

To these sources, I added interviews with eight friends—four men and four women—who all reported these top five daily hassles: worries about money, transportation problems, waiting in lines, unfair bosses, and automated phone systems that take forever and never get you an answer.

The only significant difference in the kind of hassles reported by the men and women I talked to was that several women (but not men) mentioned worries about physical safety (for example, while traveling home from school at night). When I asked my friends to report how they dealt with their stress, they seemed to confirm the Hockenbury's claim that women's stress spills over into the family and men tend to withdraw. Two men reported no psychological symptoms of stress, whereas the remaining six people (four women and two men) emphasized both psychological and physical symptoms.

These sources suggest that there might be some gender differences in the hassles that people experience and the symptoms that result from these hassles, but they might not be as major as the Hockenbury's passage led me to expect. Most of the stresses mentioned seem to be caused by having to do too much in too little time. Perhaps this is a comment on the quality of modern life, which affects both men and women equally.

Works Cited

Hockenbury, Don H., and Sandra E. Hockenbury. *Discovering Psychology*. 5th ed., Worth, 2010, p. 543.

Mayo Clinic Staff. "Stress Management: Know Your Triggers." *Mayo Clinic*, 28 Apr. 2016, www.mayoclinic.org/healthy-lifestyle/stress-management/in-depth/stress-management/art-20044151. Accessed 7 Nov. 2017.

United States, Department of Health and Human Services, Office of Disease Prevention and Health Promotion. "Manage Stress." Healthfinder.gov. 20 May 2017, https://healthfinder.gov/HealthTopics/Category/health-conditions-and-diseases/heart-health/manage-stress.

Synthesizing is important for longer writing assignments and research papers, in which you need to make connections among different works. Many courses that involve writing, such as history and psychology, require papers that synthesize information from more than one source.

WRITING
CRITICALLY

■ Summarize
■ Analyze
■ Synthesize
■ Evaluate

Evaluation

An **evaluation** is your *thoughtful* judgment about something based on what you have discovered through your summary, analysis, and synthesis. To evaluate something effectively, apply the questions from the Writing Critically box on page 13.

Here is an evaluation of "Daily Hassles."

Hockenbury and Hockenbury present important information and raise some interesting questions about how daily hassles affect our lives. In a few paragraphs, they present a great deal of information on the subject of daily hassles—what they are, who developed the scale of daily hassles, how men and women differ in their reactions to daily hassles, and how the stress of daily hassles negatively affects people. They provide numerous credible references to support their points. Other sources—such as the Mayo Clinic's website, the website *Diabetes at Work*, and a gender-based poll I conducted—provide more details about some aspects of daily hassles and raise questions about the extent to which women and men are differently affected by them. However, the Hockenburys present a good overview of the subject in a short piece of writing. I think the authors do a great job of pulling together good information for students.

When you do college-level work, you must be able to evaluate the readings and other sources you encounter. Instructors may ask you to write evaluations in order to demonstrate your ability to question and judge sources.

WRITING
CRITICALLY
■ Summarize
■ Analyze
■ Synthesize
■ Evaluate

PRACTICE 1-3 Make Connections

As you work through this exercise, refer to the Writing Critically box
on page 13.

1. **Summary:** Summarize Deborah Tannen's essay on pages 11–12.

2. **Analysis:** Write a paragraph analyzing the points Tannen presents.

3. **Synthesis:** Read additional opinion pieces or blog postings on the
    social differences between boys and girls. In one paragraph, state
    your position on the subject according to your reading of these ma-
    terials. Also, explain the range of opinions on the subject.

4. **Evaluation:** Write a paragraph that evaluates Tannen's essay.

Any time you write in response to assignments, you may want to
review the "Writing about Readings" checklist that follows.

CHECKLIST: Writing about Readings

FOCUS

☐ Carefully read the writing assignment.

ASK

☐ Does the assignment include any words that indicate the type
   of writing required (*summarize, analyze, describe, give examples
   of, compare*, and so on)?

☐ Is the writing supposed to be in response to the reading alone,
   or are you expected to bring in other sources and points of
   view?

☐ Are you supposed to quote from the reading to support your
   point?

☐ Does the assignment ask you to evaluate the reading?

WRITE

☐ Apply your critical reading skills to the material, and write a
   response to the reading that fulfills the requirements of the
   writing assignment.

2

Getting Ready to Write

Audience, Purpose, Form, and Process

Four elements are key to good writing. Keep them in mind throughout the writing process.

Four Basics of Good Writing

1 It reflects the writer's purpose and the needs, knowledge, and expectations of its intended audience.

2 It results from a thoughtful process.

3 It includes a clear, definite point.

4 It provides support that explains or proves the main point.

This chapter describes the first two basics in detail, while Chapters 3 and 4 address the final two basics. You will also learn how to begin the writing process by finding, narrowing, and exploring potential topics for writing.

Audience and Purpose

Your **audience** is the person or people who will read what you write. Whenever you write, always have at least one real person in mind as a reader. Think about what that person already knows and what he or she will need to know to understand your main idea. In most cases, assume that readers will know only what you write about your topic and main point.

When you write in formal contexts, especially in college, thinking about your audience will not necessarily come to you automatically: you will need to consider it explicitly. As you think about your audience, consider what the person knows about you and your topic and what type of writing the person expects. Think about the person's point of view.

The **purpose** of a piece of writing is the reason for writing it. Understanding your purpose for writing is key to writing successfully, particularly as writing tasks become more complex. In college, your purpose for writing often will be to show something; to summarize, analyze, synthesize, or evaluate something; or to make a convincing argument. Typically, your instructor will want you to demonstrate that you understand the content of the course. To understand the purpose of a particular assignment, be sure to read assignments and exam questions critically, highlighting words that tell you what your instructor wants to see in your writing.

Understanding your audience and your purpose helps you to select the most appropriate form and tone for your writing. Forms used by college writers include essays, lab reports, texts, emails, and résumés. Tone is the "voice" of your writing, formed by the words you use and the ways you use them, either formally or informally.

Audience, Purpose, Form, and Tone

AUDIENCE	PURPOSE	FORM/TONE
Classmates	Discuss opinions and questions about the assigned readings	Discussion board post and response (formal)
Friend	Complain about the length of the assigned reading	Text (informal)
Instructor	Request additional information about the assigned reading	Email (formal)
Instructor	Demonstrate understanding and application of three course readings	Essay (formal)

Paragraph and Essay Forms

In college, professors often assign paragraphs and essays as homework assignments, course projects, or exams. Each of them has a basic structure.

Paragraph Structure

A **paragraph** is a group of sentences that work together to make a point. A good paragraph has three necessary parts—the topic sentence, the body, and the concluding sentence. Each part serves a specific purpose.

PARAGRAPH PART	PURPOSE OF THE PARAGRAPH PART
1. The **topic sentence**	states the **main point**. The topic sentence is often either the first or last sentence of a paragraph.
2. The **body**	supports (shows, explains, or proves) the main point. It usually contains three to six **support sentences**, which present facts and details that develop the main point.
3. The **concluding sentence**	reminds readers of the main point and often makes an observation.

Essay Structure

Essays are used for more in-depth exploration of topics and include multiple paragraphs. A short essay may consist of four or five paragraphs, while a longer essay can be six paragraphs or more, depending on what it needs to accomplish—persuading someone to do something, using research to make a point, explaining a complex concept, or explaining an idea or experience.

An essay has three necessary parts—an introduction, a body, and a conclusion.

ESSAY PART	PURPOSE OF THE ESSAY PART
1. The **introduction**	states the **main point**, or **thesis**, generally in a single strong statement. The introduction may be a single paragraph or multiple paragraphs.
2. The **body**	supports (shows, explains, or proves) the main point. The body of an essay generally has at least three **support paragraphs**. Each support paragraph begins with a **topic sentence** that supports the thesis statement and continues with facts and details that develop the main point.
3. The **conclusion**	reminds readers of the main point. It may summarize and reinforce the support in the body paragraphs, or it may make an observation based on that support. Whether it is a single paragraph or more, the conclusion should relate back to the main point of the essay.

The parts of an essay correspond to the parts of a paragraph. The *thesis* of an essay is like the *topic sentence* of a paragraph. The *support paragraphs* in the body of an essay are like the *support sentences* of a paragraph. And the *conclusion* of an essay is like the *concluding sentence* of a paragraph. The diagram on pages 24–25 shows how paragraphs and essays are related.

The Writing Process

The **writing process** consists of four basic stages—generating ideas, planning and drafting, revising, and editing. Good writers do not just move through these steps in order; they move back and forth between them as they discover new facts, revise their ideas, and improve their plans. The flowchart that follows shows the steps within each stage.

THE WRITING PROCESS

Generate Ideas

CONSIDER: What is my purpose in writing? Given this purpose, what interests me? What connections can I make among ideas? Who will read what I am writing? What do they need to know?

- Determine your audience and purpose (p. 20).
- Find and explore your topic (p. 26).
- Make your point (p. 34).
- Support your point (p. 42).

Plan and Draft

CONSIDER: How can I organize and present my ideas effectively for my readers?

- Arrange your ideas, and make an outline (p. 48).
- Write a draft, including an introduction that will interest your readers, a strong conclusion, and a title (p. 53).

Revise

CONSIDER: How can I make my draft clearer or more convincing to my audience?

- Look for ideas that do not fit (p. 62).
- Look for ideas that could use more detailed support (p. 64).
- Connect ideas with transitional words and sentences (p. 66).

Edit

CONSIDER: What errors could confuse my readers and weaken my point?

- Find and correct the most serious errors in grammar (Chapter 16).
- Look for other errors in grammar and style (Chapter 17).
- Check your punctuation and capitalization (Chapter 18).

PARAGRAPH VS. ESSAY FORM

Paragraph Form

A Some ways to do good for our world do not require much time, effort, or money. My favorite way is to use click-and-give websites, where just going to the site triggers donations to it from another source (not you). Every night before I go to bed, I go to one or more of these sites. **B** The first site that I click on every night is the *Animal Rescue Site* (**www.theanimalrescuesite.com**). Each click gives food to rescued animals. **C** Another of my favorite websites is *Free Rice* (**www.freerice.com**) where I play vocabulary or grammar games. With each correct answer, grains of rice are donated to hungry people. **D** One site with lots of choices of click-and-give options is the *NonProfits* (**www.thenonprofits.com**). It lists hundreds of causes and sites, grouped under "Hunger and Poverty," "Health, Education, Misc.," and "Environment and Animals." Because I work, have a family, and take two classes, I do not have much extra time or money. **E** Going to these websites allows me to feel as if I am contributing and making a small difference, and that feels good.

Main Point: In this case, the topic sentence of the paragraph is the same as the thesis statement of the essay: that doing good can be easy.

Support for the Main Point

Details Explaining the Support: Usually, one to three sentences for each support point in paragraphs, and three to eight sentences for each point in essays.

A Topic sentence
B Support 1
C Support 2
D Support 3
E Concluding sentence

Conclusion

Essay Form

1

Some ways to do good for our world do not require much time, effort, or money. My favorite way is to use click-and-give websites, where just going to the site triggers donations to it from another source (not you). Anyone can help out in any cause they are interested in by just one quick click. Every night before I go to bed, I go to one or more of the sites. I have particular favorites, but there are hundreds to choose from.

A Thesis statement

The first site that I click on every day is the *Animal Rescue Site* (**www.theanimalrescuesite.com**). Each click gives food to rescued animals. The websites provides information about the sponsors of the site and where the donations go. It also has information about the site's projects and the animals who are rescued, a photo contest, and fun online games that you can play to trigger more donations. My favorite is Bubble Burst. People can become involved in "challenges." Most nights I have time only to click to give, which is why I go to this site every single night.

B Topic sentence 1

2

Another of my favorite websites is Free Rice (www.freerice.com) where I play vocabulary or grammar games. With each correct answer, grains of rice are donated to hungry people. The games are offered at increasingly difficult levels, and for each correct answer, you are told how many grains of rice you have given. A wooden bowl fills up with the grains as you play. When I go to this website, I feel as if I am doing good, having fun, and learning useful words.

C Topic sentence 2

One site with lots of click-and-give options is the NonProfits (www.thenonprofits.com). It lists hundreds of causes and sites, grouped under "Hunger and Poverty," "Health, Education, Misc.," and "Environment and Animals." Under "Hunger and Poverty," I go to the site named "One Click One Meal." This site says that one person dies every three seconds of starvation. A quick click will fund "One More Meal," with a donation to the World Food Programme. You can click on "WorldFoodProgramme" and read about the program, about

D Topic sentence 3

3

nutrition, and about other related information. Twenty other sites help stop hunger and poverty, and many others are available in categories such as health, education, environment, and animals. Exploring the many choices, I find that each one I click on gives me so much information as well as the opportunity to help others.

Because I work, have a family, and take two classes, I do not have much extra time or money. Still, I know there are many problems in the world, and I would like to help in some way. Going to these websites allows me to feel as if I am contributing and making a small difference, and that feels good. So try it: click and give.

E Concluding paragraph

A Thesis statement
B Topic sentence 1
C Topic sentence 2
D Topic sentence 3
E Concluding paragraph

Finding, Narrowing, and Exploring Your Topic

A **topic** is what, who, or where you are writing about. A good topic for an essay is one that interests you and that fulfills the terms of your assignment. Begin to select a topic by analyzing your assignment:

- How long should the assignment be?
- How formal is the assignment?
- How much of my grade is this assignment worth?
- What freedom do I have in choosing a topic? Is there a particular topic that I am required to write on, or am I free to choose my own topic? Is there a list of banned topics?
- Does the assignment specify a particular type of paper such as a narrative, argument, or cause and effect?

Any topic that you choose to write about should pass the following test.

QUESTIONS FOR FINDING A GOOD TOPIC

- Does this topic interest me?
- Can I find out more about it?
- Can I get involved with this topic? Is it relevant to my life in some way?
- Does it fit the assignment, focusing on a subject neither too broad nor too narrow to treat in the assigned length?

Choose one of the following broad topics or one of your own, and focus on one specific aspect of it that you think would make a good topic for a short essay.

My goals	Something I am proud of
Urban (or rural life)	College athletics
Alternatives to television	Young adult novels and
Relationships	movies
Addiction (of any type)	Viral videos

Use the general topic you have chosen to complete the practice activities on pages 28 and 32.

Narrowing a Topic

To **narrow** a topic is to focus on the smaller parts of a general topic until you find a more limited topic or angle that is interesting and specific. In real life, you narrow topics all the time: you talk with friends about a particular song rather than music, about a particular person rather than the human race, or about a class you are taking rather than every class the college offers.

In college writing, you often need to do the same thing. A professor may give you a broad topic such as "religion and culture," "cheating in our society," or "goals in life." These topics are too general to write about in a short essay, so you need to know how to narrow them. To narrow your topic, you can ask questions, use clustering to map your ideas, or make a list of specific examples.

Ask Yourself Questions

For the broad essay topic "religion and culture," one student asked the questions below to make it manageable.

GENERAL TOPIC	Religion and Culture
QUESTIONS	What religion — mine?
	Whose culture — mine? This country's? Another country's? Now or in the past?
	What kind of culture — like art? Politics?
	Serious religion? Or things like Christmas music? Maybe both?

Map Your Ideas (Cluster)

Use circles and lines to help visually break a general topic into more specific ones. Start in the center of a blank piece of paper, and write your topic. Circle your topic, and ask yourself some questions about it, such as "What do I know about it?" or "What's important about it?" Write your ideas around the topic, drawing lines from your topic to the ideas and then circling them. Keep adding ideas, connecting them with the lines and circles. This technique is called **mapping** or **clustering**. After mapping, look at each cluster of ideas, and consider using one of the narrower topics.

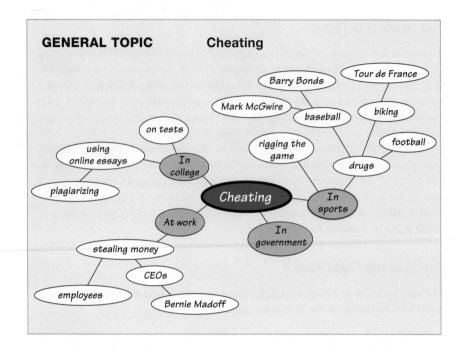

GENERAL TOPIC   Cheating

List Narrower Topics

Finally, you can take a broad topic and list as many examples related to it as you can. Don't just restate the topic (personal goals → something I want to accomplish); instead, think of specific examples that illustrate the general topic.

GENERAL TOPIC	Narrower Ideas
PERSONAL GOALS	Stop smoking
	Get a job with a higher salary
	Get a college degree
	Save money to purchase a house

PRACTICE 2–1   Narrowing a Topic

Use one of the three methods on pages 27–28 to narrow your topic. Then, write your narrowed topic below.

NARROWED TOPIC: _____

Exploring Your Topic

Once you have selected a narrow topic, *explore* it to get ideas you can use in your writing. **Invention strategies** (also called **prewriting techniques**) are ways to come up with ideas at any point during the writing process—to find a topic, to get ideas for what you want to say about the topic, and to support your ideas.

QUESTIONS FOR EXPLORING A TOPIC

- What interests me about this topic?
- Why is this topic important?
- What do I know about it, and what do I want to know?
- What do I want to say?

You can explore your narrowed topic using one or more of several invention strategies, three of which (questioning, clustering, and listing) you have already used on pages 27–28 to help you narrow your topic.

- Freewriting
- Listing and brainstorming
- Asking reporter's questions
- Discussing
- Mapping (clustering)
- Keeping a journal
- Conducting research

While exploring ideas, just think; do not judge. You can decide later whether your ideas are good or not. At this point, your goal is to get as many ideas as possible. Write down all the possibilities.

The following sections detail techniques for exploring ideas and show how one student used each one of them to get ideas about the topic "Getting a college degree."

Freewrite

Freewriting is like having a conversation with yourself on paper. To **freewrite**, just start writing everything you can think of about your topic. Write nonstop for at least 5 minutes. Do not go back and cross anything out or worry about using correct grammar or spelling; just write.

> I don't know, I don't think about goals more than just handling every day — I don't have time. The kids, my job, laundry, food, school, it's a lot. So I just get by day by day but I know that won't get me or my kids anywhere. I really do wish I could get a better job that was more interesting and I wish I could make more money and get my kids better stuff and live in a better place and not be worried all the time about money and our apartment and all that. I really do need to get that degree cause I know we'd have a better chance then. I know I need to finish college.

List and Brainstorm

List all the ideas about your topic that come to your mind. Write as fast as you can for 5 minutes without stopping.

> So hard to find time to study
>
> Good in the long run
>
> Lots of advantages
>
> Better job
>
> Better place to live
>
> More money
>
> More opportunities
>
> A big achievement — no one in my family's ever gotten a degree
>
> But they don't give me support either

Ask a Reporter's Questions

Ask yourself questions to start getting ideas. The following reporter's questions — *Who? What? Where? When? Why?* and *How?* — give you different angles on a narrowed topic, but you can also use other kinds of questions that come to you as you explore your narrowed topic.

> <u>Who?</u> Me, a single mother and student
>
> <u>What?</u> Getting a college degree
>
> <u>Where?</u> Stetson Community College
>
> <u>When?</u> Taking classes off and on now, want a degree in next couple of years
>
> <u>Why?</u> Because I want more out of life for my kids and me
>
> <u>How?</u> Working like a dog to finish school

Discuss

When you discuss ideas with someone else, you get more ideas and also feedback on them from the other person.

Team up with another person. If you both have writing assignments, first discuss one person's topic and then the other's. Ask questions about anything that seems unclear, and let the writer know what sounds interesting. Give thoughtful answers, and keep an open mind. It is a good idea to take notes when your partner comments on your ideas.

Cluster and Map

You saw an example of clustering, also called mapping, on page 28. Here is another one.

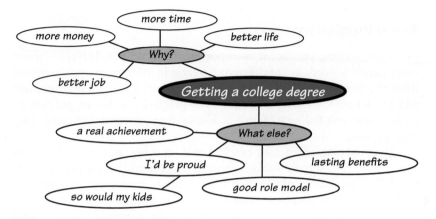

Keep a Journal

Another good way to explore ideas and topics for writing is to keep a journal. Set aside a few minutes a day to write in your journal. Your journal will be a great source of ideas when you need to find something to write about.

You can use a journal in many ways:

- To record and explore your personal thoughts and feelings
- To comment on things that happen either in the neighborhood, at work, at your college, in the news, and so on
- To examine situations you do not understand (as you write, you may figure them out)

> I've been taking courses at the college for a couple of years but not really knowing whether I'd ever finish or not. It's so hard, and I'm so tired all the time that I sometimes think it would be easier (and cheaper!) to stop or to go one semester and not another, but then it's so easy to get out of the habit. I need to decide whether getting a degree is worth all of the effort it will take, and I'm starting to think it is. I don't want to live like this forever. I want a better life.

Conduct Research

For some assignments, you will need to do research on your topic, either online or in a library. (For more on research, see Chapter 14.) If you do use research to find out some basic information about your topic, take notes and use the information you find very carefully. You must be able to document where you found the information and avoid plagiarism.

Avoid Plagiarism

In all the writing you do, it is important to avoid **plagiarism**—using other people's words as your own or handing in information you gathered from another source as your own. Your instructors are aware of plagiarism and know how to look for it. Writers who plagiarize, either on purpose or by accident, risk failing a course or losing their jobs and damaging their reputations.

To avoid plagiarism, take careful notes on every source (books, interviews, television shows, websites, and so on) you might use in your writing. When recording information from sources, take notes in your own words, unless you plan to use direct quotations. In that case, make sure to record the quotation word for word and include quotation marks around it, both in your notes and in your paper. When you use material from other sources—whether you directly quote or put information in your own words (paraphrase)—you must name and give citation information about these sources.

· ·

PRACTICE 2–2   Using Invention Strategies

Choose *two* prewriting techniques, and use them to explore your narrowed topic. Keep your readers in mind as you explore your topic. Find ideas that will be effective for both your purpose and your readers' understanding.

· ·

Writing Assignment

Review your narrowed topic (Practice 2–1) and your ideas about it (Practice 2–2). Use the checklist that follows to evaluate your topic and to understand the process of narrowing and exploring a general topic. If necessary, spend some more time clarifying your topic or generating ideas before moving on to Chapter 3.

CHECKLIST: Evaluating Your Topic

FOCUS

☐ Read the assignment carefully and consider your audience and purpose.

☐ Review the "Questions for Finding a Good Topic" on page 26.

ASK

☐ Is the topic too big for a short essay, if that is the assignment?

☐ If it is too big, what are some more limited parts of the topic?

☐ Once you have a narrowed topic, ask the "Questions for Exploring a Topic" on page 29.

☐ Do I or my audience have any assumptions or biases relating to my topic that I should be aware of? If so, what are they? (See Chapter 1, pp. 2 and 3.)

☐ What can I say about my topic? What ideas do I have about my topic?

☐ Use a prewriting technique to explore ideas about your narrowed topic.

3

Organizing Your Main
Point and Support

Giving Ideas Structure

Make a Point: Thesis Statements

The **thesis statement** of an essay states the main point you want to get across about your topic. It is your position on whatever you are writing about.

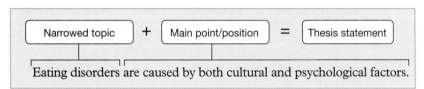

| Narrowed topic | **+** | Main point/position | **=** | Thesis statement |

Eating disorders are caused by both cultural and psychological factors.

A strong thesis statement has several basic features.

BASICS OF A GOOD THESIS STATEMENT

- It focuses on a single main point or position about the topic.
- It fits the size of the assignment.
- It is specific.
- It is something that you can show, explain, or prove.
- It is a direct statement.

| **WEAK THESIS STATEMENT** | I think college is good, and there are lots of them. |

The weak statement does not follow the basics of a good thesis statement: it focuses on two points, not one; it is very broad; the word *good* is not specific; and the words *I think* are not forceful or confident.

| **GOOD THESIS STATEMENT** | A college degree brings many potential benefits such as better jobs, more career choices, and higher salaries. |

This statement has all the basics of a good thesis statement.

A good thesis statement is essential to most good essays. Early in your writing process, you may develop a *draft thesis* (or *working thesis*), a first-try version of the sentence that will state your main point. You can revise it into a final thesis statement later in the writing process.

Focus on a Single Main Point

Your thesis should focus on one main point. If you try to address more than one main point in an essay, you will not be able to give adequate support for all the points. Also, you risk splitting your focus.

THESIS STATEMENT WITH TWO MAIN POINTS

In the next decade, <u>many high schools will have a drastic shortage of teachers,</u> and <u>high school teachers should have to take competency tests.</u>

In this example, the two points are underlined. The writer would need to explain why there will be a shortage of teachers and also why teachers should take competency tests. These are both meaty points, and any writer would have trouble supporting them equally in a single essay. Look at the revised version, below, which separates these ideas into two different thesis statements.

REVISED

In the next decade, many schools will have a drastic shortage of high school teachers.

or

High school teachers should have to take competency tests.

Although a good thesis statement focuses on a single main point, it may include more than one idea if these ideas directly relate to the main point. If you know the points or examples that you will make to support your thesis, you may preview these in the thesis statement. In the example below, the thesis statement includes some points (shown in *italics*) that support the writer's main point.

The job market for students is tight, but there are things you can do to help get a job in your field, such as *asking for an informational interview, finding a mentor, or getting an internship.*

Consider the Size of the Assignment

A thesis that is too broad is impossible to support fully in a short essay: there is just too much to cover well. A thesis that is too narrow does not give you enough to write a whole essay on.

TOO BROAD	The Industrial Revolution was important in this country.
	[The Industrial Revolution is too broad to cover in an essay.]
REVISED	During the Industrial Revolution, women workers in the textile industry played an important role in Lowell, Massachusetts.

A thesis that is too narrow leaves the writer with little to show, explain, or prove. It can also make the reader think, "So what?"

TOO NARROW	I tweeted this morning.
REVISED	Tweeting connects me to other people and their ideas.

Be Specific

A good thesis statement gives readers specific information so that they know exactly what the writer's main point is.

GENERAL	Writing is important for my job.
	[Why is writing important for your job, and what kind of job do you have?]
SPECIFIC	Although my primary job as a nurse is to care for others, I have found that my ability to write clearly is essential.
	[This thesis tells us that the job is nursing and suggests that the essay will discuss the types of writing a nurse does.]

One good way to be specific is to let your readers know what you will be discussing in your essay. In this way, your thesis prepares your reader for what is to come.

MORE SPECIFIC	As a nurse, my ability to write clearly is essential in documents such as patient reports, status notes to nurses on other shifts, and emails to other hospital staff.
	[This thesis tells the reader specific kinds of writing the essay will discuss.]

Write a Thesis That You Can Show, Explain, or Prove

If a thesis is so obvious that it does not need support or if it states a known fact, you will not be able to say much about it.

OBVIOUS	Most teenagers drive.
REVISED	The high accident rates among new teen drivers could be reduced with better and more extended driver training.
FACT	A growing number of American children are overweight.
REVISED	We must, as a nation, act to reduce obesity in our children.

Express Your Point Directly

State your thesis directly and clearly. In many academic disciplines, writers avoid thesis statements that begin, "In this essay I will show...." Rather than saying you will make the point, you should just make it. Also, academic writers usually avoid phrases such as "I believe" or "in my opinion."

WEAK	In this essay, I will prove my opinion that high school dropouts have a difficult time in life.
DIRECT	High school dropouts can expect to face surprising hardships in life.

The practices that follow will help you write a good thesis statement. The first practice helps you develop a thesis statement from a narrowed topic. The rest focus on the basics of a good thesis statement (p. 34).

PRACTICE 3–1   Developing a Thesis Statement from a Narrowed Topic

For each general topic, write a thesis statement from the narrowed topic.

EXAMPLE

GENERAL TOPIC: Foreign languages

NARROWED TOPIC: Learning a foreign language

THESIS: Learning a foreign language has many benefits.

GENERAL TOPIC	NARROWED TOPIC
Online writing	Instagram posts
Transportation	Ride-sharing apps
Childcare	Vetting an in-home daycare
Owning a car	Costs of owning a car
Television alternatives	Streaming on Netflix
Voting	Why your friends do (or don't) vote

PRACTICE 3–2   Writing Thesis Statements That Focus on a Single Main Point

Rewrite the following thesis statements so that they focus on just one of the points made. You can add information to make the statements more specific.

> **EXAMPLE:** Juggling college and other responsibilities can be challenging, and rising college costs are putting higher education out of reach for many.
>
> **FOCUSED THESIS:** Juggling college and other responsibilities can be challenging.

1. Planning for college financial aid should begin long before a student's first year of college, and prospective students should also consider how attending college will affect their family life.

2. My first job taught me the importance of cooperation, and I also learned how to manage my time effectively.

3. For several reasons, I will never own my own business, but I do have what it takes to be a top athlete.

. . . .

PRACTICE 3–3   Writing Thesis Statements That Fit the Size of the Assignment

Read the following thesis statements, and decide whether they are too broad, too narrow, or the right size for a short essay. Rewrite statements that are too broad or too narrow to better fit the size of the assignment. For statements that are the right size, write "OK."

> **EXAMPLE:** My dog will be ten years old next month. *Too narrow.*
>
> **BROADER:** *Dogs make excellent pets because they are social, loyal, and affectionate.*

1. Hinduism is a fascinating religion.

2. I love food.

3. Being a vegetarian offers a wide range of healthy food choices.

4. There are many vegetarians in this country.

5. Another gourmet coffee shop opened last week, the third one on a single block.

. . . .

. . . .

PRACTICE 3–4   Writing Thesis Statements That Are Specific

Rewrite each of the following thesis statements by adding at least two specific details.

> **EXAMPLE:** Electronic devices in high schools can be a huge problem.
>
> **SPECIFIC THESIS:** *Cell phones that ring during a high school class disrupt students' concentration and learning.*

1. I have many useful skills.

2. Studying with a partner can be helpful.

3. I have always had trouble writing.

4. Children have more allergies now than in the past.

5. After I received my first paycheck, I had many feelings.

. . . .

· ·

PRACTICE 3-12   Adding Supporting Details

For your three primary support points from Practice 3–11 (p. 44), imagine your readers asking, "What do you mean?" Add specific details to answer that question. If you have used research to find supporting details, add annotations to your outline to indicate the source of the information.

· ·

Review Support

When you have developed support for your main point, along with supporting details, use your critical thinking and reading skills to evaluate it. Does the support make assumptions? Does it reveal a bias in your point of view? Go back to Chapter 1 and remind yourself of the common logical fallacies described on pages 9–11. It is important to review your support in this way because errors in reasoning make it difficult to make your main point effectively. If you detect a bias, assumption, or logical fallacy in the support you have chosen, revise your support or add additional support to give readers a more balanced perspective.

Write Topic Sentences for Your Support Points

Your primary support points will form the topic sentences of the paragraphs that support your thesis statement. Each topic sentence should clearly relate to and show, explain, or prove your thesis.

THESIS STATEMENT	Playing a team sport taught me more than how to play the game.
TOPIC SENTENCE (paragraph 1)	I learned the importance of hard practice.
TOPIC SENTENCE (paragraph 2)	I also realized that, to succeed, I had to work with other people.
TOPIC SENTENCE (paragraph 3)	Most important, I learned to be responsible to others.

Once you develop topic sentences to support your thesis, back up your topic sentences with supporting details.

PRACTICE 3–13 Writing Topic Sentences and Supporting Details

Using the support points you generated in Practice 3–11, write topic sentences that support your thesis statement. Then list the details you came up with in Practice 3–12. When you have completed this practice, you will have developed support for an essay.

Writing Assignment 1

Develop primary support points and supporting details for the thesis you wrote on page 41 or for one of the following thesis statements.

- William Lowe Bryan said, "Education is one of the few things a person is willing to pay for and not get."
- Elderly people in this country are not shown enough respect.
- Few people know how to really listen.
- When I read _____ for my _____ class, my beliefs about _____ were challenged.

Before writing, read the following checklist.

CHECKLIST: Supporting Your Thesis

FOCUS

☐ Reread your thesis.

☐ Think about the people who will read your writing.

☐ Think about your purpose for writing.

ASK

☐ What support can I include that will show, explain, or prove what I mean?

☐ What do my readers need to know or understand to be convinced?

☐ What examples come to mind?

☐ What have I experienced myself?

☐ What information can I find on the internet, in a print source, or from people I meet and interview?

☐ What details could I use to strengthen the support?

As you arrange your ideas, consider what your purpose for writing is and what kind of organization would work best to make your main point. Some examples follow in the chart.

PURPOSE	ORGANIZATION
To describe an experience To explain how something works To explain how to do something	Chronological
To help your reader visualize whatever you are describing as you see it To create an impression using your senses — taste, touch, sight, smell, and sound To recreate a scene	Spatial
To persuade or convince someone To make a case for or against something	Importance

Make a Plan

When you have decided how to order your ideas, make a written plan—an **outline**—starting with your thesis statement. Then, state each of your primary support points as a topic sentence for one of the body paragraphs of the essay. Add supporting details to develop or explain the topic sentence. Your plan should also include a possible main point for the concluding paragraph. Although your outline serves as a good guide, it can be changed as you draft your essay.

For a diagram of the relationship between paragraphs and essays, see pages 24–25.

Also, there is no one right order for any essay. Use the order that will help you make your main point most effectively.

Outline for a Short Essay

The example that follows uses "standard" or "formal" outline format, in which numbers and letters distinguish between primary support points and secondary supporting details. Some instructors require this format. If you are making an outline for yourself, you might choose to write a less formal outline, simply indenting secondary supporting details under the primary support rather than using numbers and letters.

Some people find it useful to write full sentences as they plan so that their outline is a more complete guide for the essay; others just use words or short phrases.

Thesis statement
I.   Topic sentence (primary support point 1)
    A. Supporting detail
    B. Supporting detail (and so on)
II. Topic sentence (primary support point 2)
    A. Supporting detail
    B. Supporting detail (and so on)
III. Topic sentence (primary support point 3)
    A. Supporting detail
    B. Supporting detail (and so on)
Concluding paragraph

Writing Assignment 2

Create an outline using the thesis statement, topic sentences, and supporting details you have developed in this chapter. Arrange your ideas according to chronological order, spatial order, or order of importance. As you work on your outline, complete the checklist below.

CHECKLIST: Making an Outline

FOCUS

☐ Reread your thesis.

☐ Review your support points and details.

☐ Think about your audience and purpose.

ASK

☐ Do I have at least three supporting points for my thesis?

☐ Does each supporting point have at least one supporting detail?

☐ What order would work best for my writing purpose: chronological order, space order, or order of importance? (Review the table on page 50.)

☐ Does my instructor require me to use a formal outline format?

WRITE

☐ Put your thesis statement at the top of the outline.

☐ List your three main support points as topic sentences, following chronological order, spatial order, or order of importance.

☐ Include supporting details in complete sentences under each topic sentence.

☐ Draft a main point for your concluding paragraph.

You now have a clear main point with support, organized in a logical way. In the next chapter, you will begin drafting your paragraph or essay.

4

Drafting and Revising

Putting Your Ideas Together

A **draft** is the first whole version of your ideas in writing. Do the best job you can in writing a draft, but remember that you will have a chance to make changes later.

BASICS OF A GOOD DRAFT

- It has a thesis statement that presents the main point.
- It has a logical organization of ideas.
- It has primary support points that are stated in topic sentences that develop or explain the thesis statement.
- It has supporting details that develop or explain each topic sentence.
- It follows standard essay form (introduction, body paragraphs, conclusion) and uses complete sentences.
- The introduction captures the readers' interest and lets them know what the essay is about.
- The conclusion reinforces the main point and makes an observation or call for action.

For advice on support and more on thesis statements, see Chapter 3.

For a diagram showing the parts of an essay, see page 25, and for a complete draft of an essay, see page 60.

Writing a Draft

The explanations and practices in this section will prepare you to write a well-supported and organized essay.

Draft the Body of the Essay

Use your plan for your essay as you begin to write your draft. The plan should include your thesis statement, the primary support points for your thesis, and supporting details for your primary support points.

First, draft complete paragraphs that support your thesis. Each should contain a topic sentence (usually the first sentence in the paragraph) that presents a primary support point as well as supporting details. At this point, draft the body of your essay; you will write the introduction and conclusion later. In general, essays have at least three body paragraphs, and they may have many more, depending on your assignment and purpose.

If you are having trouble with a word or sentence as you draft, make a note to come back to it and then keep going.

· ·

PRACTICE 4–1 Writing Topic Sentences

Writing topic sentences for primary support points is a good way to start drafting the body of an essay. Convert each of the following primary support points into a topic sentence that supports the thesis. You can make up details if you want.

> THESIS STATEMENT: Being a good customer service representative in a retail store requires several important skills.
>
>   I. Being pleasant and polite [Primary support point 1]
>   A. Smiling, saying hello [Supporting detail]
>   B. Making eye contact [Supporting detail]
>
> TOPIC SENTENCE I: _____
>
>   II. Listening carefully [Primary support point 2]
>   A. Making notes [Supporting detail]
>   B. Asking questions [Supporting detail]
>
> TOPIC SENTENCE II: _____
>
>   III. Figuring out how to solve the problem [Primary support point 3]
>   A. Calling the right people [Supporting detail]
>   B. Filling out paperwork [Supporting detail]
>
> TOPIC SENTENCE III: _____

· ·

Write an Introduction

The introduction to your essay should capture your readers' interest and present the main point. Think of your introductory paragraph as a challenge. Ask yourself: How can I get my readers to want to continue reading?

BASICS OF A GOOD INTRODUCTION

- It should catch readers' attention.
- It should present the essay's thesis statement (narrowed topic + main point).
- It should give readers an idea of what the essay will cover.

The thesis statement is often either the first or the last sentence in the introductory paragraph, though you may find essays in which it is elsewhere. Here are examples of common kinds of introductions that spark readers' interest.

Start with a Surprising Fact or Idea

Surprises capture people's attention. The more unexpected and surprising something is, the more likely people are to take notice of it and read on.

> Peer pressure gets bad press, but in some cases more of it might make the world a better place. In California, psychologists recently found that they could get people to conserve electricity with a simple notice, delivered to their doorstep, telling them how their consumption compared with the neighborhood average. In the weeks that followed, homeowners who were consuming more electricity than their neighbors cut back—presumably because they were embarrassed to be out of step with the herd.
>
> —Christopher Shea, "In Praise of Peer Pressure"

Open with a Quotation

A good short quotation can definitely get people interested. It must lead naturally into your main point, however, and not just be stuck there. If you start with a quotation, make sure that you tell the reader who the speaker or writer is (unless it is a general quote like a proverb).

> In 2012, President Obama spoke to the United Nations General Assembly. He said, "The strongest weapon against hateful speech is not repression; it is more speech." It takes a special kind of speech, however, to counter the hateful words: we need slow speech—reasonable and carefully chosen words spoken after thoughtful listening. If members of your company can practice and develop slow speech, you can spare your workplace from the rancor, resignations, and even lawsuits which result from unchecked and hateful words.

Give an Example or Tell a Story

Opening an essay with a brief story or illustration often draws readers in.

> I do not know why I came to the decision to become a loser, but I know I made the choice at a young age. Sometime in the middle of fourth grade, I stopped trying. By the time I was in seventh grade, I was your typical degenerate: lazy, rebellious, disrespectful. I had lost all social graces. I was terminally hip and fatally cool.
>
> —David Flanagan, "The Choice to Do It Over Again"

Offer a Strong Opinion

The stronger the opinion, the more likely it is that people will pay attention.

> I work at a company where there are about a gazillion employees. I do not say that I know them all by name, but I know my fair share of them. I think that almost all of them know me. I would say that's the reason I've been able to go wherever it is I've made it to in this world. It is all based on one simple principle: I believe every single person deserves to be acknowledged, however small or simple the greeting.
>
> —Howard White, "The Power of Hello"

Ask a Question

A question needs an answer. If you start your introduction with a question, you engage your readers by inviting them to answer it.

> Have you ever heard of people who buy groceries for a week for a family of four but spend only a few dollars? These are the "extreme couponers," and while not everyone has the time or patience to plan and shop as they do, everyone can learn a few of their tricks to save money each week on food and other household essentials. Over time, those small savings will add up.

PRACTICE 4–2 Identifying Strong Introductions

Find a strong introduction in a newspaper, a magazine, a catalog, an advertisement — anything written. Explain, in writing, why you think it is a strong introduction.

Write a Conclusion

Your conclusion should have energy and match the force of your thesis statement; it is your last chance to drive home your main point. In fact, you should give yourself a last push at the end because people usually remember best what they see, hear, or read last. A good conclusion creates a sense of completion: it not only brings readers back to where they started but also shows them how far they have come.

BASICS OF A GOOD CONCLUSION

- It should refer to your main point.
- It should briefly summarize the support you have developed.
- It should make a final observation.

A good way to end an essay is to refer back to something in the introduction.

- If you used a quotation, use another one — by the same person or by another person on the same topic. Or refer back to the quotation in the introduction, and make an observation.
- If you stated a surprising fact or idea, go back to it and comment on it, using what you have written in the body of the essay.
- If you asked a question, ask it again, and answer it based on what you have said in your essay.
- If you started a story, finish it.
- Remind your reader of your original point, perhaps repeating key words that you used in your introduction.

Look again at three of the introductions you read earlier, each shown here with its conclusion.

START WITH AN EXAMPLE OR STORY

INTRODUCTION: I do not know why I came to the decision to become a loser, but I know I made the choice at a young age. Sometime in the middle of fourth grade, I stopped trying. By the time I was in seventh grade, I was your typical degenerate: lazy, rebellious, disrespectful. I had lost all social graces. I was terminally hip and fatally cool.

CONCLUSION: Growing up, I always heard these great turn-around stories of triumph over shortcomings. But I never thought they applied to me. Now I believe it is a choice anyone can make: to do it all over again.

— David Flanagan, "The Choice to Do It Over Again"

START WITH A SURPRISING FACT OR IDEA

> **INTRODUCTION:** Peer pressure gets bad press, but in some cases more of it might make the world a better place. In California, psychologists recently found that they could get people to conserve electricity with a simple notice, delivered to their doorstep, telling them how their consumption compared with the neighborhood average. In the weeks that followed, homeowners who were consuming more electricity than their neighbors cut back—presumably because they were embarrassed to be out of step with the herd.
>
> **CONCLUSION:** Later that same week, I read in an economics journal that freelance businessmen—I'm a freelancer—report only about 60 percent of their income, according to IRS estimates. Yet I'm scrupulous to the penny. Do I want to remain abnormal? Does anyone? I filed for an extension, so I've got some time to think about it.
>
> —Christopher Shea, "In Praise of Peer Pressure"

START WITH A STRONG OPINION

> **INTRODUCTION:** I work at a company where there are about a gazillion employees. I do not say that I know them all by name, but I know my fair share of them. I think that almost all of them know me. I would say that's the reason I've been able to go wherever it is I've made it to in this world. It is all based on one simple principle: I believe every single person deserves to be acknowledged, however small or simple the greeting.
>
> **CONCLUSION:** The day you speak to someone who has his head held down and when he lifts it up and smiles, you realize how powerful it is just to open your mouth and say, "Hello."
>
> —Howard White, "The Power of Hello"

PRACTICE 4–3 Analyzing Conclusions

After reading the preceding paired introductions and conclusions, indicate the techniques used in each conclusion to refer back to its introduction.

· ·

PRACTICE 4-4   Identifying Good Introductions and Conclusions

In a newspaper, magazine, or any other written material, find a piece of writing that has both a strong introduction and a strong conclusion. Answer the following questions about the introduction and conclusion.

1.   What method of introduction is used?

2.   What does the conclusion do? Does it restate the main idea? Sum up the points made in the piece? Make an observation?

3.   How are the introduction and the conclusion linked?

· ·

· ·

PRACTICE 4-5   Writing a Conclusion

Read the following introductory paragraphs, and write a possible conclusion for each one. Your conclusions can be brief, but they should each include the basics of a good conclusion (p. 57) and consist of several sentences.

1.   When it comes to long-term love relationships, I very much believe Anton Chekhov's statement, "Any idiot can face a crisis; it's the day-to-day living that wears you out." When faced with a crisis, couples often pull together. A crisis is a slap in the face that reminds you of who and what is important in your life. It is the routine necessities of living that can erode a relationship as couples argue over who does the laundry, who does the cleaning, or cooking, or bill paying. The constant skirmishes over day-to-day living can do more serious damage over the long term than a crisis.

2.   Why do so many people feel that they must be available at all times and in all places? Until recently, the only way you could reach someone was by telephone or by mail. Now if you do not have a smartphone for texting, Instagram and Twitter accounts, and call waiting, people trying to reach you get annoyed. I resent the loss of privacy. I do not want to be available twenty-four hours a day.

· ·

Title Your Essay

Even if your title is the *last* part of the essay you write, it is the *first* thing that readers read. Use your title to get your readers' attention and to tell them what your essay is about. Use concrete, specific words to name the topic of your essay.

BASICS OF A GOOD ESSAY TITLE

- It makes readers want to read the essay.

- It does not repeat the wording in your thesis statement.

- It may hint at the main point but does not necessarily state it outright.

- It is usually not a complete sentence.

One way to find a good title is to consider the type of essay you are writing. If you are writing an argument (as you will in Chapter 13), state your position in your title. If you are telling your readers how to do something (as you will in Chapter 8), try using the term *steps* or *how to* in the title. This way, your readers will know immediately both what you are writing about and how you will present it. For example, "Five Steps to Financial Independence" may be a more inviting and more accurate title for a process analysis essay than "Financial Independence."

Sample Student Essay: Draft

Following is a draft of a student essay. The revised essay appears on page 70.

Identifying
information

Introductory
paragraph

Thesis
statement

Primary
support 1

Primary
support 2

Deshon Briggs
Professor Riva
EN 099
October 15, 2017

One day, my teacher wrote "You are the change in your life" on the board. She said that statement related to our going to college and making our lives better. She gave us a writing assignment: to explore the statement that was due in four weeks. I did not really know what she was talking about but figured I had plenty of time to think about it. <u>I learned that I really can be the change in my life.</u>

<u>I took my son to play basketball at the park near us, and he gave me grief when I threw my Coke can off to the side.</u> He got a bag from my car and picked up my can. He started picking up others, and I helped. A guy I know came by with his kids, and we all started picking up cans and bottles. There were a lot.

<u>I had the idea to go to the local freecycle.org and posted that we wanted a big trash can for bottles and cans for the park.</u> I had a bunch of offers and other guys said they would help with clean-up. We set up a schedule. My son and I got the idea of returning the bottles and cans for the deposit money that we could use to get a new basketball net. We did that.

→

After a few weeks, the local paper called me and wanted to interview my son and me about the stuff we had done at the basketball court. We got our pictures in the paper, and we got some more people interested and some people made donations. Now we have enough money to get a bench.

Primary support 3

At this point, the court looks great, we met a lot of other people, and people gave us a lot of respect. It was great. And this is my paper for my English class, how my son and I were the change in our lives, starting with just picking up a Coke can.

Concluding paragraph

Point for conclusion

Writing Assignment

Write an outline and a draft using the thesis statement and support you developed in Chapter 3 or using one of the following thesis statements. Use the checklist below as you work.

- With the advent of so many new technologies, teenagers no longer do much traditional dating.
- Although cartoons are typically intended to entertain, they may also have important messages.
- Living with roommates requires patience.

CHECKLIST: Writing a Draft Essay

FOCUS

☐ Review your support.

ASK

☐ Is my thesis clear?

☐ Are there topic sentences for each body paragraph?

☐ Do I have supporting details for each topic sentence?

☐ Is my support arranged in a logical order?

☐ What introductory technique will get my readers' attention and make my point stand out?

☐ How can I use the conclusion for one last chance to make my point?

☐ How can I link my conclusion to my introduction? What is the strongest or most interesting part of the introduction that I might refer back to in my conclusion?

☐ Will my title make readers want to read my essay?

WRITE

☐ Write a draft essay.

Revising Your Draft

Revising is rewriting your drafts to make your ideas clearer, stronger, and more convincing. When revising, you might add, cut, move, or change whole sentences or paragraphs.

Editing is correcting problems with grammar, style, usage, and punctuation. While editing, you usually add, cut, or change words and phrases instead of whole sentences or paragraphs.

Revising (covered in this chapter) and editing (covered in Chapters 16, 17, and 18) are two different ways to improve a paper. Most writers find it difficult to do both at once. It is easier to look first at the ideas in your essay (revising) and then to look at the individual words and sentences (editing).

No one gets everything right in a draft—even professional writers need to revise. The tips below will help you with the revision process.

TIPS FOR REVISING

- Take a break from your draft—set it aside for a few hours or a whole day.
- Read your draft aloud, and listen to what you have written.
- Imagine yourself as one of your readers.
- Get feedback from a friend, a classmate, or a colleague (see the last section of this chapter).
- Get help from a tutor at your college writing center or lab.

Revise for Unity

Unity in writing means that all the points are related to your main point: they *unite* to support your main point. Sometimes writers drift away from their main point, as the writer of the following paragraph did with the underlined sentences.

Online dating services have many benefits, but users should be aware of the possible negatives as well. One benefit of online dating services is that people do not have to cruise bars to meet people. The websites offer subscribers potential matches, and the first contact is via email. Contact via email or text allows users to get to know each other a little before meeting. Sometimes a couple of exchanges can reveal that meeting is not necessary, so not

→

only do users get to avoid cruising, they save time by eliminating bad matches. The services also try to match compatible people by comparing profiles, so the likelihood of having something in common is greater than in a random encounter. With all the online dating services available, people can choose ones that appeal to people with specific interests and preferences. <u>A good place to meet is a cheap restaurant. Most people like Italian food or burgers, so those types of places are safe</u>. Also, online dating services offer many choices of screened possible dates, more than anyone could meet in a bar in months. On the negative side, online dating services can be expensive, and there are no guarantees of a good match. Also, although the companies do minor screening, nothing prevents a person from lying. People often lie about their age, weight, and appearance. Arranging a date through a dating service can put more pressure on people than meeting in a natural way because people sometimes have unreasonably high expectations. Online dating services can be successful, but people should be realistic about what to expect.

PRACTICE 4–6   Revising for Unity

The following essay includes four sentences that are off the main point. Underline those sentences. The main point in the essay is in boldface type.

A recent survey of the places students prefer to study revealed some strange results. We would expect the usual answers, such as a library, bedroom, desk, and kitchen, and the survey respondents did in fact name such areas. But some people prefer less traditional places.

One unusual place cited was a church. The respondent said it was a great spot to study when services were not taking place because it was always quiet and not crowded. Some churches are locked during the day because of vandalism. Other churches have had big problems with theft.

Another unusual study area was the locker room during a football game. A problem is that the person would miss the game. Except for half-time, the large area was empty. The person who studied there claimed that there was a high energy level in the locker room that, combined with the quiet, helped him concentrate. I wonder what the smell was like, though.

The most surprising preference for a place to study was the bleachers by the pool of a gym. The light was good, said the student, she loved the smell of chlorine, and the sound of water was soothing.

The results may seem strange—a church, a locker room, and a pool—but they do share some characteristics: quiet, relative solitude, and no interruptions, other than half-time. Perhaps we should all think about new places that might help us study.

Revise for Support and Detail

Support is the evidence, examples, or facts that show, explain, or prove your main point. **Primary support points** are the major ideas developed in the paragraphs that make up the body of your essay. **Supporting details** are the specifics that explain your primary support to your readers.

For more on primary support points and supporting details, see Chapter 3.

When you read your draft essay, ask yourself: Do I provide enough information for my reader to understand the main point? Do I present enough evidence to convince my reader of that point? Look for places where you could add more support and detail, and examine your writing for obvious biases or errors in logic (see pp. 9–11).

Read the two paragraphs that follow, and note the support the writer added to the second one. Notice that she did not simply add to the paragraph; she also deleted some words and rearranged others to make the story clearer to readers. The additions are underlined; the deletions are crossed out.

FIRST DRAFT

This morning I learned that my local police respond quickly and thoroughly to 911 calls. I meant to dial 411 for directory assistance, but by mistake I dialed 911. I hung up after only one ring because I realized what I had done. A few seconds after I hung up, the phone rang, and it was the police dispatcher. She said that she had received a 911 call from my number and was checking. I explained what happened, and she said she had to send a cruiser over anyway. Within a minute, the cruiser pulled in, and I explained what happened. I apologized and felt stupid, but I thanked him. I am glad to know that if I ever need to call 911, the police will be there.

REVISED TO ADD SUPPORT AND DETAIL

    This morning I <u>tested the 911 emergency system and found</u> <u>that it worked perfectly. Unfortunately, the test was a mistake.</u> ~~learned that my local police respond quickly and thoroughly~~ ~~to 911 calls.~~ I meant to dial 411 for directory assistance, but <u>without thinking</u> ~~by mistake~~ I dialed 911. I <u>frantically pushed the</u> <u>disconnect button</u> ~~hung up~~ after only one ring because I realized <u>my error.</u> ~~what I had done.~~ <u>As I reached for the phone to dial 411,</u> ~~A few seconds after I hung up,~~ it rang like an alarm. ~~the phone~~ ~~rang, and it was the police dispatcher.~~ The police dispatcher <u>crisply announced</u> ~~She said~~ that she had received a 911 call from my number and was checking. I <u>laughed weakly and</u> explained what happened, <u>hoping she would see the humor or at least the</u> <u>innocent human error. Instead, the crispness of her voice became</u> <u>brittle as</u> ~~and~~ she said she had to send a cruiser over anyway. <u>I</u> <u>went to meet my fate.</u> Within a minute, the cruiser pulled in, and <u>a police officer strode toward me.</u> I explained what <u>had</u> happened, apologized, <u>and thanked him humbly. I felt guilty of stupidity, at</u> <u>the least.</u> ~~and felt very stupid, but I thanked him.~~ <u>We learn from</u> <u>our mistakes, and in this case</u> I am glad to know that if I ever need to call 911, the police will be there.

. . . .

PRACTICE 4–7 Revising for Support

Read the following essay, and write in the space provided at least one additional support point or detail for each body paragraph and for the conclusion. Indicate where the added material should go in the paragraph by writing in a caret (^).

    Anyone who has owned a dog knows that there is a special bond between dogs and humans. Even without speech, dogs seem to understand humans' words and emotions. Dogs have been beloved family pets for a very long time, but they are also being used effectively in new educational, workplace, and therapeutic settings.

—————————————————————————————

    Dog rescue organizations often bring dogs into schools to talk about the dogs' resilience and responsiveness to good care. For example, Greyhound Rescue, an organization that saves dogs from death after they are too old to race or when a track is being closed, is active in schools. Students meet the dogs and learn about caring for them and ways to help them. After visits, some students become volunteers at the organization.

—————————————————————————————

Dogs work hard, too. They are sometimes brought into hotels to check for bedbugs, to airports for security checks, and to hospitals and nursing homes for patient therapy. There are also programs where chronically ill children are visited weekly by the same dog. The dogs seem to sense the children's pain or weakness, and their visits give the children something to look forward to. The dogs have the same effect on nursing home residents.

Dogs are also brought into prisons to be trained by prisoners. Sometimes inmates train these dogs as seeing-eye dogs for blind people. Other times prisoners ready abandoned puppies for adoption. Many violent prisoners have been successful trainers. The sad part is that they cannot keep the dogs they have trained.

It is said that dogs are man's best friend. They are trusting companions who love unconditionally. They are able to communicate and help where words sometimes do not.

Revise for Coherence

Coherence in writing means that all the support connects to form a whole that makes sense, with one sentence or idea leading smoothly to the next. In other words, even when the support is arranged in a logical order, it still needs "glue" to connect the various points.

A piece of writing that lacks coherence sounds choppy and is hard for the reader to follow. Revising an essay for coherence helps readers see how one point leads to another. The best way to improve coherence is to add transitions.

Transitions are words, phrases, and sentences that connect ideas so that writing moves smoothly from one point to another. Transitions can connect sentences and ideas within a paragraph and also connect one paragraph to another. The following box lists some, but not all, of the most common transitions and their purpose.

The essay on page 68 shows how transitions link ideas within sentences and paragraphs and connect one paragraph to the next. It also shows another technique for achieving coherence: repeating key words and ideas related to the main point. The transitions and key words in this piece are underlined. As you read, imagine what would happen if the transitions and repetitions were removed. How would your ability to read the piece be affected?

Common Transitional Words and Phrases

INDICATE SPACE RELATION			
above	below	near	to the right
across	beside	next to	to the side
at the bottom	beyond	opposite	under
at the top	farther	over	where
behind	inside	to the left	

INDICATE TIME ORDER			
after	eventually	meanwhile	soon
as	finally	next	then
at last	first	now	when
before	last	second	while
during	later	since	

INDICATE IMPORTANCE			
above all	in fact	more important	most
best	in particular	most important	worst
especially			

SIGNAL EXAMPLES			
for example	for instance	for one thing	one reason

SIGNAL ADDITIONS			
additionally	and	as well as	in addition
also	another	furthermore	moreover

SIGNAL CONTRAST			
although	in contrast	nevertheless	still
but	instead	on the other hand	yet
however			

SIGNAL CAUSE OR CONSEQUENCE			
as a result	due to	owing to	since
because	finally	so	therefore

AN ANTI-WORK CONSPIRACY

I thought I would never make it to work today. I had an important meeting, and it seemed as if everything was <u>conspiring</u> against me. <u>The conspiracy started before I even woke up.</u>

<u>I had set my alarm clock, but it did not go off, and therefore I did not wake up on time.</u> <u>When</u> I did wake up, I was already late, not just by a few minutes but by an hour and a half. To save time, I brushed my teeth <u>while</u> I showered. <u>Also,</u> I figured out what I was going to wear. <u>Finally,</u> I hopped out of the shower ready to get dressed. <u>But the conspiracy continued.</u>

<u>The next act of the conspiracy</u> concerned my only clean shirt, which was missing two buttons right in front. <u>After finding a sweater that would go over it, I ran to the bus stop.</u>

<u>When I got to the stop,</u> I discovered that the buses were running late. <u>When one finally came,</u> it was one of the old, slow ones, and it made stops about every ten feet. <u>In addition,</u> the heat was blasting, but I could not take off my sweater because my shirt was gaping open. <u>Now I was sweating,</u> and perspiration was running down my scalp and neck. <u>At least, I thought, I will dry off by the time the bus gets to my work.</u>

<u>In fact, I</u> did dry off a little, but the conspiracy did not end there. <u>When</u> I <u>finally</u> got to work, the elevator was out of service, <u>so</u> I had to walk up ten flights of stairs. I was drenched, late, and inappropriately dressed. <u>By the time I got to my desk,</u> I knew that the hardest part of the day was behind me.

- -

PRACTICE 4–8   Adding Transitional Sentences

Read the following essay. Then, write a transitional sentence that would link each paragraph to the one following it. You may add your transitional sentence at the end of a paragraph, at the beginning of the next paragraph, or in both places.

Many teenagers today do not date in the traditional sense — one boy and one girl going on dates or "going steady." Instead, they go out in groups rather than as couples. This new pattern gives many parents a sense that their sons and daughters are safe from premature sex and sexually transmitted diseases.

_____

_____

Although teenagers do not pair off romantically, they are getting plenty of sex, just not with people they care about. They care about their friends and do not want to risk ruining friendships, so they "hook up" with strangers they meet while out at night or online. "Hooking up" means having sex with someone, and many teens hook up only with people they have no other contact with, preferably from different schools or towns.

Although teenagers often think that sex without emotional involvement will avoid heartbreak and breakups, many teens, both girls and boys, admit that it is difficult not to develop feelings for someone they are physically intimate with. If one person begins to feel an attachment while the other does not, a distancing occurs: that hurts. It is a breakup of a different sort.

Teenagers have always experimented with ways to do things differently than their parents did. Trying new ways to do things is an important stage in teenagers' development. Experimentation is normal and sometimes produces better ways of doing things. According to most teens, however, the "hook-up" is not the answer to heartbreak: it is just another road to it. Perhaps teenagers are destined to experience some pain as they try out what "love" means.

Sample Student Essay: Revised

Below is a revised version of Deshon Briggs's essay on page 60. His revisions are highlighted in blue. As you read, consider whether his changes are effective. What additional suggestions would you make?

Deshon Briggs   Briggs 1
Professor Riva
EN 099
October 29, 2017

Title added ———————————————— Be the Change

Added detail ———— On the first day of my English class last spring, my teacher wrote "You are the change in your life" on the board. She said that ~~statement related to our going to college and making our lives better.~~ we had already taken a step toward change by coming to college to improve our lives. She said that we would be revisiting the theme of "people connecting to their communities" in our assignments and discussions and that we should be alert to ways that people are making a difference. She also gave us a writing assignment to explore ~~the statement that was due~~ ~~in four weeks.~~ and find ways that we could make the statement true in our own lives. The paper would not be due for four weeks, but we should start taking action now. I did not really know what she was talking about but figured I had plenty of time to think about it. In those four weeks, though, I learned that I really can be the change in my life.

The weekend after we got the assignment, I took my son to play basketball at the park near us, and he gave me grief when I threw my Coke can off to the side. He said in his school they were learning about how litter is bad for the earth. He got a bag from my car and picked up my can. Then he started picking up others, and I helped. Once we started, I was surprised how many bottles and cans there were that I just had not noticed before. ~~While~~ we were working, a guy I know came by with his kids, and we all started picking up cans and bottles. ~~There were a lot.~~ We filled three big bags, just with bottles and cans. But then we kept going, filling another bag ~~with paper~~ and other litter. When we were done, we brought the bags home, threw away the trash, and took the cans and bottles to the supermarket to redeem the deposit money.

That night, I had the idea to go to the local freecycle.org and post that we wanted a big trash can for bottles and cans for the park. By the next morning, I had ~~a bunch of offers~~ seven offers of free trash cans and ~~other guys~~ four other guys with sons said they would help with clean-up. We set out the trash cans and labeled one for bottles and cans, one for other trash. Then we set up a schedule. The people responsible for pick-up would take the day's

→

Annotations (left margin):
Added detail
Added Details
Transition
Revised Thesis
Transition
Added Detail
Transitions Detail
Transition
Added Details
Transitions
Transitions
Added Details

collection for deposit money and get rid of the trash. ~~My son and I got the idea of returning the bottles and cans for the deposit money that we could use to get a new basketball net. We did that~~ With the money we collected, we got a new basketball net and a bench. We felt proud of ourselves.

    After a few weeks, the local paper called me and wanted to interview my son and me about ~~the stuff we had done at~~ our "campaign to improve" the basketball court. We got our pictures in the paper, and ~~we got some more people interested~~ some people who read about what we had done made donations. ~~Now we have enough money to get a bench.~~ Since then, we have made more improvements, and the court and park around it are clean. Someone had the idea of starting a community garden in the park, and now whole families come there. There are some picnic tables, and it is a wonderful and safe family recreation area. ~~The court looks great, we met a lot of other people, and people gave us a lot of respect. It was great.~~ My son and I have met many new people as we created our own little piece of paradise from what was just a junky basketball court in a park that no one used. And this is my paper for my English class: how my son and I ~~were~~ learned that we are the change in our lives. ~~starting~~ It all started with just picking up a Coke can.

Added Detail

Transition

Added Details

Revised conclusion

Writing Assignment

Revise an essay using the draft you developed earlier in this chapter. Before revising, read the following checklist.

CHECKLIST: Revising Your Essay

FOCUS

☐ After a break, reread your draft with a fresh perspective.

ASK

☐ What is my point or position? Does my thesis statement clearly state my main point?

☐ Does my essay have the following?

    – An introductory paragraph

    – Three or more body paragraphs

    – A topic sentence for each paragraph that supports the main point

    – A forceful concluding paragraph that reminds readers of the main point and makes an observation

→

☐ Does my essay have unity?
- Do all of the support points relate directly to the main point?
- Do all of the supporting details in each body paragraph relate to the paragraph's topic sentence?
- Have I avoided drifting away from the main point?

☐ Do I have enough support?
- Taken together, do the topic sentences of each paragraph give enough support or evidence for the main point?
- Do individual paragraphs support their topic sentences?
- Would more detail strengthen my support?

☐ Is my essay coherent?
- Have I used transitional words to link ideas?
- Have I used transitional sentences to link paragraphs?

REVISE

☐ Revise your draft, making any improvements you can. Be sure to look for bias or errors in reasoning.

Peer Reviewing

Peer review is the process of exchanging feedback on pieces of writing with your fellow students, colleagues, or friends. Getting comments from a peer is a good way to begin revising your essay.

Other people can look at your work and see things that you might not — parts that are good as well as parts that need more explanation or evidence. The best reviewers are honest about what could be better but also sensitive to the writer's feelings. In addition, they are specific. Reviewers who say a paper is "great" without offering further comment do not help writers improve their work.

BASICS OF USEFUL FEEDBACK

▪ It is given in a positive way.
▪ It is specific.
▪ It offers suggestions.
▪ It may be given orally or in writing.

To get useful feedback, find a partner and exchange papers. Each partner should read the other's paper and jot down a few comments. The first time someone comments on what you have written, you may feel a little embarrassed, but you will feel better about the process once you see how your writing benefits from the comments. You may also feel uncomfortable making suggestions to others, so to begin, you might paraphrase the most important point you read or heard ("So you are saying that …") and ask for confirmation ("Is that right?").

Peer reviewers can also consider the following questions as they read.

QUESTIONS FOR PEER REVIEWERS

1. What is the main point?
2. After reading the introductory paragraph, do you have an idea of what the essay will cover, and why?
3. How could the introduction be more interesting?
4. Is there enough support for the main point? Where might the writer add support?
5. Are there confusing places where you have to reread something to understand it? How might the writer make the points, the organization, or the flow of ideas clearer or smoother?
6. Does the writer have assumptions or biases that weaken the writing? What are they?
7. How could the conclusion be more forceful?
8. What do you most like about the essay? Where could it be better? What would you do if it were your essay?
9. What other comments or suggestions do you have?
10. How do you think the audience for the writing will respond to the thesis, and its support?

PRACTICE 4–9 Practicing Peer Review

Exchange drafts of the writing you are doing for this chapter (or for another class) with a partner or small group. Use the questions above to practice giving feedback. Before you begin, consider asking your peer reviewers one or two specific questions about the draft. Knowing your concerns will help your reviewers focus during the peer review.

5

Narration

Writing That Tells Stories

Understand What Narration Is

Narration is writing that tells a story of an event or experience.

> ### Four Basics of Good Narration
>
> **1** It reveals something of importance to your reader (main point).
>
> **2** It includes all the major events of the story (primary support).
>
> **3** It uses details to bring the story to life for your audience (secondary support).
>
> **4** It presents the events in a clear order, usually according to when they happened (logical organization).

In the following passage, each number corresponds to one of the Four Basics of Good Narration.

4 Events presented in the order they happened.

1 Thanksgiving is a time of repeating old traditions, such as gathering with family and friends and eating special foods like turkey, cranberry relish, and pumpkin pie. Every year, my family and I go to my older sister's and brother-in-law's house, and we enjoy the whole traditional experience. But it was there that I also learned how unexpected new traditions can enter the mix and make a holiday even more meaningful.

2 My sister's son Jacob had spent a semester in Niger, a desert country in central Africa. There he made a good friend, Ibrahim, who later moved to the United States to study science and engineering. My sister and brother-in-law invited Ibrahim to Thanksgiving every year, so gradually we all came to know this warm and friendly person.

He would ask questions about Thanksgiving traditions, which were new and unfamiliar to him. We would ask questions about his country, which was unfamiliar to us. **3** In response he would often say, "Well, where I am from, whenever we gather, we drink a strong, sweet, green tea called *atai*." It was as though, to him, this tea seemed strangely missing from the party.

2 One year he brought with him everything necessary to make the tea in the traditional way of his country: **3** two small metal pots with lids; tea leaves; sugar; special small glasses, like shot glasses; a tiny wire grill; and charcoal. He made the tea on my sister's back porch, though the weather was drizzly and cold. The process was complicated, and involved boiling the tea a long time, then pouring it from high up, to cool it. Patience is a necessary ingredient.

4 Events presented in the order they happened.

2 When the tea was finally ready, we all hesitatingly took sips from the little glasses, expecting to try it, set it aside, and think "that will be that." **3** But the tea was so pleasingly tasty—smoky and sweet—and so strikingly different that this custom quickly became an essential and beloved Thanksgiving tradition. **2** Now Ibrahim carefully makes this tea every year and serves it at the end of the big meal, and the holiday would not seem right otherwise.

1 I give thanks to Ibrahim for enlarging my world and proving that, when it comes to excellent customs, there is plenty of room at the table for one more.

You can use narration in many practical situations. Consider the following examples.

COLLEGE	In a U.S. history course, you trace, in your own words, the specific sequence of events that led the United States to enter World War II.
WORK	A customer becomes angry with you and lodges a complaint with your boss. You recount—in writing—what happened.
EVERYDAY LIFE	Your wallet is stolen, and you file a written account with the police reporting exactly what happened.

First Basic: Main Point in Narration

Whenever you write a narration, have a *purpose* in mind, whether that purpose is to explain what happened, to prove something, or simply to entertain someone. If your purpose is not clear to you, it will not be clear to your readers. To clarify your purpose, complete this sentence: I am telling this story in order to _____.

Also consider who your *audience* is and what they know and do not know about your story. Finally, be clear on your *main point*—what is important about the narration. Generally, college instructors will want your main point to indicate what is important to you about a story. For clarity, state the main point in the first paragraph, and remind readers of it at the end of your narration.

Take another look at the passage under the Four Basics of Good Narration (p. 74).

> ... I also learned how unexpected new traditions can ... make a holiday even more meaningful.

This statement emphasizes the event's importance to the writer.

In writing a narrative, make sure your topic sentence (for paragraphs) and thesis statement (for essays) communicate your general topic and the main point you are making about the topic.

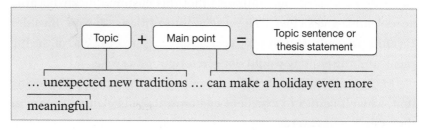

Second and Third Basics: Support in Narration

To **support** your main point, you will present and explain the major events in the story and describe relevant details. As you write a narrative, you will have decisions to make—what to include, what to leave out, and what perspective you will take on events. Your **point of view** determines how you will present the major events and details of the story and how you will support your main point.

The **major events** of a story are your primary support in narration, and they will usually become the topic sentences for the body paragraphs in your essay. Ask yourself what the major events are and what makes them important. To help your readers experience the events as you did, give supporting details that bring the experience to life.

For example, one student stated the main point of an event in the following thesis: *the theft of my wallet this morning showed me how easy it is for criminals to deceive unsuspecting victims.* The student then did some listing to come up with the major events and details about those events.

MAJOR EVENTS (primary support)	SUPPORTING DETAILS (secondary support)
Woman bumped into me.	Light bump, but she dropped her folder of papers, and they scattered.
I bent down to help her collect the papers.	Wind was blowing, so I had to work fast.
A man stopped and asked if he could help.	I didn't get a good look at him because I was trying to get the papers, but he stood close to me and hung around for a minute just watching us. Then, he just left without saying anything.
Woman thanked me, and I said no problem.	She had her head down and walked off fast.
When I went to get coffee, I realized the wallet was gone.	I broke into a sweat at the café and had that horrible panicked feeling.
I realized that the man and woman were working together.	Looking back on the details, it was clear how carefully they had planned the theft.

As you tell your story, you might want to include direct speech or **dialogue,** the words that you or other people said. If you report exactly what was said, use quotation marks, as in the following example.

For more on using quotation marks, see Chapter 18.

> The woman said, "Oh, I'm so sorry! I'll never be able to get these papers before they blow away, and my boss will have a fit."

Using direct speech like this can bring a narrative alive.

Fourth Basic: Organization in Narration

Because narration tells a story of "what happened," it often uses **chronological (time) order**. Start at the beginning of the story, and describe the events in the sequence in which they occurred.

For more on chronological order, see page 48.

Time transitions (words and phrases like *next* and *meanwhile*) are important in a narrative because they make the order of events clear to readers. Writers of narration use these common transitions not only within a paragraph—to move from one detail about the event to the next—but also between paragraphs to move from one major event to the next.

For more in transitions, see page 67.

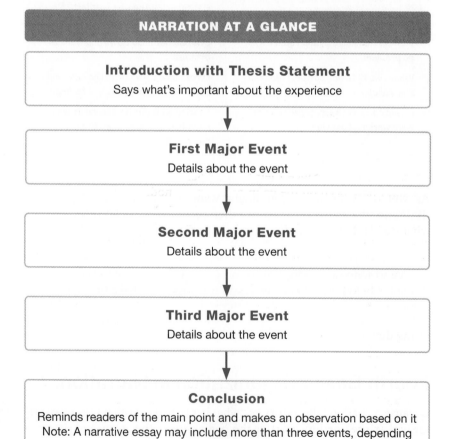

Common Time Transitions

after	eventually	meanwhile	soon
as	finally	next	still
at last	first	now	then
before	last	second	when
during	later	since	while

NARRATION AT A GLANCE

Introduction with Thesis Statement
Says what's important about the experience

↓

First Major Event
Details about the event

↓

Second Major Event
Details about the event

↓

Third Major Event
Details about the event

↓

Conclusion
Reminds readers of the main point and makes an observation based on it
Note: A narrative essay may include more than three events, depending on your purpose.

Read and Analyze Narration

Read the following three examples of narration—from college, the workplace, and everyday life—and answer the questions that accompany them. For each essay, review the Four Basics of Good Narration (p. 74) and practice the critical reading process explained in Chapter 1.

Narration in College

A student wrote the following essay for a college writing course. The assignment was "Write an essay describing an important decision in your life."

Jordan Brown

A Return to Education

GUIDING QUESTION

How does Brown feel about his return to college?

1   For me, college has been an experience marked by anticipation, fear, and pride. I sometimes find myself still surprised that I am really here. The journey to get here has been a long one, but if I can put my fears behind me, I believe I will be able to accomplish something that I can really be proud of.

2   Being able to go to college is something that I have been anticipating for many years. Since I left high school and the California Bay Area behind, I have been on the go in one way or another. After graduation, I felt that I wasn't ready for the commitments or responsibilities of college. Instead, I enlisted in the army. The army provided me with the maturity and self-discipline that I desperately needed in my life; however, being in the army also provided me with very little time or money to go to college, so I put it off until "a later date."

3   After the army, I sought a higher-paying job, first becoming a truck driver. This job provided me with money but no time. Now I work for the railroad, and with my apprenticeship behind me, I have some free time for the first time in my life.

4   What I have been anticipating for years is finally here. I now have the time and money for college, but do I have the ability? It has been eleven years since I last sat in a classroom. This made me question myself: Can I do this? Will I succeed? Will I fail? Am I even capable of learning in a classroom environment? Although I had these questions, I knew that the only way to face my fears was to attack them head-on. I reminded myself that the only thing I could do is try.

CRITICAL READING
■ Preview
■ Read
■ Pause
■ Review

(See pp. 4–11.)

PAUSE: Why did Brown join the army? Was it a good decision for him?

PAUSE: How does Brown's first sentence here relate to the first paragraph? What questions does he have?

PAUSE: Why was Brown nervous?

5   When I first walked into Front Range Community College, I was nervous. I couldn't help but notice how young everyone looked. I got to my study skills class, sat down, and looked around. I felt out of place. Most of the people in the class looked as if they had just graduated from high school. When we did our introductions, however, I learned that one of the women sitting across the room had graduated from high school eleven years ago. I started to feel a little younger.

PAUSE: How do the other students help Brown feel better?

6   When I got to my philosophy class, I watched the other students come in and noticed that not everyone looked like a kid. This class looked very much like an American melting pot, with students of many ages and cultures. As we went around the room introducing ourselves, I felt very much more confident about my decision to try college. Many students were even older than I was. A woman sitting near me, who looked about my mom's age, said she was in college because all of her kids were in college now. She told us that she wanted a college education and a better job. An older gentleman across the room said that he was a business executive from Germany. His job had become boring, and he was looking for something more challenging. By the end of the introductions, I was convinced that this "college thing" might just work.

PAUSE: How does Brown's first sentence here relate back to his thesis statement?

7   Since I have gone back to school, there has been a lot of pride surrounding me. My parents can't stop talking about me and how proud they are. My family and friends are excited for me and congratulate me on my decision. I am also proud of myself for making the tough decision to go back to school. I know that when I get my degree, I will have something to be truly proud of.

PAUSE: How does Brown tie his conclusion to his introduction?

8   I still have fears and uncertainties. But I also have positive anticipation and hope. Now, I know that I am on the right course. I know that as long as I have stamina and determination, nothing can stop me from achieving my dream of getting my degree in mechanical engineering.

CRITICAL THINKING
■ Summarize
■ Analyze
■ Synthesize
■ Evaluate
(More on p. 12.)

For more on peer review, see p. 72.

1. **Summarize.** Briefly summarize Brown's essay, including his *main point* and *purpose* and the *major events* in his story. What is his point of view?

2. **Analyze.** Does Brown's *support* all relate to his main point? Is it logically organized? Does he give you enough details? How do the topic sentences relate specifically to the thesis statement? Did the title give you an idea of what the essay would be about?

3. **Synthesize.** How does Brown's experience relate to your own or to other things you have thought about, read, or heard?

4. **Evaluate.** Does Brown achieve his purpose? Does his essay have the Four Basics of Good Narration (see p. 74)? If Brown were a student in your writing class, what questions and comments would you have for him as part of the peer review process?

Narration at Work

The following is an excerpt from an article, published in the *Chronicle of Higher Education*, that the author wrote in her profession as a journalist.

Monique Rizer

Journalist and Development Associate

When Students Are Parents

GUIDING QUESTION

How has being a parent and student affected Rizer's decisions?

CRITICAL READING
- Preview
- Read
- Pause
- Review

(See pp. 4–11.)

1   Crammed behind my desk, I fidgeted and shifted my eyes to observe the other students in the room. I tried not to look the way I felt—like I didn't belong there with them. I couldn't help noticing that all the other women were wearing shorts, sandals, flirty summer dresses: appropriate clothes for a warm September day. I tugged at the baggy clothes hiding my postpartum weight. I thought of my six-week-old son and hoped I'd make it home to nurse him at the scheduled time. The thought of him reminded me that however odd I felt, I was going to stay in college this time.

PAUSE: Have you felt out of place in college or other places?

2   It was the summer of 1998. I was a twenty-year-old new mother and wife, and it was my first day of class, though not my first day of college. I'd begun my long journey through higher education three years before, but my plans to attend full time after high school graduation were put on hold when financial difficulties forced my family of eight to move. I then found a local community college and felt prepared to start again, but instead the registration papers sat abandoned in my car, where I practically lived since home was a 32-foot trailer filled with seven other people. In the summer of 1996, I packed my bags and left to live on my own; I enrolled again the next spring and had my son in July 1998. I knew I had to stay in school and go full time. I wanted more for my son and myself, even though I wasn't sure what exactly "more" was at the time.

PAUSE: How do Rizer's purpose and audience affect her choice of details in this paragraph?

3   Focusing on my son helped me to persist in college during difficult times, and there were many. I did not have time to socialize with other students because when I was not in class, I had to rush to take care of the details of life as a mother. Grocery shopping, cooking, arranging for child care, taking my son to the doctor when he was sick, seemed to take every minute. I was exhausted every day, and finding the time and mental energy to study and do homework often seemed an overwhelming challenge. But I stuck with it, determined to finish, to do what my mother had not done. When she had me at nineteen, she quit college and never returned.

PAUSE: Study the use of commas in this paragraph. How do the commas help readers understand Rizer's narrative?

4   What helped me finish college, even after my marriage and the birth of my second son, was meeting other students who were also parents. I realized other people were in my situation, too, and probably felt just as stretched. As I met other mothers, we offered to baby-sit for each other or to get together with our children so that they could play, and we could study. All of us wanted more for our children than we had had, and that kept us going.

PAUSE: Do you have enough information to understand how Rizer got through college? If not, what additional information would you like to see?

5   My commitment to finish college has paid off. Now, I have a bachelor's in journalism from Gonzaga University and a master's in information management from Syracuse University. During my years in school, my son kept me focused and ignited my ambition to be a better student. In my experience, there is no better motivation to finish college and to appreciate the full experience than a child whose future depends on your decisions. I had to continue to use my education to give him a better life and to set an example for him to follow.

6   I feel a tremendous sense of accomplishment: I've learned so many intangible lessons about myself; I've decided that I want to help other young parents achieve their educational goals; and I see a better future for my boys (I have two now). And I keep telling my mom that she doesn't have to live vicariously through me: she can return to college any time she wants. Being a student and a parent is challenging, but nothing is more rewarding than providing a bright future for your children.

1.   Briefly summarize Rizer's essay, including her *main point* and *purpose* and *the major events* in her story.

2.   Carefully examine the Four Basics of Good Narration (p. 74) and determine specifically whether Rizer's workplace writing is a good narrative. Make notes to support your opinion.

3.   What is your reaction to Rizer's essay? What would you say to her or ask her if you had the chance?

Narration in Everyday Life

The following address was originally broadcast on National Public Radio.

Howard White

The Power of Hello

GUIDING QUESTION

What is the power of hello in White's experience?

CRITICAL READING
■ Preview
■ Read
■ Pause
■ Review
(See pp. 4–11.)

1   I work at a company where there are about a gazillion employees. I do not say that I know

Ethan Miller/Getty Images

he holds high rank

Doesn't know many co-workers

them all by name, but I know my fair share of them. I think that almost all of them know me. I would say that's the reason I've been able to go wherever it is I've made it to in this world. It is all based on one simple principle: I believe every single person deserves to be acknowledged, however small or simple the greeting.

nice guy

2   When I was about 10 years old, I was walking down the street with my mother. She stopped to speak to Mr. Lee. I was busy trying to bulls-eye the "O" in the stop sign with a rock. I knew I could see Mr. Lee any old time around the neighborhood, so I did not pay any attention to him. After we passed Mr. Lee, my mother stopped me and said something that has stuck with me from that day until now. She said, "You let that be the last time you ever walk by somebody and not open up your mouth to speak, because even a dog can wag its tail when it passes you on the street." That phrase sounds simple, but it has been a guidepost for me and the foundation of who I am.

Gave a memory example

PAUSE: Why does White tell this story?

3   When you write an essay like this, you look in the mirror and see who you are and what makes up your character. I realized mine was cemented that day when I was ten years old. Even then, I started to see that when I spoke to someone, they spoke back. And that felt good.

PAUSE: What does the first sentence mean?

4   It is not just something I believe in; it's become a way of life. I believe that all people deserve to feel someone acknowledge their presence, no matter how humble they may be or even how important. At work, I always used to say hello to the founder of the company and ask him how our business was doing. But I was also speaking to the people in the café and the people who cleaned the buildings, and asked how their children were doing. I remembered after a few years of passing by the founder, I had the courage to ask him for a meeting. We had a great talk. At a certain point, I asked him how far he thought I could go in his company. He said, "If you want to, you can get all the way to this seat."

PAUSE: Why do you think the founder feels this way about White?

5   I have become vice president, but that has not changed the way I approach people. I still follow my mother's advice. I speak to everyone I see, no matter where I am. I have learned that speaking to people creates a pathway into their world, and it lets them come into mine, too.

PAUSE: Paraphrase the lesson that White learned.

6   The day you speak to someone who has his head held down and when he lifts it up and smiles, you realize how powerful it is just to open your mouth and say, "Hello."

1.   Briefly summarize White's essay.

2.   What is the author's *purpose*?

3.   How does White use *details* to make the narrative vivid and engaging for his readers?

4.   Does White's story reflect the Four Basics of Good Narration (p. 74)?

5. Where does White use quotes? How does the use of these quotes support his main idea?

6. Write three questions that you would ask if you were writing a quiz on White's essay (and be able to answer your own questions).

Write a Narrative Essay

Write your own narrative essay on one of the following topics or on a topic of your own choice. Use **NARRATION AT A GLANCE** as a basic organizer (p. 78), and follow the Writing Guide: Narration checklist as you write and revise.

COLLEGE	Write about your first experience of college, as Jordan Brown did. • Participate in a social event or club-sponsored activity at your college. Tell the story of your experience to encourage other students to participate.
WORK	• Tell the story of something positive you did at work (some achievement). • Write a narrative that explains an obstacle that you or your employer faced. Make sure your narrative explains the challenge, how it was addressed, and what the results were.
EVERYDAY LIFE	• Recount a time when you took a risk. • Following White's model, tell the story of a lesson you learned, how you learned it, and how it has affected your life.

WRITING GUIDE: Narration

STEPS IN NARRATION	HOW TO DO THE STEPS
☐ Focus.	• Think about your audience and what is important about your story.
☐ Explore your topic. See Chapter 2.	• Narrow your topic. • Prewrite, recalling what happened. Why is the story important?

(Continued)

STEPS IN NARRATION	HOW TO DO THE STEPS
☐ **Write a thesis statement.** Topic + <u>Main point</u> = (Thesis) See Chapter 3.	• Say what is important about the story — how it affected you or others.
☐ **Support your thesis.** See Chapter 3.	• Recall the major events. • Provide background information that your readers will need. • Describe the events with specific details.
☐ **Write a draft.** See Chapter 4.	• Arrange the events chronologically. • Consider using one of the introductory techniques in Chapter 4, and include your thesis statement in your introduction. • Write topic sentences for each major event. • Write a paragraph for each event giving details about them.
☐ **Revise your draft.** See Chapter 4.	• Read to make sure that all events and details show, explain, or prove what is important about the story. • Add important events or details that occur to you. • Add time transitions. • Improve your introduction, thesis, and conclusion.
☐ **Edit your revised draft.** See Chapters 16 through 18.	• Correct errors in grammar, spelling, word use, and punctuation.
☐ **Evaluate your writing.**	• Does it have the Four Basics of Good Narration (p. 74)? • Is this the best I can do?

Reflect on the Process

Look at your writing from this chapter, from your prewriting through revision and editing, and consider these questions:

1. What was the most difficult part of the process for you? Why?

2. Did the feedback you got on your initial draft provide you with information you could use to make changes in your draft? If not, what can you do to improve the feedback you get next time? What specific questions do you need your reviewers to answer for you?

3. What will you do differently the next time you write a narrative essay?

4. Talk to someone who has taken courses in your major or who is working in your field. How is narration used in your major or career? What kinds of narrative writing tasks can you expect in the future?

6

Illustration

Writing That Shows Examples

Understand What Illustration Is

Illustration is writing that uses examples to show, explain, or prove a point.

> **Four Basics** of Good Illustration
>
> **1** It makes a clear point (main point).
>
> **2** It gives specific examples to show, explain, or prove the point (primary support).
>
> **3** It gives vivid details to support the examples (secondary support).
>
> **4** It arranges support by order of importance or emphasis (logical organization).

In the following paragraph, each number corresponds to one of the Four Basics of Good Illustration.

What is the strongest predictor of your health? **1** It may not be your income or age but rather your literacy. **2** People with low literacy skills have four times greater annual health costs than those with high skills. Why is literacy so important? **3** Most Americans read at an eighth- or ninth-grade level, and 20 percent read at just a fifth-grade level or below. However, most health-care materials are written above the tenth-grade level. **3** As many as half of all patients fail to take medications as directed, often because they don't

4
Examples organized by order of importance to illustrate both the problem and a solution.

understand the instructions. [2] Americans can improve their health literacy by asking their doctor or pharmacist three questions: [3] (1) "What is my main problem?" (2) "What do I need to do?" and (3) "Why is it important to do this?" If you're still confused, don't hesitate to ask your doctor, nurse, or pharmacist to go over the information again.

— "Literacy and Health," *Parade*, 18 January, 2004

Whenever we explain something, we use examples to show what we mean. Here are some ways you might use illustration.

COLLEGE	In a criminal justice course, you discuss and give examples of the most common plea agreements.
WORK	In applying for a job, you create a cover letter with examples of projects you have coordinated in order to show your leadership skills.
EVERYDAY LIFE	You complain to the phone company that your cell phone is not working properly, and you provide three examples.

First Basic: Main Point in Illustration

Look at the opening sentences in the paragraph with the colored shading (p. 87).

> *What is the strongest predictor of your health?* It may not be your income or age but rather your literacy.

In this case, the topic—the strongest predictor of your health—is in the opening sentence, which is followed by a surprising *main point*—that literacy might be a predictor of health. Because the point is surprising, the reader will be interested in reading on to find out how it could be true. The writer demonstrates the main point by giving examples.

Often, a thesis statement in illustration includes the topic and your main point.

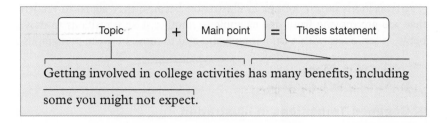

Getting involved in college activities has many benefits, including some you might not expect.

Second and Third Basics: Support in Illustration

In illustration, the **examples** show, explain, or prove your stated main point. A student who had written the thesis *Homeschooling is beneficial to both the child and the parent* focused her prewriting on finding examples of benefits of homeschooling. Here are some examples from her brainstorming.

individualized to child	parent and child have control
parent and child together	more flexibility
at child's own pace	considers child's learning style
one-on-one	education is part of regular life

An illustration essay usually uses several examples as **support points**. The writer of the prewriting on homeschooling selected "individualized to child" as one support point and asked herself, "What do I mean? How? In what ways?" to find supporting details.

She also chose "parent and child have control" as another major example that would support the thesis. She then asked herself, "How do they have more control?" and listed potential supporting details.

- control over materials used (what books, what computer programs, what approach)
- control over time of instruction (what hours of the day, based on child's natural rhythms, vacations — not tied to a school's calendar)

Fourth Basic: Organization in Illustration

Illustration often uses **order of importance** to organize several examples, saving the most vivid, convincing example for last.

For more on order of importance, see page 49.

Transitions are important in illustration because they signal to readers that you are moving from one example to another. Use transitions to move between sentences within a paragraph and also to move between paragraphs.

Common Transitions in Illustration

also	finally	for instance	in addition
another	for example	for one thing	one example ...
			another example

ILLUSTRATION AT A GLANCE

Introduction with Thesis Statement
Says what you want readers to know about the topic

↓

First Example
Details about the example

↓

Second Example
Details about the example

↓

Third Example (Often the Most Powerful)
Details about the example

↓

Conclusion
Reminds readers of the main point and makes an observation based on it
Note: An illustration essay may include more than three examples,
depending on your purpose.

Read and Analyze Illustration

Read the following three examples of illustration—from college, the workplace, and everyday life—and answer the questions that accompany them. For each essay, review the Four Basics of Good Illustration (p. 87) and practice the critical reading process explained in Chapter 1.

Illustration in College

The following is part of a report that Luz Medina wrote when she served as a student representative to the Division of Student Affairs at her college. Her job was to survey some other students and present a list of suggestions for new services that would help students.

GUIDING QUESTION

What does Luz Medina learn from her interviews?

To: Vice President, Student Affairs
From: Luz Medina
Re: Suggestions for student services

CRITICAL READING
- Preview
- Read
- Pause
- Review

(See pp. 4–11.)

1   To complete this report, I interviewed twenty-five students, asking them the following questions: (1) Do you know about the student services that are available on this campus? (2) What service or organization would help your college experience and why? (3) Would you be willing to help set up this program? I have attached the complete responses to these questions, but here I will summarize what I found. The responses were both surprising and well worth considering in the future.

PAUSE: How is the first sentence linked to the thesis statement?

2   To my surprise, most of the students I interviewed were not aware of the many programs that are already available to them. For example, several of the students said that they did not know what to do if they were thinking about dropping out. I told them about our Succeeding Together program and gave them the website that lists the people and services that are designed just for these situations. I encouraged them to go to these sites for help, telling them that the college works hard to help keep students from dropping out.

PAUSE: What is Medina's purpose? Who is her audience?

3   Another area in which we have many services that students do not know about is in preparing for a job search. Most students knew that there is an office of career planning, but they thought it just posted job announcements. They did not know about great programs like the Virtual Job Fair or the many mini-seminars on interviewing, making a good first impression, or one-on-one counseling to match students with employers. They also did not know about the program that gives very specific career counseling that matches student interests with careers and then helps students plan what courses will best help them get started in the career.

PAUSE: What examples does Medina give of her topic sentence?

4   There were many other services students did not know about. Although they are listed online and we offer an orientation, I think we, as a committee, should figure out how to more successfully let students know what resources they have on this campus.

5   The students offered some good suggestions for new services. One is that we devise an instant-messaging system for communication with advisers. Students said that often they have to wait to see their advisers when they have a question that would take only a minute to ask and answer. One student compared it to standing in a long line to buy a package of gum: it doesn't seem worth the wait.

6   Two other good suggestions regard the problems students often have with transportation and child care. Students suggested that there be a college-sponsored online bulletin board that students can go to find rides at various times. Students looking for transportation could find other students with cars who would be willing to give students rides for a small fee. The students also suggested a similar child-care bulletin board that might help parents connect to baby-sit for each other.

PAUSE: How are paragraphs 6 and 7 related to paragraph 5?

7   A final suggestion that two students made was to have professors record their lectures so that they could be downloaded for students who had to miss a class. Students said that they could already get the homework assignments for a missed class, but they had no way to get the lecture material.

PAUSE: How does Medina tie paragraph 8 to the introductory paragraph?

8   Students were surprised that the college already has so many resources, and they gave serious and thoughtful suggestions for new and needed services. I am sorry to report that only five of the twenty-five students said that they would be willing to help set up a new service, but at least those few are willing. Interviewing other students was an interesting project for me, making me think about the importance of student-affairs programs and giving me experience gathering and analyzing information.

1. **Summarize**. Briefly summarize Medina's essay (which is itself a summary), including her main point and purpose and the major examples she gives. Who is her intended audience?

2. **Analyze**. Do Medina's examples all relate to her thesis statement? How do her topic sentences state what the paragraph will be about? What word does she repeat to link the thesis and support?

3. **Synthesize**. What is Medina's conclusion? What do you know about student services at your college? Ask three other students the same question and include them in your response.

CRITICAL READING
- Summarize
- Analyze
- Synthesize
- Evaluate

(More on p. 12.)

4. **Evaluate**. Does Medina achieve her purpose? Does her essay have the Four Basics of Good Illustration (see p. 87)? What effect did her essay have on you, and why?

Illustration at Work

The following is from an address that Juan Gonzalez made to a group of new students when he was Vice President for Student Affairs at the University of Texas, Austin.

Juan Gonzalez

Complete Learning

GUIDING QUESTION

What is the purpose of Student Affairs?

Courtesy Juan Gonzalez

Juan Gonzalez
Vice Chancellor of Student
Affairs, University of California,
San Diego

CRITICAL READING

■ Preview
■ Read
■ Pause
■ Review

(See pp. 4–11.)

1   **A**s new students, you are embarking on an incredibly exciting and challenging time, a time of expanding knowledge, relationships, viewpoints, and achievements. In my role as vice president, I am constantly striving to match that energy level so that we can offer the highest level of service on this very diverse campus. I frequently marvel at college students who seem to have an unlimited amount of energy that allows them to attend classes, read and study, maintain a social life, run for political office, pursue a hobby, play an intramural sport, volunteer for a worthy cause, hold down a job. We in the Division of Student Affairs strongly encourage activities outside the classroom that enrich the academic experience, as we recognize that a university education is enhanced through involvement in our campus community.

PAUSE: Why is Gonzalez surprised by students?

2   Last November, a group of Student Affairs staff, students, and faculty began work on creating a strategic plan for the division. They have been laboring diligently on this document, and I am excited to share with you the fruit of that labor, our newly developed Student Affairs Strategic Plan, which has as its motto "Student Affairs: Where Life and Learning Intersect."

PAUSE: How does Gonzalez address his audience in paragraph 2? What do we learn about that audience?

3   This phrase encapsulates the driving force behind the Division of Student Affairs. We exist, in essence, to help students succeed and grow, and we believe that growth and success must be measured in many ways. Academic success is one gauge of how well students are performing, but there are a variety of indicators other than grades. Those who take the most from their college experience are those who recognize that learning happens both inside and outside the classroom.

PAUSE: How does Gonzalez define success?

4   In fact, I recently had our units count the services they offer that are collaborative efforts with the academic side of the family, and a rough survey yielded 140 programs. This idea of integrated learning carries through most of what we do, whether it is a program to recruit the best students from around Texas like the Honors Colloquium, the increasingly

PAUSE: What do the capital letters in this paragraph tell you about the examples Gonzalez uses?

popular "Academic Community Centers" for studying and advising on site in the residence halls, Summer Orientation, or the professor-led Freshman Reading Round-Up book discussions.

Our Vision Statement

5   Our vision statement lights the path we are following to where we aspire to be:

> The Division of Student Affairs at The University of Texas at Austin seeks to become the premier organization of its kind. We envision a network of programs and services that excels in meeting students' out-of-classroom needs, complementing their academic experiences, and building community on a diverse campus. In doing so, we will contribute to developing citizens and leaders who will thrive in and enrich an increasingly complex world.

PAUSE: How does this paragraph relate to the introductory paragraph?

Our Mission

6   Our mission, or the explanation of what we do, is described this way:

> The Division of Student Affairs facilitates students' discovery of self and the world in which they live. We enhance students' educational experiences through programs and services that support academic success. We provide for fundamental needs, including shelter, nourishment, and a sense of security. We create environments that foster physical, emotional, and psychological wellness, and advance healthy lifestyles. Student Affairs builds communities, both real and virtual, that encourage inclusiveness, invite communication, and add to the cultural richness of the institution. We focus on personal development, including career decision making, problem solving, and group dynamics, challenging students to work both independently and as part of a team.

PAUSE: What does the vocabulary in this paragraph tell you about the purpose and audience of this piece? Point to specific examples.

7   The work group that wrote the strategic plan also composed a defining phrase to encapsulate Student Affairs: "Our passion is complete learning." These, I hope you will agree, are stirring words. We take our responsibility for providing an environment that is inclusive and promotes a healthy lifestyle seriously. We are committed to supporting you as you achieve your goals at this university.

PAUSE: What is "complete learning"?

Our Core Values

8   Sharing a fundamental belief in the value of Student Affairs and its ability to transform lives, we will pursue our vision by

- Focusing on the lifelong learning and personal growth of all members of the university community;
- Engendering a community that is inclusive, accessible, and secure;

- Conducting ourselves and our programs with the highest integrity;
- Enhancing our services by creating opportunities to collaborate and nurture partnerships;
- Challenging ourselves to move beyond the status quo and pursue higher levels of excellence with determination and enthusiasm;
- Strengthening a tradition of quality, compassion, and an unwavering belief in students and ourselves;
- Demonstrating the innovation and courage to adapt to changing conditions; and
- Realizing that both action and vision are necessary for a better future.

9 Our society benefits by having everyone educated, and education is a process that requires everyone to be engaged in the advancement of all peoples. The well-being of our state requires the next generation of leaders and scholars to understand our new world. This understanding means looking at the process of education as more than four years in college, the material in textbooks, or the contents of a classroom lecture but as a way to improve the world.

PAUSE: What is education, according to Gonzalez?

1. Who is the audience for Gonzalez's illustration? What is his purpose?
2. Carefully reread the Four Basics of Good Illustration (p. 87) and determine if Gonzalez's essay is a good example of illustration. Make notes to support your opinion.
3. What do you know about the services that are offered on your campus? If you know little, find out more, and comment on whether your college offers services like those that Gonzalez refers to.
4. Why does Gonzalez include the vision statement, mission statement, and core values in his address? Would the address be effective without these examples? Explain.
5. In your own words, state what you think Gonzalez says about what a good education is. Does he give you good examples? Do you agree with what he says?

Illustration in Everyday Life

The following is from the *New York Times*.

Rob Walker

Stuck on You

GUIDING QUESTION

What examples of bumper stickers does Walker give?

CRITICAL
READING
■ Preview
■ Read
■ Pause
■ Review
(See pp. 4–11.)

PAUSE:
Why doesn't
Walker
want to be
mistaken for a
Yankee?

1   My friend Scott once laughed in my face when I told him I did not like driving a car with Massachusetts plates in Texas. I am from Texas, you see, and when I visit my native state in a rental car, I don't want to be mistaken for a Yankee. Scott, incredulous and logical, pointed out that it really did not make the slightest difference what inferences drivers on the roads I traveled might make about my geographical roots because I would never have any real-life dealings with them. Who cares what strangers in other cars think about you? One answer is that a lot of people must care or there would be no such thing as bumper stickers.

PAUSE: What
is the purpose
of the
comment in
parentheses
in this
paragraph?
Why is it in
parentheses?

2   That doesn't mean that my friend didn't have a point, though: How much thought do we really put into the rather extraordinary number of identity signals that zoom by on highways or inch along in commuter traffic? It's possible that from time to time a Misfits or McCain message hits its mark, and somebody, somewhere, gives a thumbs up to another driver. (It's also plausible that some stickers inspire fellow motorists to extend another digit as a form of acknowledgment.) But the overwhelming majority of signals sent via bumper sticker almost certainly float unnoticed into the ether for the simple reason that nobody much cares. It's sad, really.

PAUSE: What
are tribal-
affiliation
stickers?

3   In addition to tribal-affiliation stickers—I Like This Band; I Root for That Sports Team; I Graduated From the Following Institution of Higher Learning—many bumper stickers attempt the more ambitious business of broadcasting some point of view on a matter of public contention, geopolitical policy, or even a philosophical mode of being. It's even more sad to conclude that nobody thinks about those either, but it turns out that somebody does or at least has: Jack Bowen, who teaches philosophy at Menlo School in Atherton, California. In a recent book called *If You Can Read This: The Philosophy of Bumper Stickers,* he not only thinks about bumper stickers but takes them seriously, evaluating the underlying worldviews they express.

PAUSE: What
political point
of view does
the sticker
reveal?

4   Consider, for example, the sticker "Against Abortion? Then Don't Have One!" The political point of view there is obvious enough. But, Bowen says, if we delve deeper, we find the suggestion that morality itself is up for grabs, resolved on a person-by-person, situation-by-situation basis. "This is not at all what we want to say morality is," he says. "It would make the idea of morality completely pointless." He says he takes issue with about 70 percent of the broader conclusions implied by the many bumper stickers he evaluates.

PAUSE: Why
does he say
that bumper
stickers "end
conversa-
tions"? How
does this
characteriza-
tion relate to
road rage?

5   Now, do we really need a philosopher to reveal that bumper stickers are simplistic? Probably not. We know that bumper stickers are about declaration, not dialogue; designed to end conversations, not start them. Possibly the most revelatory research to date on the subject was a 2008 Colorado State University study concluding that drivers who put bumper stickers and other decorations on their vehicles are 16 percent more likely to engage in road rage. It wasn't the message on the "territory markers,"

as a researcher called bumper stickers in an interview with *Nature News,* but the number of them that "predicted road rage better than vehicle value, condition or any of the things that we normally associate with aggressive driving."

6   Bowen concedes all this. But when he appears on radio call-in shows and the like to promote his book, he has learned that "people are really fired up about bumper stickers." Tellingly, however, the people he hears from almost never engage him with counter-interpretations of their own stickers (or even admit to having them). Instead they want explanations for messages they find baffling—or aggravating. "My Child Is an Honors Student" turns out to be one message that ticks off a surprising number of people. As it happens, that one used to vaguely annoy Bowen too, but when he reflected on it for the book, he concluded that it was a perfectly reasonable thing to have on a car and not deserving of the "My Child Beat Up Your Honor Student" response stickers it has inspired.

PAUSE: What questions do callers ask Bowen?

7   Still, the general reaction to this benign message suggests that when the signals we send are noticed, we might not be happy with how they are received. This brings us to the most puzzling sticker Bowen evaluates: "Don't Judge Me." He argues that passing judgment is not such a bad thing. But this sticker struck me as an even more extreme version of my own silly worries about license-plate signifiers: Why would someone go out of the way to demand neutrality from strangers? And yet this beguiling paradox of a message might capture what bumper stickers are really about. Probably no one thinks about the signals sent along the highway more than those sending them. And bumper stickers are all about announcing judgments, not accepting them.

PAUSE: What sentence in paragraph 7 answers a question asked in paragraph 1?

PAUSE: What is a paradox? Why does Walker say this paradox is "beguiling"?

1.   Briefly summarize Walker's essay. What is his *purpose*?

2.   What *examples* does he give of bumper stickers?

3.   What stereotype does Walker start the essay with? Is this strategy effective? What does it tell readers about Walker?

4.   What *transitions* does Walker use to move readers through his examples?

5.   What is another good title for Walker's essay?

6.   What types of bumper stickers have you seen? What attitudes do they express?

Write an Illustration Essay

Write your own illustration essay on one of the following topics or on a topic of your own choice. Use ILLUSTRATION AT A GLANCE as a basic organizer (p. 90), and follow the Writing Guide: Illustration checklist as you write and revise (p. 98).

COLLEGE	• Discuss some of the activities, services, and programs offered on your campus. Choose a specific audience (new students, prospective students, a student council) and a purpose (encouraging enrollment, getting students involved, or making changes).
	• Write about something you learned in another course, and give examples to explain it to a friend who has not taken the course.
WORK	• Tell someone applying for a job like yours what his or her typical responsibilities might be.
	• Demonstrate to an interviewer the following statement: "I am a detail-oriented employee."
EVERYDAY LIFE	• Write a letter to your landlord about how your apartment's maintenance needs to be done more regularly.
	• Write a letter to your town council. Identify at least three examples of improvements that the town could make to improve the quality of life for residents in the area.

WRITING GUIDE: Illustration

STEPS IN ILLUSTRATION	HOW TO DO THE STEPS
☐ Focus.	• Think about your topic and what your audience knows about it.
☐ Explore your topic. See Chapter 2.	• Prewrite to give examples of your topic.
☐ Write a thesis statement. Topic + Main point = Thesis See Chapter 3.	• Write a working thesis that includes your topic and main point about it. You might also include some examples you will give in your support paragraphs.
☐ Support your thesis. See Chapter 3.	• Choose at least three examples that demonstrate your main point. • Consider what details about the examples your reader needs to know.

(Continued)

STEPS IN ILLUSTRATION	HOW TO DO THE STEPS
☐ **Write a draft.** See Chapter 4.	• Arrange your examples in order of importance or time. • Write topic sentences for each major example. • Write a paragraph for each example, giving details about the examples.
☐ **Revise your draft.** See Chapter 4.	• Make sure that your examples and details all relate to your main point. • Add transitions. • Improve your introduction, thesis, and conclusion.
☐ **Edit your revised draft.** See Chapters 16 through 18.	• Correct errors in grammar, spelling, word use, and punctuation.
☐ **Evaluate your writing.**	• Does it have the Four Basics of Good Illustration? (p. 87) • Is this the best I can do?

Reflect on the Process

Look at your writing from this chapter, from your prewriting through revision and editing, and consider these questions:

1. What was the most difficult part of the process for you? Why?

2. Did the feedback you got on your initial draft provide you with information you could use to make changes in your draft? If not, what can you do to improve the feedback you get next time? What specific questions do you need your reviewers to answer for you?

3. What will you do differently the next time you write an illustration essay?

4. Talk to someone who has taken courses in your major or who is working in your field. How is illustration used in your major or career? What kinds of illustration writing tasks can you expect in the future?

7

Description

Writing That Creates Pictures with Words

Understand What Description Is

Description is writing that creates a clear and vivid impression of the topic. Description translates your experience of a person, place, or thing into words, often by appealing to the senses—sight, hearing, smell, taste, and touch.

Four Basics of Good Description

1 It creates a main impression — an overall effect, feeling, or image — that brings the person, place, or object to life for the reader (main point).

2 It uses specific examples to support the main impression (primary support).

3 It supports those examples with details that appeal to the five senses (secondary support).

4 It organizes supporting examples and details, usually according to space or order of importance (logical organization).

In the following paragraph, each number corresponds to one of the Four Basics of Good Description.

4
Supporting details are presented in spatial order.

1 Nojoqui Falls is a special place to me because its beauty provides a break from human worries. **2** At the start of the trail leading to the falls, the smell and sound of oak trees and pine trees make visitors feel they are up for the journey. **3** The sun hitting the trees makes the air fresh with a leafy aroma. Overhead, the wind blows through the leaves, making a soft noise. **2** Closer to the waterfall, the shade from the trees creates a shielding blanket. **3** When the sun comes out, it fills the place with light, showing the vapor coming out of the trees and plants. **2** To the left of the trail are rocks that are positioned perfectly for viewing the waterfall. **3** Water splashes as it hits the rocks. **2** The waterfall itself is beautiful, like a transparent, sparkling window of diamonds. **3** The water is so clear that objects on the other side are visible. It is like a never-ending stream of water that splashes onto the rocks. **1** The total effect of these sights, sounds, and smells is a setting where daily cares can be set aside for a while.

4 Supporting details are presented in spatial order.

— Liliana Ramirez, student

Being able to describe something or someone accurately and in detail is important both in college and in other settings. Describing something well involves using specific, concrete details. Here are some ways that you might use description:

COLLEGE	For a science lab report, you describe the physical and chemical properties of an element.
WORK	You write a letter to your office manager describing the unacceptable conditions of the office refrigerator.
EVERYDAY LIFE	You describe a jacket that you left at the movies to the lost-and-found department.

First Basic: Main Point in Description

In descriptive writing, your **main point** conveys the main impression you want your readers to see. Take another look at the paragraph starting on page 100. What if the topic sentence had been the following?

> I love Nojoqui Falls.

You would not know why the writer likes the place from reading this sentence. But the actual topic sentence conveys a main impression of the falls and lets you know why this place is important to the writer.

> Nojoqui Falls is a special place to me because its beauty provides a break from human worries.

This statement provides a preview of what is to come, helping the audience read and understand the description.

The thesis statement in description essays typically includes the topic and the main impression about it that the writer wants to convey.

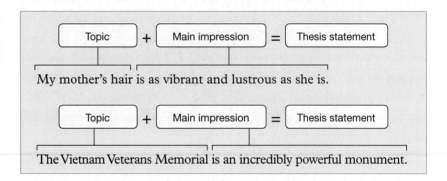

Second and Third Basics: Support in Description

Good description uses specific, concrete details to create the sights, sounds, smells, tastes, and textures that support and show your main impression.

SIGHT	SOUND	SMELL
Colors	Loud/soft	Sweet/sour
Shapes	Piercing/soothing	Sharp/mild
Sizes	Continuous/off-and-on	Good (like what?)
Patterns	Pleasant/unpleasant (how?)	Bad (rotten?)
Brightness	High/low	New (like what?)
Does it look like anything else?	Does it sound like anything else?	Does it smell like anything else?

TASTE	TOUCH
Good (What does *good* taste like?)	Hard/soft
Bad (What does *bad* taste like?)	Liquid/solid
Bitter/sugary	Rough/smooth
Metallic	Dry/oily
Burning/spicy	Textures
Does it taste like anything else?	Does it feel like anything else?

As you think about the main impression you want to convey, ask yourself: what sensory details might bring this subject to life? Add additional details to convey each sensation more accurately or vividly.

Fourth Basic: Organization in Description

Description may use any of the orders of organization, depending on the purpose of the description. If you are describing what someone or something looks like, you might use **spatial order**, the most common way to organize description. If you are describing something you want to sell, you might use **order of importance**, ending with the feature that would be most appealing to potential buyers.

For more on spatial order and order of importance, see page 49.

Use transitions to help readers move smoothly from detail to detail.

Common Transitions in Description

TRANSITIONS TO SHOW SPATIAL ORDER	TRANSITIONS TO SHOW ORDER OF IMPORTANCE
above/underneath	even more
beyond	more
in front of/behind	the most
to the left/right	the most intense
	the strongest

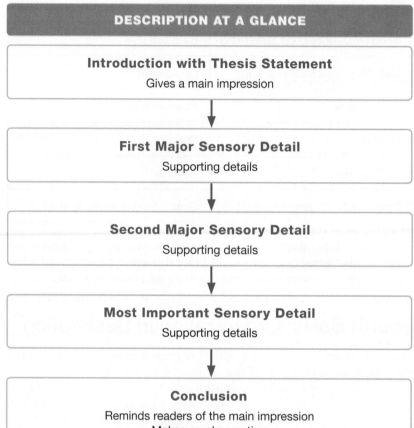

DESCRIPTION AT A GLANCE

Introduction with Thesis Statement
Gives a main impression

↓

First Major Sensory Detail
Supporting details

↓

Second Major Sensory Detail
Supporting details

↓

Most Important Sensory Detail
Supporting details

↓

Conclusion
Reminds readers of the main impression
Makes an observation
Note: A descriptive essay may include more than three major sensory details, depending on your purpose.

Read and Analyze Description

Read the following three examples of description—from college, the workplace, and everyday life—and answer the questions that accompany them. For each essay, review the Four Basics of Good Description (p. 100) and practice the critical reading process explained in Chapter 1.

Description in College

The following description essay was written by a student for a course assignment in her first college writing course. She was asked to describe an important photograph.

Florence Bagley

Photograph of My Father

GUIDING QUESTION

What does Bagley see in the photo of her father?

CRITICAL READING
▪ Preview
▪ Read
▪ Pause
▪ Review

(See pp. 4–11.)

1   This old black-and-white photograph of my father fills me with conflicting emotions. He died young, and this photo is one of the few that my family has of him. The picture seems to show a strong, happy man, young and smiling, but to me it also reveals his weakness.

2   Looking at this picture of my father, I feel how much I have lost. In it, my father is sitting upright in a worn plaid easy chair. It was "his" chair, and when he was at work, I'd curl up in it and smell his aftershave lotion and cigarette smoke. His pitch-black hair is so dark that it blends into the background of the photo. His eyes, though indistinct in this photo, were a deep, dark brown. Although the photo is faded around my father's face, I still can make out his strong jaw and the cleft in his chin. In the photo, my father is wearing a clean white T-shirt that reveals his thick, muscular arms. Resting in the crook of his left arm is my younger brother, who was about one year old at the time. Both of them are smiling.

PAUSE: Underline the sensory details in this paragraph. What mood do these details create?

3   However, when I study the photo, my eyes are drawn to the can of beer that sits on the table next to him. Against my will, I begin to feel resentful. I have so many wonderful memories of my father. Whether he was carrying me on his shoulders, picking me up from school, or teaching me to draw, he always made time for me. All of these memories fade when I see that beer. From what I remember, he always made time for that beer as well. The smell of beer was always on him, the cool, sweating can always within reach.

PAUSE: How has the mood changed? What transition signals the change?

4   In this photo, my father appears to be a strong man; however, looks are deceiving. My father died at the age of thirty-seven because he was an alcoholic. I was eleven when he died, and I really did not understand that his drinking was the reason for his death. I just knew that he left me without a father and the possibility of more memories. He should have been strong enough to stop drinking.

PAUSE: What conflicting feelings does the picture create?

5   In spite of the resentment I may feel about his leaving me, this photo holds many loving memories as well. It is of my father—the strong, wonderful man and the alcoholic—and it is the most precious thing I own. Although I would much rather have him here, I stay connected to him when I look at it.

1.   **Summarize.** Briefly summarize Bagley's essay, including her main impression and major support. What is her purpose? How does she feel about the photo and her father?

CRITICAL
READING

■ Summarize
■ Analyze
■ Synthesize
■ Evaluate

(See p. 12.)

2. **Analyze**. How do the second and third paragraphs create different impressions? How do these paragraphs and paragraph 4 support the main impression in the first paragraph?

3. **Synthesize**. How does Bagley's essay prove the saying, "Photographs can be deceiving"? Find a photograph that deceives. How can you apply what you know about reading visuals to Bagley's essay and the photo you have found?

4. **Evaluate**. Does Bagley achieve her purpose? Can you visualize her father? Does her essay have the Four Basics of Good Description (see p. 100)? What questions do you have for the author? Would you like any additional information?

Description at Work

The following is a passage from the novel *Still Water Saints*. Note that there is no thesis statement because this is not an essay but rather part of a novel.

Alex Espinoza

CRITICAL
READING

■ Preview
■ Read
■ Pause
■ Review

(See pp. 4–11.)

From *Still Water Saints*

GUIDING QUESTION

What kinds of sensory details does Alex Espinoza use?

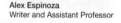

Alex Espinoza
Writer and Assistant Professor

Courtesy Alex Espinoza

PAUSE: What impression do you have of the area so far? Which specific words create this impression?

1   The iron security gate unfolded like the bellows of an accordion as Perla pulled it along the rail in front of the door. She snapped the padlock shut, turned around the corner of the building, and headed home. Her house was close, just across the empty lot next to the shopping center. Wild sage and scrub grew beside the worn path that cut through the field. Boys sometimes rode their bikes there, doing tricks and wheelies as they bumped over mounds and breaks, falling down, laughing and scraping their knees, their faces coated with grime. Their tires left thin tracks that looped around the salt cedar trees, around the soiled mattresses and old washers and sinks that were dumped there.

2   People told of a curse on these grounds, of a group of monks traveling through Agua Mansa in the days when California was still a part of Mexico, back before states were shapes on a map. They said a tribe of Indians massacred the monks; they skinned them and scattered their body parts around the lot for the crows. Still others said Mexican settlers had been lynched from the branches of the cedars by Anglos who stole their land for the railroads. Seeing a piece of stone, Perla wondered about the monks

and those men dangling from branches. *A tooth? Part of a toe?* Empty soda cans and wrappers were caught under boulders and discarded car parts. *What would the monks think about having a tire for a headstone, a couch for a marker?* She thought of her husband, Guillermo, of his tombstone, of the thick, green lawns of the cemetery where he was buried.

3   When she reached her house and stepped inside, the air was warm and silent. Perla put her purse down on the rocking chair near the front door and went around, pushing the lace curtains back and cracking open the windows. She breathed in the scent of wood smoke from someone's fireplace down the street, a smell that reminded her of her father toasting garbanzo beans. She went into the kitchen and looked for something to eat.

4   Dinner was a bowl of oatmeal with two slices of toast, which she took out to the patio. The night was cold, and the steam from the oatmeal rose up and fogged her glasses as she spooned it in her mouth. Police sirens wailed down the street, and dogs answered, their cries lonely and beautiful. She looked up, and in the flashing lights saw a set of glowing red eyes.

5   Perla flicked on the porch light. It was an opossum, its fur dingy and gray, the tips and insides of its ears bright pink. It stood motionless, behind the trunk of the organ pipe cactus, staring at her. It climbed to the top of the fence, making a low, faint jingle as it moved. Perla looked again; a small brass bell was tied to a piece of red yarn knotted around the opossum's tail. She took her spoon and threw it. When it hit the bottom of the fence, the animal darted, the clatter of the bell frantic. The opossum disappeared behind the branches of the avocado tree and down the other side of the fence into the empty lot, the ringing growing fainter and fainter.

6   From under the kitchen sink, behind the pile of cloths and old sponges she could never bring herself to throw away, was a bottle of rum. She poured some into a cup and took a drink. Then she took another. The warmth calmed her nerves.

7   She imagined the ghosts of the dead monks and the lynched men rising up from the ground, awakened by her thoughts. Curls of gray smoke at first, they slowly took human form. They walked in a straight line, one in front of the other. A slow progression followed the opossum's tracks through the lot and back home.

8   She took another drink and closed her eyes. That animal was a messenger. It was letting her know that something was out there. It was coming.

1.   What is Espinoza's purpose?

2.   What does he assume readers know about Agua Mansa?

3.   How does the final paragraph contrast with the introductory one in terms of the impressions they create?

4.   How are you left feeling about the place? Why? Choose several details that give you that impression.

Margin notes:

PAUSE: How does this paragraph change the mood? Point to specific words that indicate the shift.

PAUSE: How does the impression change here? Why?

PAUSE: How does the last sentence of this paragraph change the mood of the scene?

PAUSE: Underline the sensory details in this paragraph.

PAUSE: What impression does the final paragraph create?

Description in Everyday Life

The following is a letter that Jennifer Orlando wrote for a **helium.com** contest.

Jennifer Orlando

CRITICAL
READING

■ Preview
■ Read
■ Pause
■ Review

(See pp. 4–11.)

Rattlesnake Canyon: A Place of Peace and Beauty

GUIDING QUESTION

What impression does Orlando create?

PAUSE:
What do you expect the rest of the essay will be about? Which words provide clues for the reader?

1   Today I went for a hike in Rattlesnake Canyon in my hometown of Grand Junction, Colorado. I had been a little down and I just wanted to get out and forget my troubles. Instead, though, I came back happy and feeling really lucky to be alive. Rattlesnake Canyon is incredibly beautiful, peaceful, and restorative.

2   The hiking path is lined with gorgeous desert plants that go on for acres. There are many varieties of cactus, many with long white spines reaching out of the green "leaves." I never thought of cactus as being colorful, but they can be purple or about five shades of green. Some of them have "flowers" that look like huge, bright red radishes. Others have tiny yellow flowers growing beside the sharp spines, and still others have lavender flowers sprouting. There are all kinds of yellow flowering plants—some pale, and some darker, like an egg yolk. Swarms of yellow butterflies flutter around them, dancing in and out of the branches. I just started laughing when I saw them; it was so perfect. My favorite plant is sage, again lots of different kinds. Some have billions of little purple flowers, and they are about four feet tall. Others are a silvery green, and when you run your hand over the leaves, they give off this savory scent that is barely sweet and makes me think of my mother's stuffing at Thanksgiving. It is sage, the herb. The air just smells all herby from sage, juniper, and other smells I cannot identify. Some low bushes have bright red flowers—some scarlet, some rust, and some orangy. The desert plants are beautiful. The desert is so much more than just sand.

PAUSE: What impression does paragraph 2 create? Underline details that contribute.

3   As I went along, I was surrounded by the huge rocks of the canyon, like a mini-Grand Canyon. At the base, the rocks are a dark, rusty color. As they rise up, they have about ten different layers of color—from a kind of light grey, to darker grey, to pale red, and finally to a brilliant red that shines in the sunlight from flecks of mineral in them. Those layers of rock reveal the many different climates the area has experienced over billions of years, including being underwater several times. I was literally surrounded by these looming rocks, thousands of feet high.

PAUSE:
How are the sensory details in this paragraph organized?

4   Best of all, though, is the sky. The towering, multicolored cliffs are met by the bluest sky imaginable. There were no clouds, and this blue was dark and beautiful against the red of the rock. The sun was bright, as it usually is here, and everything was so big, so colorful, so intense that I felt lucky to be alive. There is something about all this beauty that has been here for billions of years that makes you feel as if your problems are unimportant: it gives peace.

5   Rattlesnake Canyon and places like it give us perspective on our lives. The beauty and eternity of nature assure us that so much in our lives is small compared with our surroundings. It opens our senses if we allow it to: we see, smell, hear, and feel more closely. These places restore our faith in forces that far surpass us in power and endurance. I left the canyon with my spirit restored. Nature is open to everyone, and we should take the time to let it work its wonders on our humanity.

PAUSE:
What final impression does Orlando create?

1.   Summarize Orlando's description of Rattlesnake Canyon and its effect on her.

2.   What details and impressions contribute to the effect?

3.   What experience have you had of a place affecting you, either positively or negatively? What details caused your feeling?

4.   Study Orlando's use of color words. How does she modify basic color words (red, yellow, blue) to help the reader see them more clearly?

Write a Description Essay

Write your own description essay on one of the following topics or on a topic of your own choice. Use DESCRIPTION AT A GLANCE as a basic organizer (p. 104), and follow the Writing Guide: Description checklist as you write and revise (p. 110).

COLLEGE	• Describe your favorite place on campus so that a reader understands why you like to be there. • Describe an event, place, device, or experiment that you learned about in one of your courses.
WORK	• Describe a product your company makes, or a service it provides. • Describe a specific area at work that you see every day but have not really noticed. Look at it with new eyes.
EVERYDAY LIFE	• Describe a family heirloom or a traditional food that is important in your family. Consider your extended family or future generations as an audience. • Describe a local landmark, such as a well-known restaurant, a monument, or historic site.

WRITING GUIDE: Description	
STEPS IN DESCRIPTION	**HOW TO DO THE STEPS**
☐ **Focus.**	• Think about what you want to describe and who your readers are.
☐ **Explore your topic.** See Chapter 2.	• Make sure your topic can be described in a short essay. • Prewrite to generate sensory images and details.
☐ **Write a thesis statement.** Topic + <u>Main impression</u> = Thesis See Chapter 3.	• Decide your purpose for writing a description and what picture you want to create for your readers.
☐ **Support your thesis.** See Chapter 3.	• Add images and details that will bring what you are describing to life for your audience. • Use your senses to create the images.
☐ **Write a draft.** See Chapter 4.	• Arrange your main point and the images that help create it in a logical order. • Write topic sentences for the supporting images and details that show them.
☐ **Revise your draft.** See Chapter 4.	• Reread your essay, adding vivid details. • Add transitions to help show your reader your main impression of your topic. • Improve your introduction, thesis, and conclusion.
☐ **Edit your revised draft.** See Chapters 16 through 18.	• Correct errors in grammar, spelling, word use, and punctuation.
☐ **Evaluate your writing.**	• Does it have the Four Basics of Good Description (p. 100)? • Is this the best I can do?

Reflect on the Process

Look at your writing from this chapter, from your prewriting through revision and editing, and consider these questions:

1. What was the most difficult part of the process for you? Why?

2. Did the feedback you got on your initial draft provide you with information you could use to make changes in your draft? If not, what can you do to improve the feedback you get next time? What specific questions do you need your reviewers to answer for you?

3. What will you do differently the next time you write a description essay?

4. Talk to someone who has taken courses in your major or who is working in your field. How is description used in your major or career? What kinds of description writing tasks can you expect in the future?

8

Process Analysis

Writing That Explains How Things Happen

Understand What Process Analysis Is

Process analysis explains either how to do something (so your readers can do it) or how something works (so your readers can understand it). Both types of process analysis present the steps involved in the process.

> ### Four Basics of Good Process Analysis
>
> **1** It explains a process so that readers can perform the steps or understand how something works (main point).
>
> **2** It presents the essential steps in the process (primary support).
>
> **3** It gives details about each step (secondary support).
>
> **4** It arranges the steps, usually in chronological order (logical organization).

In the following paragraph, each number corresponds to one of the Four Basics of Good Process Analysis.

4 Steps arranged in chronological order.

1 Two teenagers, Robbie and Brittany Bergquist, wanted to help American soldiers in combat zones call home, so in 2004 they founded the organization Cell Phones for Soldiers, which has proved to be extremely successful. **2** First, Robbie and Brittany pooled their own money, a total of $14. Realizing that would not go far, they then decided to hold fund-raising events. **3** Next, they enlisted friends and family to help them organize a series of bake sales and car washes. As people learned about their efforts, more joined them, and they began to raise serious money to purchase phones. 2 Second, they started another fund-raising initiative: recycling old cell phones. 3 They collected old phones and brought them to a recycling company. With this money, they purchased minutes on phone cards for the soldiers. Then, they organized volunteers to wrap and send the cards to soldiers who had heard about their work and had contacted them. 2 To date, they have provided over 60 million minutes of phone time. 3 Robbie and Brittany continue their efforts to include not only soldiers overseas but also returning veterans who are in the hospital.

4 Steps arranged in chronological order.

Whenever you give someone directions about how to do something or explain how something works, you are using process analysis. Here are some ways you might use process analysis.

COLLEGE	In an information technology course, you write an essay explaining the process for implementing a new data management system.
WORK	The office has a new security system, and you are asked to write a memo to employees explaining how to access their work areas during and after normal business hours.
EVERYDAY LIFE	You write directions telling your child how to operate the washing machine.

First Basic: Main Point in Process Analysis

Your **purpose** in process analysis is to explain a process so that readers can either do it themselves or understand how it works. Your **main point** lets your readers know what you think about that process—for example, whether it is easy or complicated.

The website *MapQuest.com* can get you from where you are to where you want to go in several easy steps.

A thesis statement for a process analysis usually identifies the process and the point you want to make about it. The thesis should also suggest what you want your readers to know or learn about the process.

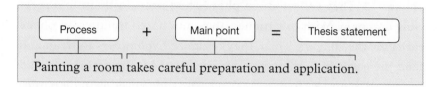

In process analysis, include your thesis statement in your introduction so that readers know from the start what the process and the purpose are.

Second and Third Basics: Support in Process Analysis

A clear process analysis presents all the essential steps in the process; these steps constitute the **major support**. Each step is explained by supporting details. For example, the writer of the thesis *Successful weight loss is a challenge, but it starts with some simple steps* might use the following essential steps and details to explain the steps.

ESSENTIAL STEPS

STEP 1: Get rid of the junk food in your home and commit not to buy any.

SUPPORTING DETAILS

It is tempting but is not nutritional

It includes chips, candy, and any other unhealthy foods you snack on

Do not shop when you are hungry

Stay away from the junk food aisles

STEP 2: Keep a list of everything you eat each day.

SUPPORTING DETAILS

When you are tempted, wait 5 minutes before eating

Write down each item just before or just after you eat it

Include everything, even just tastes

→

STEP 3: Weigh yourself just once a week.

SUPPORTING DETAILS

Not daily because weight fluctuates

Record your weight

STEP 4: Reward yourself, but not with food.

SUPPORTING DETAILS

Call a friend to share your success

Go to a movie you want to see

Fourth Basic: Organization in Process Analysis

Because process analysis explains how to do something or how something works, it usually uses **chronological (time) order**. Start with the first step, and then explain each step in the order that it should occur.

For more on chronological order, see page 48.

Add transitional words and sentences to your essay to help readers follow each step in the process.

Common Transitions in Process Analysis

after	eventually	meanwhile	soon
as	finally	next	then
at last	first	now	when
before	last	second	while
during	later	since	

PROCESS ANALYSIS AT A GLANCE

Introduction with Thesis Statement
Includes the process you are describing

↓

First Step in Process
Details about the first step (how to do it or how it works)

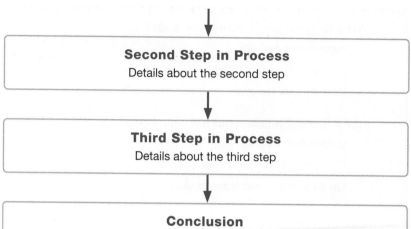

Read and Analyze Process Analysis

Read the following three process analysis essays—from college, work, and everyday life—and answer the questions that accompany them. For each essay, practice the critical reading process explained in Chapter 1.

Process Analysis in College

CRITICAL
READING
■ Preview
■ Read
■ Pause
■ Review

(See pp. 4–11.)

Daniel Flanagan

The Choice to Do It Over Again

GUIDING QUESTION

What did Flanagan do over?

PAUSE:
Why does
Flanagan
refer to
"your" typical
degenerate?

PAUSE:
What does
the second
sentence
mean?

1   I do not know why I came to the decision to become a loser, but I know I made the choice at a young age. Sometime in the middle of fourth grade, I stopped trying. By the time I was in seventh grade, I was your typical degenerate: lazy, rebellious, disrespectful. I had lost all social graces. I was terminally hip and fatally cool.

2   Not long after that, I dropped out of school and continued my downward spiral. Hard physical labor was the consequence for the choices I made as an adolescent. At the age of twenty-one, I was hopelessly lost and

using drugs as a way to deal with the fact that I was illiterate and stuck in a dead-end job carrying roof shingles up a ladder all day.

3　　But now I believe in do-overs, in the chance to do it all again. And I believe that do-overs can be made at any point in your life, if you have the right motivation. Mine came from a surprising source.

4　　It was September 21, 2002, when my son Blake was born. It's funny that after a life of avoiding responsibility, now I was in charge of something so fragile. Over the years, as I grew into the title of Dad, I began to learn something about myself. In a way, Blake and I were both learning to walk, talk, work, and play for the first time. I began my do-over.

PAUSE: Why did Flanagan decide to change his life?

5　　It took me almost three years to learn how to read. I started with my son's books. Over and over, I practiced reading books to him until I remembered all the words in every one of them. I began to wonder if it were possible for me to go back to school. I knew I wanted to be a good role model, so after a year-and-a-half and a lot of hard work, I passed my GED test on my son's fourth birthday. This may not sound like much, and I am not trying to get praise for doing something that should have been done in the first place, but all things considered it was one of the best days in my life. Today, I am a full-time college student, studying to become a sociologist.

PAUSE: Underline the steps in Flanagan's do-over.

6　　Growing up, I always heard these great turn-around stories of triumph over shortcomings. But I never thought they applied to me. Now I believe it is a choice anyone can make: to do it all over again.

1.　**Summarize.** Briefly summarize Flanagan's essay, including the process he describes and the major steps.

2.　**Analyze.** How does the title set up the essay? Why do you think Flanagan placed his thesis somewhere other than the first paragraph? How is his concluding sentence tied to his thesis statement?

3.　**Synthesize.** What has Flanagan learned about choices? How does this relate to other stories and choices you have experienced or read about?

4.　**Evaluate.** What is Flanagan's purpose for writing, and does he achieve it? Does he give enough information? Is the process he went through clear? Does his essay use the Four Basics of Good Process Analysis (p. 112)?

CRITICAL THINKING
- **Summarize**
- **Analyze**
- **Synthesize**
- **Evaluate**

(More on p. 12.)

Process Analysis at Work

The following is from a report that a nurse prepared for a patient's file to document the steps taken to treat her. The report shows that when a nurse on the team and a resident disagreed as to the treatment called for, the nurse called for another opinion. This type of communication is frequent among medical personnel.

Patty Maloney

Clinical Nurse Specialist

CRITICAL
READING
■ Preview
■ Read
■ Pause
■ Review

(See pp. 4–11.)

**COMBINING
MODES:**
If you have
already
studied
illustration,
note that
illustration is
used here to
give examples
of steps in
the process.
Also, note
that the report
uses narration
within the
process.

PAUSE: What
do you think
will happen
next?

**pneumo-
thorax:** a
collapsed
lung caused
by air leaking
into the space
between the
lung and
chest wall

Patient Report

GUIDING QUESTION

How did Maloney and others save a child's life?

1   **Patient:** (name), female, age 8, with tumor and disease progression

2   **Symptoms at arrival:** Child had not eaten much for two days and was withdrawn and uncommunicative.

3   **Treatment process:** First, we needed to determine if the child was in immediate danger or in need of further medications for pain control. We took her vital signs, which were within the range of normal for her, with a slightly elevated heart rate. Then we interviewed the child's mother to see if she had administered any breakthrough pain medication during the last 24 hours. We gave the child a short-term pain medication.

4   As a next step, we had a discussion with the doctor in the unit, and we then administered a breakthrough pain medication. We closely monitored the patient's vital signs, particularly noting if the heart rate came down. We were documenting the signs every hour formally but also checked on the child's status in the Intensive Care Unit every 15 minutes.

5   During one check, one of our nurses noted that the child looked pale, and her breathing was somewhat shallow. The nurse knew that the child had fragile lungs and felt that she was at risk of a **pneumothorax** and of collecting fluid causing a possible rupture of the lung lining and collapse of the lung. Following procedure, the nurse immediately alerted the resident, who felt that the child was fine and suggested that nothing but continued observation was necessary.

6   The nurse disagreed with the resident's diagnosis and at that point sent another nurse to page the attending physician for another opinion. In the meantime, while waiting for the attending, the nurse called for an X-ray. She then pulled the cart over to the patient in preparation for inserting a tube into the lung cavity to reinflate the lung. When the attending physician arrived and was briefed, he agreed with the nurse's diagnosis. The tube was quickly inserted, and the collapse of the lung was avoided.

7   The child continues in observation in the ICU. Her condition is stable.

1.   Briefly summarize Maloney's report.

2.   Although a description of a treatment process, the report does not give many details. What is the purpose of the report? What does the lack of detail tell you about the intended audience?

3.   How would the report differ if its purpose was to teach new nurses how to do a particular procedure?

4. Write a possible thesis statement for the report.

5. Write a possible concluding statement.

Process Analysis in Everyday Life

Michael Gates Gill was born into a wealthy family, grew up in a mansion, attended Yale University, and had a job as Creative Director of the largest advertising agency in the world. After losing his job, getting divorced, losing most of his money, and being diagnosed with a brain tumor, he took a job at Starbucks that turned his life around and led him to write the best-seller *How Starbucks Saved My Life*, from which the following excerpt is taken. (For this reading, you do not need to underline the major support or circle transitions.)

Michael Gates Gill

How I Learned to Be a Barista

GUIDING QUESTION

What are the steps that Gill learns, and what else does he learn during his first day?

Courtesy of Darien Library, CT

barista:
Italian for "bartender." Starbucks servers are called *baristas.*

CRITICAL READING
■ Preview
■ Read
■ Pause
■ Review

(See pp. 4–11.)

1   **"G**et out to the registers, Mike," my boss Crystal encouraged me. "And be sure to make eye contact and connect with conversation."

I had heard those words on the training video, but I was more concerned with just handling the cash so that I did not make a perfect fool of myself. Unfortunately, now the kids from school arrived.

Joann came over to me, though, and helped me put the drawer in.

PAUSE:
Why was Gill concerned about the kids from school coming in?

"The computer will show you the correct change, and the great thing is that the Guest will see the numbers, too, so they can catch you if you get it wrong. You will do fine, Mike."

5   "But I'm terrible with money."

"So were my first two husbands. Just let the register do the work."

I smiled. That was a good mantra.

A guy stepped up to my register to order. He had no idea that he was dealing with a person who had never done this before.

"I want a Tall Mocha."

10   I called down to Tawana, an attractive but combative barista on the espresso bar: "Tall Mocha."

PAUSE: So far, what steps in the process has Gill presented?

"Tall Mocha," Tawana called back to me, confirming that she had gotten the order right.

I looked at the register. On the screen I read the words "Tall" and "Mocha," just like on the computer training module. I jabbed at them with my finger. Sure enough, it worked, and the price came up on my screen.

The guy handed me five dollars.

The screen displayed the option "Five dollars" in a box, so I punched the box.

15   Then, the register opened, and the screen displayed the exact change I should hand the guy: $2.73. I dug out the change from my drawer. The guy looked at it and stuck it in his pocket and made his way to the espresso bar to pick up his drink.

PAUSE: What steps does the register do for the barista?

My screen, about the size of a small television, read, "Close your drawer."

I closed my drawer, and said to myself, *Hey, you can do this!*

Then, the next Guest stepped up, a young lady who was clearly pregnant.

"Just a Decaf Tall Coffee," she said.

PAUSE: Why does Gill include so much dialogue (in quotation marks)?

20   I punched in Tall, took her money, gave her the change, closed the drawer, and turned to get a cup of coffee for her. Fresh coffee was right behind me, with the cups. I gave one to her.

She gave me a big smile, as though I were already a friend. "My name's Rachel. I have another child on the way. I have to stick to Decaf for a while. Can't wait to get back on the hard stuff."

PAUSE: What has Gill just realized?

I had a sudden realization that people might treat me the way they were said to treat bartenders.... They wanted to engage with someone serving them the good stuff. The afternoon went surprisingly well, despite the constant stream of customers.

As evening fell, it got even busier, but Joann came over a couple of times to help me out. The line moved smoothly, with people ordering Single Pump Mocha or Tall Latte. I was supposed to call out the size, name of drink, and any "customizing" such as One Tall One Pump Mocha. Often I would get the order wrong and start with One Pump Mocha, forgetting to call the size ... or call for a Tall Latte forgetting to mention the Guest wanted it with skim milk. Sometimes, Guests would order Single Pump Mocha, or they would order a drink backward, starting with the milk, then the syrup, then the size, and I would repeat what they said and call it out to Tawana. Tawana would correct me at the top of her lungs, putting the order in the right way. It was humiliating for me, but I learned fast.

PAUSE: How does Tawana help Gill learn the job?

Also, it was a gift to me that Tawana had such a large, commanding voice. I had been worried about getting the orders straight, and I never missed Tawana's powerful calls. And I found that by leaning over the register, closer to the Guests, I could also hear them clearly.

25   "Ask if you have any questions," Joann said. "Just ask."

And I did. I found that the Guests didn't seem to mind helping me get their request just right.

That night, around 7:00 p.m., I was surprised to see the store grow really busy. I had thought coffee was something you picked up on the way to work, but it clearly was now an essential pick-me-up on the way home as well. I noticed a businessman enter the store and join the growing line. When I had been on the *other* side of the bar, I had worked so hard just to get a prospective client like this well-dressed man to return a call. Now, my customers were literally waiting in line for my services, I thought to myself. How funny.

The businessman stepped up in line and told me, "Double Macchiato."

This was Starbucks language. I had a hard time figuring out what it translated to on the cash register screen. I started to feel flushed as I punched at various combinations incorrectly.

30   "You are new here, right?" the man asked. I looked at him. Was he going to complain to Crystal and get me fired on my first day at the register?

But he smiled at my look of panic.

"Don't worry, you'll get it."

He actually took the time to encourage me. Wow. I looked back at the screen with a renewed clarity of mind. Double Macchiato. Hit Tall, then Macchiato. Simple.

The businessman wasn't the only one to try to set me at ease.

35   "Welcome to the neighborhood," one lady said.

Another guy with an open shirt who looked like a hippie commented, "I'm glad to see they are hiring older people."

Older?! Okay, so I wasn't so happy with this comment, but I appreciated his attitude. There was no denying it: I was older, at least a generation or two older than most **Partners** so it was good to be welcomed even if it was for my conspicuous seniority.

Around eight o'clock, it started to get even busier. I had not realized that people had made Starbucks a part of their nightlife. Crowds of young people were piling in to share time with one another over their Lattes.

Focus, I reminded myself: You know how this works. *Punch the right button, call out the order, make the right change, smile.*

PAUSE:
What has Gill learned about people getting coffee?

Partners:
what Starbucks baristas are called

1.   Briefly summarize Gill's process.

2.   Were you surprised by anything in the essay? What and why?

3. In addition to the critical skills needed to do his new job, what else did Gill observe and learn?

4. Write three questions that might be on a quiz on this essay (and be prepared to answer them).

5. Does Gill's essay have the Four Basics of Good Process Analysis (p. 112)? Why or why not, specifically?

6. Of the three essays in this chapter, which do you think is the most effective model of process analysis? Is it the same one you like best? Why or why not?

Write a Process Analysis Essay

Write your own process analysis essay on one of the following topics or on a topic of your own choice. Use **PROCESS ANALYSIS AT A GLANCE** as a basic organizer (p. 123), and follow the Writing Guide: Process Analysis checklist as you write and revise (p. 112).

COLLEGE	• Explain how to apply for financial aid or study for a test. For your audience, consider a student who is attending college for the first time.
	• Using your answers to the "Reflect on the Process" questions in Chapters 5–7, write an essay that explains your writing process.
WORK	• Explain how to do one of your major tasks at work. Write for a coworker who might substitute for you one day.
	• Explain how to get fired or how to get promoted.
EVERYDAY LIFE	• Explain a process for waking up or getting to sleep.
	• Write a blog post that explains how to break up with someone.

WRITING GUIDE: Process Analysis

STEPS IN PROCESS ANALYSIS	HOW TO DO THE STEPS
☐ Focus.	• Think about a process and its essential steps.
☐ Explore your topic. See Chapter 2.	• Make sure your process can be explained in a short essay. • Prewrite to decide on the steps and how you will explain them to your audience.
☐ Write a thesis statement. Process + Main point = Thesis See Chapter 3.	• Decide what you want your readers to know or learn about this process and write a thesis statement.
☐ Support your thesis. See Chapter 3.	• List all of the essential steps and details to describe them for your readers. • Imagine you are not familiar with the process. Would you understand it from the support you have listed, or do you need more explanation?
☐ Write a draft. See Chapter 4.	• Arrange the steps in a logical order (often chronological). • Write topic sentences for each essential step and paragraphs that describe them in detail.
☐ Revise your draft. See Chapter 4.	• Ask another person to read and comment on your draft. • Read to make sure that all the steps are there and relate to the topic. • Add transitions (often chronological). • Improve your introduction, thesis, and conclusion.
☐ Edit your draft. See Chapters 16 through 18.	• Correct errors in grammar, spelling, word use, and punctuation.
☐ Evaluate your writing.	• Does it have the Four Basics of Good Process Analysis (p. 112)? • Is this the best I can do?

Reflect on the Process

Look at your writing from this chapter, from your prewriting through revision and editing, and consider these questions:

1. What was the most difficult part of the process for you? Why?

2. Did the feedback you got on your initial draft provide you with information you could use to make changes in your draft? If not, what can you do to improve the feedback you get next time? What specific questions do you need your reviewers to answer for you?

3. What will you do differently the next time you write a process analysis essay?

4. Talk to someone who has taken courses in your major or who is working in your field. How is process analysis used in your major or career? What kinds of process analysis writing tasks can you expect in the future?

9

Classification

Writing That Puts Things into Groups

Understand What Classification Is

Classification is writing that organizes, or sorts, people or items into categories.

The **organizing principle** for a classification is *how* you sort the people or items, not the categories themselves. The organizing principle is directly related to the **purpose** of your classification. For example, you might sort clean laundry (your purpose) using one of the following organizing principles (how you achieve your purpose) — by ownership (yours, your roommate's, and so on) or by where it goes (closet, top drawer, bottom drawer, etc.).

Four Basics of Good Classification

1. It makes sense of a group of people or items by organizing them into categories according to a single organizing principle (main point).

2. It sets up logical and comprehensive categories (primary support).

3. It gives detailed explanations or examples with details of what fits into each category (secondary support).

4. It organizes information by time, space, emphasis, or importance depending on its purpose (logical organization).

In the following paragraph, each number corresponds to one of the Four Basics of Good Classification.

1 All people do not learn in the same way, and it is helpful to know what learning style you prefer. How do you naturally take in and absorb new information? The VARK learning styles inventory is a thirteen-item questionnaire that reveals which learning style a person favors. **2** The first of its four learning styles is visual (V). **3** Visual learners absorb information best by looking at images or by drawing or diagramming a concept. For example, a visual learner may learn more by studying a flowchart of information rather than reading that same information in paragraph form. **2** The second learning style is auditory (A). **3** Auditory learners take in information most efficiently by hearing and listening. They remember information that they hear better than they remember information that they read. Even reading aloud is better than reading silently because hearing is key. Auditory learners benefit from discussion with others rather than working alone silently. **2** The third learning style is read/write (R). **3** Read/write learners learn best by reading written material. They also benefit from writing about what they have read. For example, many read/write learners study by reading and then writing a summary of what they have just read. Many people who are not naturally read/write learners have used that learning style in school because schools are oriented toward reading and writing. For example, a person whose score on the VARK is split evenly between auditory and read/write is probably an auditory learner who has learned to use a read/write learning style for school. **2** The final learning style is kinesthetic (K). **3** Kinesthetic learners learn by doing and by being active. For these learners, experiments in science may be easier to understand than reading a chapter in a book, listening to a lecture, or looking at an image. Kinesthetic learners often need to create activity in order to learn well: they may make flash cards, walk around as they study, or make a static activity interactive in some other way. All learners benefit from learning techniques such as highlighting and making notes, though different kinds of notes work for different learning styles. All learners are active learners: they learn best when they actively involve themselves in a task rather than passively observe it. Taking a learning styles inventory is both fun and useful, particularly for students.

4 Major support organized in the order of the VARK acronym.

Whenever you organize or sort things to make sense of them, you are classifying them. Here are some ways that you might use classification:

COLLEGE	In a nursing course, you discuss three types of antibiotics used to treat infections.
WORK	For a report on inventory at the office, you list the types of supplies used in the office and report how many of each type you have in stock.
EVERYDAY LIFE	You look at the types of payment plans that are available for your car loan.

First Basic: Main Point in Classification

The **main point** in classification uses a single **organizing principle** to sort items into useful categories that help achieve the **purpose** of the classification. The diagram below shows how movies on online services are classified.

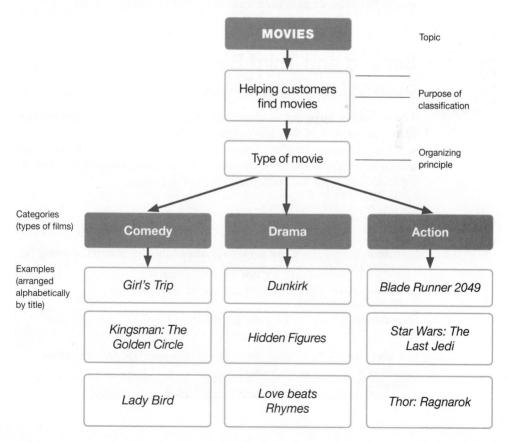

The following examples show how thesis statements for classification express the organizing principle and purpose.

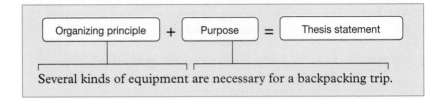

In addition to the purpose and organizing principle, a thesis statement in a classification may also include the categories that will be explained.

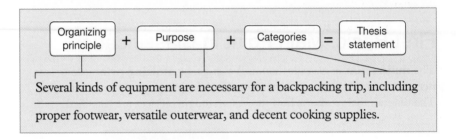

Second and Third Basics: Support in Classification

The **primary support** in classification consists of the **categories** that serve the purpose of the classification.

    The categories in classification are the "piles" into which the writer sorts a topic (the items to be classified). These categories will become the topic sentences for the body paragraphs of the essay.

TOPIC	College costs
THESIS STATEMENT	Tuition is only one of the many costs of going to college.
ORGANIZING PRINCIPLE	Types of costs other than tuition
PURPOSE	To show the different kinds of costs and their significance
CATEGORIES/ PRIMARY SUPPORT	Fees, costs of course materials, transportation expenses

The **supporting details** in classification are **examples** or explanations of what is in each category. The examples in classification are the various items that fall within each category. These are important because readers may not be familiar with your categories.

> **CATEGORY:** Fees
>
> > **EXAMPLES/SUPPORTING DETAILS:** General student fee assessed to each student, lab fees, technology fees, parking fees
>
> **CATEGORY:** Costs of course materials
>
> > **EXAMPLES/SUPPORTING DETAILS:** Costs of books, lab manuals, software, notebooks
>
> **CATEGORY:** Transportation expenses
>
> > **EXAMPLES/SUPPORTING DETAILS:** Costs of gas, parking, train and bus fare

Fourth Basic: Organization in Classification

Classification can be organized in different ways (*time order*, *space order*, or *order of importance or emphasis*) depending on its purpose.

PURPOSE	LIKELY ORGANIZATION
To explain changes or development over time	Time
To describe the arrangement of groups in physical space	Space
To analyze parts of an issue or problem To focus on a specific feature of groups	Importance Emphasis

As you write your classification, use **transitions** to move your readers smoothly from one category to another.

> ## Common Transitions in Classification
>
> | | |
> |---|---|
> | another | for example |
> | another kind | for instance |
> | first, second, third, and so on | last, lastly |
> | | one example, another example |

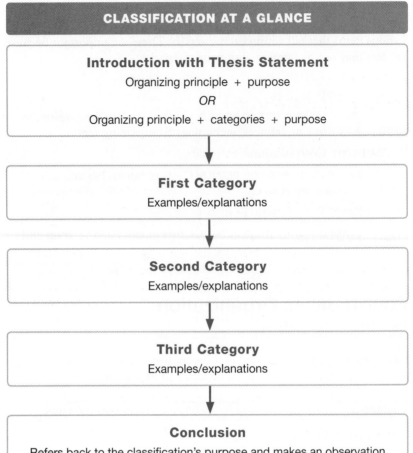

CLASSIFICATION AT A GLANCE

Introduction with Thesis Statement
Organizing principle + purpose
OR
Organizing principle + categories + purpose

First Category
Examples/explanations

Second Category
Examples/explanations

Third Category
Examples/explanations

Conclusion
Refers back to the classification's purpose and makes an observation
Note: A classification essay may include more than three categories,
depending on its purpose.

Read and Analyze Classification

Read the following three examples of classification—from college,
the workplace, and everyday life—and answer the questions that accompany them.

For each essay, review the Four Basics of Good Classification
(p. 125) and practice the critical reading process explained in Chapter 1.

Classification in College

The following student essay was written for an English class.

Josef Ameur

Videogame Genres

GUIDING QUESTION

What types of videogame genres does Ameur describe?

CRITICAL READING
■ Preview
■ Read
■ Pause
■ Review

(See pp. 4–11.)

1   **V**ideo games are an easily accessible way to cure the effects of bore-dom. Ever since the late 1970s, video games have been extremely popular. They started out as arcade units, costing 25 cents to $1 per play. Kids would spend hundreds of dollars playing these games. The accessibility of video games has evolved over time from pay-to-play arcade units to personal home TV consoles. The genres of games have also evolved over time: shooter, role-playing, and strategy are just a few.

PAUSE: Underline the sentence where Ameur presents his categories.

2   Shooters are one of the oldest genres of games. This genre was born in arcade games such as *Asteroids* and *Galaga*. The early shooters were quite simple, and everything was on a two-dimensional plane. *Asteroids* consisted of a small spaceship avoiding asteroids by dodging and shoot-ing at them. In *Galaga*, the players shot at enemy alien ships. Eventually, shooters evolved into third- and first-person shooters. In third-person, the player's view is from above, looking down at the character. In first-person, the player looks through the character's eyes. These shooters involve a character holding a gun shooting at enemies. Military, Sci-Fi, and Sur-vival are a few sub-genres.

3   Role-playing games (RPGs) started out on paper. *Dungeons & Drag-ons* was one of the more popular paper RPGs. Paper RPGs gave birth to computer-based ones. The benefit of computer-based RPGs is that with an internet connection, they can be played with millions of other people. Players and their friends can create and control characters who live in a fantasy world. These characters are often class-based with classes such as thief, warrior, mage, and ranger. Players micromanage the attributes of their characters: charisma, strength, and magic, to name a few. Players embark on epic quests, slay beasts, find treasure, and fight in great battles.

PAUSE: How does Ameur develop his categories — through definitions, explanations or examples?

4   Strategy games are similar to RPGs, but they are on a much larger scale. In strategy games, players often control a historic civilization. The three main components of strategy games are economy, military, and pol-itics. There are usually several types of resources that the players man-age such as gold, stone, wood, and food. Players control the villagers, assigning them to gather resources. In the military aspect of this genre, players control the army and train different types of soldiers, taking into

consideration the strengths and weaknesses of the different units. Politics determines allies and enemies and who wars with whom. In strategy games, there is no such thing as peace.

PAUSE: What sentence ties the conclusion to the thesis statement?

5   Many genres of games have been created to explore and play, but all video games offer the same core benefit: they offer a brief moment in time to escape the world around you. Video games not only cure boredom, but they also offer an experience that can rival that of books or films.

1. **Summarize**. Briefly summarize Ameur's essay, including what he is classifying and what categories he uses.

CRITICAL THINKING
▓ Summarize
▓ Analyze
▓ Synthesize
▓ Evaluate

(More on p. 12.)

2. **Analyze**. What is Ameur's organizing principle? Are the categories useful to Ameur's purpose of explaining videogame genres? Are all of the details clearly related to each category? How does Ameur's conclusion remind readers of his purpose?

3. **Synthesize**. What else do you know about the topic? Do you agree that the reason people play video games is to relieve boredom? What other ways are there to relieve boredom?

4. **Evaluate**. Does Ameur achieve his purpose? Does he need to provide additional categories? Does he need to provide additional information within categories? If so, where? Do you agree that playing video games rivals the experience of reading a book or seeing a film? Does the essay have the Four Basics of Good Classification (see p. 125)?

Classification at Work

The following was written for a presentation at the American Institute of Certified Public Accountants.

Rebeka Mazzone

Director, Rhode Island Region

Serving on a Nonprofit Board Need Not Be Onerous

Rebeka Mazzone
Director, Rhode Island Region

Essdras M Suarez/The Boston Globe via Getty Images

CRITICAL READING
▓ Preview
▓ Read
▓ Pause
▓ Review

(See pp. 4–11.)

GUIDING QUESTION

What kinds of practices will help nonprofits?

1   **D**oing good by serving on the board of nonprofit organizations, always laudable, is more demanding as public scrutiny of nonprofit financial management increases. But the job need not be onerous. A board member with a solid financial background can help a nonprofit achieve a sounder financial footing which will in turn help maintain its independence by

minimizing potential legislative intrusion. Several types of sound financial management practices can benefit nonprofit organizations.

PAUSE: What is Mazzone classifying?

2   *Documenting accounting and financial management practices.* Organizations cannot know what needs improving until they understand how they currently operate. Everything the organization does should be inventoried and documented, including fund-raising, accounting, generating financial reports, interactions between senior management and the board, and when these actions occur.

3   *Budgeting as part of strategic planning.* Budgeting provides an opportunity to link the organization's operational plans with its strategy and financial success and growth. Before plunging into the budget process and assigning costs to program activities, all program and project managers should understand and discuss the organization's strategy. The time spent educating, communicating, and planning will get everyone to agree on organizational goals and how to achieve them.

PAUSE: According to Mazzone, what should the budgeting process do?

4   *Managing the operating budget and audited financial statements.* Frequently, management and the board look at cash budgets. Outsiders, including lenders, look at audited statements and can get a different picture. For example, depreciation expenses and vacation accruals can turn a $10,000 surplus on an operating budget into a $50,000 loss on an audited statement of activities.

5   *Budget a surplus.* Being around for the long term requires building reserves. Budget an annual surplus, even a minimal amount, to ensure that adequate resources exist to guard against unexpected shortfalls.

PAUSE: How do these sound business practices relate to everyone?

6   *Project cash flow.* An organization should have three to six months of current assets (cash, accounts receivable, and short-term investments) on hand. This policy and practice ensures enough cash to meet obligations throughout the year. It will help manage accounts receivable and accounts payable and the timing of budgeted expenditures.

PAUSE: How does Mazzone link the conclusion to the introduction?

7   With the nonprofit sector pumping more than $50 billion into the Massachusetts economy each year, solid financial management of nonprofit organizations is not simply nice to have. It is mandatory, and it need not be onerous for a person with financial acumen.

1.   Briefly summarize Mazzone's presentation, including what she is classifying and what categories she uses.

2.   What is her purpose? (Consider the meaning of the word *onerous* and the title of the essay in your answer.)

3.   Who is Mazzone's intended audience? How can the vocabulary used in the essay help you identify the audience?

4.   Do you think Mazzone achieves her purpose? Why or why not?

Classification in Everyday Life

CRITICAL
READING
■ Preview
■ Read
■ Pause
■ Review
(See pp. 4–11.)

Dylan Marcos

Bad Roommates

GUIDING QUESTION

What kinds of bad roommates does Marcos classify?

PAUSE: What is Marcos's purpose? What do you think his organizing principle is?

1   **O**ver the past few years, I have learned a lot about bad roommates. Although I doubt that I have encountered all types, I certainly know more now than I did before. I'll pass on to you some of what I have experienced, so you can try to avoid the following types of roommates — the romeos, the slugs, and the criminals.

2   The romeos are usually great guys and lots of fun, when they happen to be single — but they are usually not. They always seem to have girlfriends, who basically become nonpaying roommates. The women are mostly nice, but they change the apartment in big ways. First, we have to watch how we act. We can't walk around half-dressed in the morning, for example. Also, we have to get used to sharing: the girlfriends spend hours at a time in the bathroom, doing their hair and putting on make-up. There are always more dishes in the sink when they are around, more food disappears, and even shampoo goes faster than normal. The romeos do not seem to understand that having semipermanent guests in the apartment really changes the way we live.

PAUSE: What does the first sentence tell you about the order of organization in this essay?

3   Another type, the slug, is even harder to live with than the romeo because the slugs are slobs. They never wash the dishes or put away food, they leave a trail of dirty clothes behind them, and they completely destroy the bathroom every time they use it. Slugs pretty much live in front of the television, so you will probably never have a chance to watch what *you* want. The slug is also sloppy about paying rent and bills. Although he usually has the money, he has to be reminded — no, hounded — before he will actually pay what he owes.

4   The worst type of roommate is the criminal, for obvious reasons. I've had only one of these, but one was more than enough. He was a nice guy for about two weeks — clean, not around too much, but good to have a beer with when he was there. One day, though, I came home after work to find that he was gone, along with everything valuable in the apartment — our laptops, iPods, some cash, a bunch of CDs, and my favorite leather jacket. Although we called the police, I know I will never get back anything he stole.

5   What I have learned from my experience is that, when I interview *potential* roommates, I should ask for at least two references, preferably from former roommates, so I can weed out the romeos, slugs, and

criminals. That should keep my living situation sane—at least until I meet someone who seems great at first but turns out to fall into another, equally bad category. I'll keep you posted.

PAUSE: How does Marcos tie the conclusion to the introduction?

1. What is Marcos's topic, and what categories does he use?

2. Does he give enough detail about each category for you to understand it as he does?

3. How does Marcos organize information within each paragraph? Are there clear transitions?

4. Does the essay have the Four Basics of Good Classification (p. 125)?

5. What other categories would you add based on your experience or that of other people you know?

Write a Classification Essay

Write your own classification essay on one of the following topics or on a topic of your own choice. Use **CLASSIFICATION AT A GLANCE** as a basic organizer (p. 130), and follow the Writing Guide: Classification checklist as you write and revise (p. 136).

COLLEGE	• Classify the types of degree programs or career pathways at your college. • Explain the types of students at your college (or in a particular class).
WORK	• Write a classification of customers or clients for new coworkers. • Write a classification of the communication styles in your workplace.
EVERYDAY LIFE	• Explain types of resources available to students in your area. • Write a classification of restaurants in your town.

WRITING GUIDE: Classification

STEPS IN CLASSIFICATION	HOW TO DO THE STEPS
☐ Focus.	• Think about your topic and how you can sort it so that your audience will understand the categories.
☐ Explore your topic. See Chapter 2.	• Prewrite to find possible categories to use and examples that will explain each category.
☐ Write a thesis statement. Organizing principle + Purpose = ⸨Thesis⸩ Or Organizing principle + Categories = ⸨Thesis⸩ See Chapter 3.	• Include your topic and either the method you are using to sort (the organizing principle) or the categories you will describe.
☐ Support your thesis. See Chapter 3.	• Choose useful categories that will achieve your purpose. • Consider what your readers need to know to understand the categories.
☐ Write a draft. See Chapter 4.	• Arrange the categories logically. • Write topic sentences for each category and paragraphs giving examples of each of the categories.
☐ Revise your draft. See Chapter 4.	• Add any examples that will help your readers understand. • Add transitions. • Improve your introduction, thesis, and conclusion.
☐ Edit your revised draft. See Chapters 16 through 18.	• Correct errors in grammar, spelling, word use, and punctuation.
☐ Evaluate your writing.	• Does it have the Four Basics of Good Classification (p. 125)? • Is this the best I can do?

Reflect on the Process

Look at your writing from this chapter, from your prewriting through revision and editing, and consider these questions:

1. What was the most difficult part of the process for you? Why?

2. Did the feedback you got on your initial draft provide you with information you could use to make changes in your draft? If not, what can you do to improve the feedback you get next time? What specific questions do you need your reviewers to answer for you?

3. What will you do differently the next time you write a classification essay?

4. Talk to someone who has taken courses in your major or who is working in your field. How is classification used in your major or career? What kinds of classification writing tasks can you expect in the future?

10

Definition

Writing That Tells What Something Means

Understand What Definition Is

Definition is writing that explains what a term or concept means.

> ### Four Basics of Good Definition
>
> **1** It presents a clear definition of a term for a specific purpose (main point).
>
> **2** It presents defining characteristics, features, or examples of the term (major support).
>
> **3** It uses details to help readers understand the characteristics, features, or examples (secondary support).
>
> **4** It arranges support by order of importance or emphasis, according to the purpose (logical organization).

In the following paragraph, each number corresponds to one of the Four Basics of Good Definition.

1 *Internet addiction* is chronic, compulsive use of the internet that interferes with the addicts' lives or their relationships with others. **2** For example, addicts may spend so much time online that they are unable to perform as expected at home, work, or school. **3** These addicts may spend hours surfing the Web, playing games, or emailing friends and family. **2** In more serious cases, the internet addiction can cause financial problems, or worse. **3** For example, online shoppers who go to extremes can find themselves in debt and, as a result, damage their credit, not to mention personal

4
Examples arranged in order of importance.

relationships. **2** Still other internet addictions involve potentially dangerous or illegal activities. **3** These activities can include meeting people online, gambling, viewing pornography, and engaging in cybersex. However, for internet addicts, the problem usually isn't *how* they use the internet; the problem is that they cannot stop using it, even if they want to.

Many situations require you to explain the meaning of a term, particularly how you are using it.

COLLEGE	On a U.S. history exam, you define the term *carpetbagger*.
WORK	You describe a coworker as a "slacker" to a human resources staffer, and the staffer asks what you mean exactly.
EVERYDAY LIFE	You explain the term *fair* to your child in the context of games or sports.

First Basic: Main Point in Definition

In definition essays, your **main point** typically defines your topic. The main point is directly related to your **purpose**, which is to get your readers to understand the way that you are using a term or concept in your essay. Although writers do not always define a term or concept in a thesis statement, it helps readers if they do.

A thesis statement in definition can follow a variety of different patterns, two of which include the term and its basic definition.

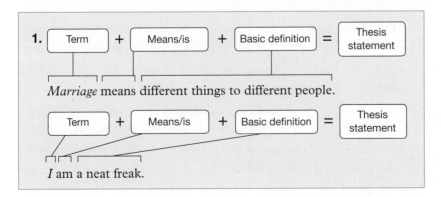

1. Term + Means/is + Basic definition = Thesis statement

Marriage means different things to different people.

Term + Means/is + Basic definition = Thesis statement

I am a neat freak.

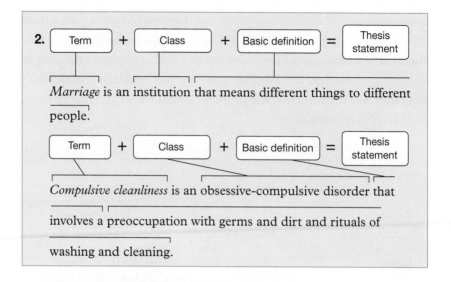

In essays based on the previous thesis statements, readers would expect the italicized terms and concepts to be defined through examples that show the writer's meaning.

Second and Third Basics: Support in Definition

If a friend says, "Summer in the city is awful," you do not know what she means by *awful*. Is it the weather? The people? The transportation? Until your friend explains what she means, you will not know whether you would agree that summer in the city is awful.

Support in definition provides specific examples of terms or concepts to help explain what they mean. Read the two thesis statements that follow and the lists of examples that could be used as support for them.

THESIS	Today, marriage means different things to different people.
SUPPORT	A union of one man and one woman
	A union of two people of either sex
	A union that is supported by state law
	A union that is supported by both civil and religious laws

→

THESIS	I am a neat freak.
SUPPORT	I clean compulsively.
	I am constantly buying new cleaning products.
	My cleaning habits have attracted the notice of friends and family.

In both of these examples, the writer would then go on to develop the examples with details.

THESIS	I am a neat freak.
SUPPORT	I clean compulsively.
	DETAILS: I clean in the morning and at night, and cannot let a spot on the counter go for a second.
SUPPORT	I am constantly buying new cleaning products.
	DETAILS: Every week, I buy new products, have a closet full of them, and believe every new sales pitch.
SUPPORT	My cleaning habits have attracted the notice of friends and family.
	DETAILS: My kids used to appreciate the clean house; now they complain that I am compulsive; friends tease me, but I wonder if they think I go too far.

Fourth Basic: Organization in Definition

The examples in a definition essay are often organized by **importance** or the impact they will have on readers. Save the most important example for last. As you write, add transitions to connect one example to the next.

Common Transitions in Definition

another	for example
another kind	for instance
first, second, third, and so on	

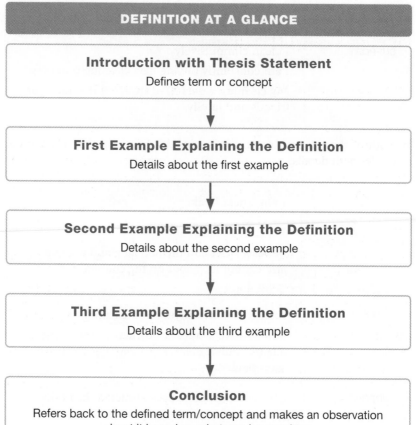

DEFINITION AT A GLANCE

Introduction with Thesis Statement
Defines term or concept

↓

First Example Explaining the Definition
Details about the first example

↓

Second Example Explaining the Definition
Details about the second example

↓

Third Example Explaining the Definition
Details about the third example

↓

Conclusion
Refers back to the defined term/concept and makes an observation
about it based on what you have written
Note: A definition essay may include more than three examples,
depending on your purpose.

Read and Analyze Definition

Read the following three examples of definition—from college, the work-place, and everyday life—and answer the questions that accompany them.

For each essay, review the Four Basics of Good Definition (p. 138) and practice the critical reading process explained in Chapter 1.

Definition in College

The following essay was written for an English class. Note the use of out-side sources and the documentation of them at the end.

Benjamin Mills

Of Nerds and Nerdiness

GUIDING QUESTION

Does Mills believe that "nerd" has a single, "right" definition?

CRITICAL
READING
■ Preview
■ Read
■ Pause
■ Review

(See pp. 4–11.)

1   I have always been a nerd, in almost every way that someone can visualize one. From elementary school, I was in the gifted program, I got great marks in most of my classes, and I had a reading level beyond my far older classmates. I love to read; I play, listen to, and compose some music; I have always been an avid gamer—there are many things that have put me in the "nerd" category—and never being particularly social didn't help, either. More than once has a classmate asked me for some tutoring in math or science courses, editing papers, etc., because my reputation as a nerd precedes me. However, it is as much a boon as a bane; being a nerd carries certain expectations and an abundance of meanings.

PAUSE: Based on the introduction, what do you think the writer's purpose is?

2   From many dictionary sources and from a lifetime of context, I have distilled three prime definitions of the word "nerd." The first is very broad: a person who is boring, socially awkward, and/or unfashionable. This definition lacks detail and could very well describe half of the occupants of planet Earth. The second is less broad: an intelligent person with single-minded, nonsocial, or antisocial interests or hobbies. It is more pointed, and it reveals the way nerds are treated in the real world. And the third is more specific: a person contemptible in certain social groups (such as the "jocks" referred to by Lipsyte in the essay, "Jock Culture") for having the aforementioned characteristics (similar to the "pukes" described by Lipsyte; 350).

PAUSE: How are the three definitions given by Mills different? Which one is closest to your definition of the term?

3   These three definitions work in tandem to help distinguish so-called "nerds" from other people (as all labels, of course, are meant to do). However, the way a word is used in context is where it gains meaning; definitions only work insofar as everyone agrees that the word means what it means and use it as such. Being able to derive connotation from context is key, and one can use the same process for any broad label, as is displayed in Gloria Naylor's essay, "The Meanings of a Word," when she breaks down a racial epithet to demonstrate how words meant as pejoratives can be used as terms of endearment or status within a certain discourse community (478). "Nerd," for example, if one watches movies or shows from the 90's, has always been an insult, of sorts—a way to immediately and irrefutably cut someone off from social interaction with certain people (usually the "jock" sort, in such shows). From those who are very definitely not nerds, "nerd" is a derogatory word, something to put people down and shut them up. It also generates a certain bias, as one finds in other attempts to "poison the well"—a logical fallacy that

PAUSE: What connotations of "nerd" are presented in this paragraph? Have you heard "nerd" used in this way?

attempts to discredit someone by using irrelevant information to cause the audience (in a school setting, fellow classmates) to lose trust or interest in the opponent (in the same setting, the nerd) because they are no longer favorable.

4   From other nerds, however, it can mean something else entirely—not an insult or generalization at all. In the context of a high school band, for example, being a band nerd is a good thing—any band nerd worth his brass is proud of how much of a band nerd he is. The same is true for gamers and computer nerds and geeks alike (one could call a "geek" someone who is a nerd with regards to certain subjects like *Star Wars* or *The Lord of the Rings*, etc.). This is where one could find conflict with the first and second definitions of "nerd" that I have provided: to other nerds, they are anything but antisocial or boring, not unfashionable or single-minded. They're just nerdy.

PAUSE: What connotation of *nerd* does Mills present in this paragraph? Are you familiar with this view of nerds?

5   In recent years, being a nerd has also shifted from being a blanket pejorative for undesirables to a more-or-less good thing—at least partly due to the massive influx of superhero movies to the box office. Now, instead of being shunned for your prowess at a particular video game or card game or board game, be it classic or new, you could instead make thousands of dollars by playing it professionally (or at least somewhere where someone else can watch you, like an online platform). Rather than being rejected for your massive knowledge of a fictional universe, you can become the fastest of friends with many people. There are now nerds everywhere—or at least they are less hesitant to announce themselves as such.

6   Unfortunately, as words tend to do when used all the time, the word "nerd" has lost most of its meaning. Rarely is it used as an insult, anymore, and it is used so frequently that anyone and anything can be a nerd. Be it a term of endearment or an ironic insult to a friend or the way the word has been used in the past—the ability of those to identify themselves by this term is essentially lost. A matter of years ago, one could call oneself a nerd and others would have a decent notion of how one operates in the world. Now, if someone calls themselves a nerd, "So what?" is a valid response. "What kind of nerd?" also follows, because there are practically an infinite number of ways to be a nerd. Nerdiness now requires context. Band nerds are different from gamers, who are different from techs, who are different from binge-watchers. Those who wish to identify themselves as nerds must now actually qualify their nerdiness to other nerds. When did a group of social outcasts develop the ability to cast out their fellow nerds? Is there a word for an outcast among outcasts?

PAUSE: What changes has Mills noted in the way "nerd" is used today? Have you seen similar changes?

7   It is also unfortunate that when someone hears the word "nerd," to many, it still evokes a picture of a pale face lit only by a computer screen, sitting in the dark recesses of their parents' basement. This caricature of nerds causes non-nerds to assume someone who is, perhaps, a brilliant biology student also has amazing skills at handling computers. I, for example, am at least competent in chemistry and mathematics, but I

can barely function with a computer and know nothing about technical diagnoses, but some will still come to me for tech advice because of their conception of nerds (it also does not help that I am as ghostly pale as the caricature I described). There is also the grand expectation of academic exceptionalism among nerds—if a self-described nerd does poorly on a test, there is shock among the nerd's peers. How can a nerd have a C in calculus? What do you mean "you failed a class"? Aren't nerds supposed to be super smart? Just because someone has an affinity for astrophysics or computer programming does not indicate perfect (or even necessarily good) academic performance. Nor does it necessarily indicate weakness or lack of dexterity—there is no blanket truth about nerds.

8   Essentially, in modern discourse on the subject of what is and is not a nerd, one must come to the understanding that there is a point where we all must agree to disagree; not all nerds must be a certain thing or behave a certain way nor must they all be proud of their nerdiness at all times. One type of nerd is not necessarily superior to another, and feuding bands of geeks do not describe what it means to be a nerd in full. Context is everything, and hopefully, with context, all nerds can come to a sense of peace and fulfilment in knowing what a nerd means to them—appreciate what it means to others.

Works Cited

Lipsyte, Robert. "Jock Culture." *The Bedford Reader*, 12th ed., Ed. X. J. Kennedy et al., Bedford/St. Martin's, 2014, pp. 349–353.

Naylor, Gloria. "The Meanings of a Word." *The Bedford Reader*, 12th ed., Ed. X. J. Kennedy et al., Bedford/St. Martin's, 2014, pp. 476–479.

For more on documenting sources using MLA style, see Chapter 14.

1.   **Respond.** Mills provides several definitions for "nerd" in his essay. Do you think one of these definitions is better than the others? If so, which one? How would you change his definition?

2.   **Summarize.** Briefly summarize Mills's essay, including the term he is defining, his definition, his examples, and his thesis.

3.   **Analyze.** How does the final line of the first paragraph organize the rest of the essay?

4.   **Synthesize.** Mills refers to an essay by Robert Lipsyte — "Jock Culture" (www.thenation.com/article/jocks-vs-pukes/). Read Lipsyte's essay. How does Lipsyte's characterization of "pukes" connect to Mills's definition of "nerds"?

5.   **Evaluate.** Does Mills give you a clear idea of how he understands the term *nerd*? What is his point of view? Do you think he is biased? If so, how? Does his essay have the *Four Basics of Definition* (p. 138)?

CRITICAL THINKING
- Summarize
- Analyze
- Synthesize
- Evaluate

(More on p. 12.)

Definition at Work

The following is a mission statement for a sign company.

Gary Knoblock

Customer Orientation

Courtesy Gary Knoblock

GUIDING QUESTION

What does customer-oriented mean to Knoblock?

CRITICAL
READING
■ Preview
■ Read
■ Pause
■ Review

(See pp. 4–11.)

1   The fundamental principle of Lightning Quick (LQ) Signs is customer orientation. While most companies claim that they are customer-oriented,

Gary Knoblock
Business Owner

most have no idea what that really means. I tell my employees that I would like to have a customer giggle at the completion of the job, delighting in the product and service we have delivered, his every expectation met and exceeded. For all of us at LQ Signs, *customer-oriented* means that from start to finish to follow-up, the customer comes first.

2   Our customer orientation begins before the job begins. Before doing anything, we interview the customer to learn what his or her needs are and to determine the most cost-effective route to meet those needs. No job for us is "standard." Each is unique.

3   Our customer orientation means that we produce high-quality products quickly. We keep signs simple because our customers want their prospective customers to be able to read the sign in a glance. We use the most current digital printing processes to produce sharp, readable signs quickly. Because we have previously determined, with the customer, the most cost-effective method of producing the signs, the high quality and rapid return do not come at extra cost.

4   Our customer orientation means that our products are thoroughly checked for flaws and installed at the customer's convenience. Our signs leave our workshop in perfect condition, as the customer has ordered. Our well-trained team of installers works with the customer to determine the installation schedule.

PAUSE: What are three examples of customer-oriented practices?

5   Finally, our customer orientation means that the job is not complete when the sign is in place. We follow up every sale to make sure that the product is in top shape and that the customer is pleased.

6   LQ Signs is truly customer-oriented, from start to finish to follow-up. Our customers are our partners.

1.   What is Knoblock's purpose?

2.   Briefly summarize the essay, including the term being defined and the definition and examples.

3.   Is Knoblock likely to be biased? Why or why not?

4.   Does he do a good job of explaining the term?

Definition in Everyday Life

The following appeared originally in the *Boston Globe*.

Baxter Holmes

My Date with Fifteen Women

GUIDING QUESTION

How does the experience of judging a beauty pageant change Holmes's definition of *beauty*?

CRITICAL
READING
■ Preview
■ Read
■ Pause
■ Review

(See pp. 4–11.)

1   There is a lot more to a beauty pageant than meets the eye. I know, after judging one myself. Beauty is a vague term often defined by first impressions. If you like what you see, it is beautiful. If not, it is not. For many people tuning in to the Miss America pageant, that will be their definition. It certainly was mine, until I judged a preliminary pageant for Miss New Hampshire last summer.

2   How did a twenty-one-year-old sportswriter on summer break from college get to be a tiny part of this glamorous slice of Americana? Given proper guidance on the rules, pretty much anyone can become a judge, and a former journalism professor of mine who has been involved in pageantry since 1986 signed me up to be on the panel for the twenty-second annual Miss Kingston/Miss Seacoast scholarship pageant, partly because he thought it would be a good experience for me. He also thought it would be fun. So did I. It wasn't.

3   As I entered the blue-gray antique home in Kingston, New Hampshire, where a preliminary session of private interviews would take place, I saw fifteen young women, all seventeen to twenty-one years old. I walked through the crowd, knowing I would be judging which one was most deserving of a scholarship; to me, in my own common sense terms, that meant picking who was most beautiful. It seemed so cool at the outset—there are far worse ways for a heterosexual male to spend a Sunday—but once I saw them and they saw me, it was terrifying. I was not the only judge (there were seven of us, all men), but because communication among judges is limited to avoid bias, I felt alone.

4   They walked in one by one, and, in ten-minute segments, we asked questions. It wasn't hard to decide who was the most physically attractive, but in those first ten minutes, I began to understand just how grossly misunderstood this whole pageantry thing is. Being a role model—and a pretty one at that—is hardly enough to win and advance. (The winners of this event would go on to prepare for the 2009 Miss New Hampshire contest, which leads to the Miss America pageant.) Each of the contestants had innumerable academic and extracurricular honors. Each had a thoroughly developed plan for advancing good causes, like awareness of Lyme disease, depression, and low self-esteem; or for donating blood; helping

PAUSE:
How would you define *beauty*? How does Holmes prepare readers for his thesis?

PAUSE: Why did seeing the contestants terrify Holmes?

PAUSE: Why does Holmes's definition of beauty start to change?

the elderly; or volunteering at local schools. To be sure, none of them was perfect. But they were mighty impressive human beings. And yet, what most of the typical observers will remember from a pageant is the swimsuit competition. If only they knew. After the interviews, the judges sat on a screened-in patio and ate lunch. I felt sick. Over and over in each interview, my definition of beauty was shattered, and I was ashamed.

5   That night, the pageant moved to a nearby café for the talent, swimsuit, onstage questioning, and evening-wear events. The contestants sang beautifully, danced gracefully, played violins and flutes, and recited poetry. They looked elegant in evening wear and articulated as best they could intelligent answers to the onstage questions, which were created by my former professor, a charming emcee if there ever was one.

6   And then the swimsuit competition began. On my drive to Kingston, I had looked forward to this event like Christmas morning. Now, I dreaded it. After seeing the contestants' smarts, skills, poise, and dedication, I couldn't help but wonder: what does a swimsuit have to do with any of this? Later, after the judging, I talked to KeriAnn Lynch, a former winner of this pageant, and Lindsey Graham, who was crowned Miss Seacoast that night, about whether pageants should drop this segment. Lynch said she "wouldn't shed a tear," while Graham said it would be a disservice if they did, because the contestants "need to represent what healthy is."

> **PAUSE:** Why does Holmes dread the swimsuit segment? Why did he include the voices of two winners on this issue?

7   But I guess that is a debate for another time. Each contestant crossed the stage in about fifteen seconds. I jotted a number from one to ten, and we moved on. The winners were crowned, and there was a dinner back at the blue-gray home. There, Graham told me she would not have gotten through college without the nearly $30,000 she has won in pageants. She also admitted the difficulty of presenting herself. "You walk around in life trying not to think of people's opinions," she said, "but it's really hard when they are literally in front of you with numbers, judging you."

True enough, but it is not so easy on the other side, either. Beauty is not a simple matter.

1.   Briefy summarize Holmes's essay including the term he is defining and how his experience affects his definition.

2.   What is his purpose in writing? Do you think he achieves it?

3.   What does Holmes mean by his thesis, "There is a lot more to beauty than meets the eye"? What else is there? How does he tie his conclusion to his thesis statement?

4.   Do you think the swimsuit competition in beauty pageants should be eliminated? Why or why not?

5.   Think of other situations where you or others are judged by "what meets the eye." What are they? What is the danger in judging by what meets the eye?

Write a Definition Essay

Write your own definition essay on *one* of the following topics or on a topic of your own choice. Use **DEFINITION AT A GLANCE** as a basic organizer (p. 142), and follow the Writing Guide: Definition checklist below as you write and revise.

COLLEGE	• Define an important term or concept from another course you have taken. • Define cheating. If possible, interview both instructors and students as you develop your definition.
WORK	• Define a term you use at work, one which might not be familiar to those outside your workplace. • Define harassment, using both your company's policy manual and interviews with coworkers.
EVERYDAY LIFE	• Choose a current term related to social media use such as *troll* or *go viral*. Define the term and include relevant examples. • Define *road rage*.

WRITING GUIDE: Definition

STEPS IN DEFINITION	HOW TO DO THE STEPS
☐ Focus.	• Think about the term you are going to define and how to get your readers to understand the term as you do.
☐ Explore your topic. See Chapter 2.	• Prewrite to get possible definitions and examples that will explain the definition.
☐ Write a thesis statement. Term + Definition = Thesis See Chapter 3.	• Include the term or concept you are defining and a basic definition of it.

(Continued)

STEPS IN DEFINITION	HOW TO DO THE STEPS
☐ **Support your thesis.** See Chapter 3.	• Choose examples of the definition and details about the examples that will show your reader how you "see" the term.
☐ **Write a draft.** See Chapter 4.	• Arrange your examples. • Write topic sentences for each example and paragraphs that give details about them.
☐ **Revise your draft.** See Chapter 4.	• Make sure the examples explain your definition. • Think about what other details your readers might need to understand your definition. • Add transitions. • Improve your introduction, thesis, and conclusion.
☐ **Edit your revised draft.** See Chapters 16 through 18.	• Correct errors in grammar, spelling, word use, and punctuation.
☐ **Evaluate your writing.**	• Does it have the Four Basics of Good Definition (p. 138)? • Is this the best I can do?

Reflect on the Process

Look at your writing from this chapter, from your prewriting through revision and editing, and consider these questions:

1. What was the most difficult part of the process for you? Why?

2. Did the feedback you got on your initial draft provide you with information you could use to make changes in your draft? If not, what can you do to improve the feedback you get next time? What specific questions do you need your reviewers to answer for you?

3. What will you do differently the next time you write a definition essay?

4. Talk to someone who has taken courses in your major or who is working in your field. How is definition used in your major or career? What kinds of definition writing tasks can you expect in the future?

Comparison and Contrast

Writing That Shows Similarities and Differences

Understand What Comparison and Contrast Are

Comparison is writing that shows the similarities among subjects—people, ideas, situations, or items; **contrast** shows the differences. In conversation, we often use the word *compare* to mean either compare or contrast, but as you work through this chapter, the terms will be used separately.

Four Basics of Good Comparison and Contrast

1 It compares and/or contrasts for a purpose — to help readers make a decision, to help them understand the subjects, or to show the writer's understanding of the subjects (main point).

2 It presents several parallel, important points of comparison/contrast (primary support).

3 It develops points of comparison/contrast fairly, with supporting details for both subjects (secondary support).

4 It arranges points either point-by-point or whole-to-whole (logical organization).

In the following paragraph, which contrasts the subjects, each number corresponds to one of the Four Basics of Good Comparison and Contrast.

1 My current boyfriend is a major improvement over my ex-boyfriend in terms of how he treats me. **2** One difference is their manners and courtesy. **3** My current boyfriend opens the door when I get in the car as well as when I get out. In contrast, my ex-boyfriend never opened the door of the car or any other door. **2** My current boyfriend likes to tell me that he loves me. **3** For example, we went to the beach, and he screamed that he loved me to the four winds so everyone could hear. My ex, on the other hand, always had a ready excuse for why he couldn't say that he loved me, ever. However, he wanted me to tell him I loved him all the time. **2** Another difference between the two is that my boyfriend spends money on me. **3** When we go out to a restaurant, he pays for the meal. My ex just never seemed to have money to pay for dinner or anything else. He would say he forgot to bring his wallet, and I would have to pay for the food. **2** To me, the most important difference between the two guys is that my current boyfriend is honest. **3** He never lies to me about anything, and he makes me feel confident about our relationship. In contrast, I never could tell if my ex was lying or telling the truth because he often lied about his family and other things, and I never knew what to believe. To sum it all up, my current boyfriend is a gentleman, and my ex was a pig.

4 Uses point-by-point organization (see p. 154).

—Liliana Ramirez, student

Many situations require you to use comparison and contrast.

COLLEGE	In a business course, you compare and contrast practices in e-commerce and traditional commerce.
WORK	You compare and contrast two health insurance options offered by your company in order to select the one that is best for you.
EVERYDAY LIFE	Before choosing a telephone plan, you compare and contrast the rates, services, and options each offers.

First Basic: Main Point in Comparison and Contrast

A comparison and contrast essay shows readers how two or more subjects are alike or different. The **purpose** of a comparison and contrast essay may be to have readers understand the subjects or to help them make a decision.

In comparison and contrast, your **main point** expresses similarities or differences in your subjects. For example, in the paragraph on page 152, Liliana Ramirez contrasts the different ways that her two boyfriends treated her. Her purpose is to help readers understand why one became her "ex."

Typically, thesis statements in comparison and contrast essays present the central subjects and indicate whether the writer will show similarities, differences, or both.

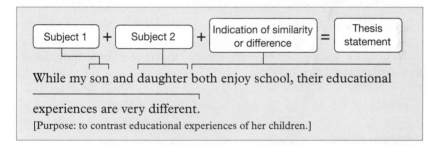

While my son and daughter both enjoy school, their educational experiences are very different.
[Purpose: to contrast educational experiences of her children.]

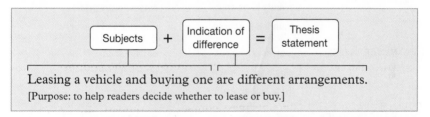

Leasing a vehicle and buying one are different arrangements.
[Purpose: to help readers decide whether to lease or buy.]

To determine your thesis in a comparison and contrast essay, decide whether you want to show similarities, differences, or both. To make this decision, you need to think about what your purpose is—what you want your readers to understand—and what will be meaningful to those readers.

Second and Third Basics: Support in Comparison and Contrast

The **support** in comparison and contrast demonstrates your main point by showing how your subjects are the same or different. To find support, many people make a list with multiple columns—one for the points that will serve as the basis of the comparison or contrast and one for each of the subjects.

For example, one student wrote the following thesis statement, which indicates that his essay will focus on the differences between the ages of twenty and forty.

> *The ages of twenty and forty are both enjoyable, but they represent very different stages in life.*

To support this thesis, the student needs to find several points of contrast between twenty and forty. He generates the following list.

> DIFFERENCES BETWEEN TWENTY AND FORTY
>
> appearance
>
> place in life
>
> perspective

Then, for each point of comparison, the student lists some details that explain the differences.

	AGE TWENTY	AGE FORTY
APPEARANCE	smooth skin	some wrinkles
	trendy haircut	classic hairstyle
	rounded features	well-defined features
PLACE IN LIFE	just starting out	established
	single, no children	married with children
	living at home	own home
PERSPECTIVE	self-centered	more thoughtful
	choices to make	many choices made
	uncertainty	wisdom

Fourth Basic: Organization in Comparison and Contrast

A comparison and contrast essay can be organized in two basic ways: a **point-by-point** organization first compares or contrasts one point between the two subjects and then moves to the next point of comparison or contrast. A **whole-to-whole** organization first presents all the points of comparison or contrast for one subject and then all the points for the second. To decide which organization to use, consider which of the two will best serve your purpose of explaining similarities or differences to your readers. Once you choose an organization, stick with it throughout the essay.

The two organization types look like this.

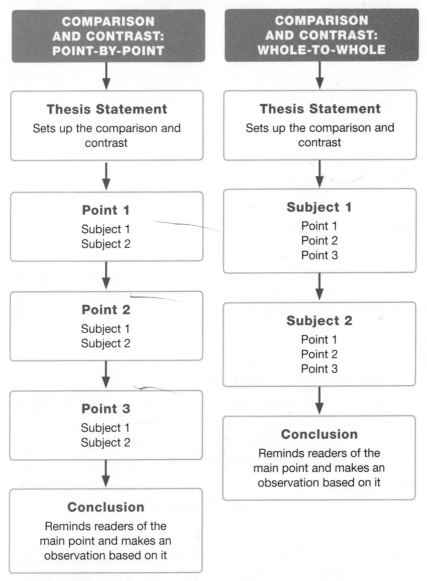

Note: whether you use point-by-point or subject-by-subject to organize a comparison and contrast essay, you may discuss more than three points of comparison and/or contrast, depending on your purpose.

Using **transitions** in comparison and contrast essays is important to move readers from one subject to another and from one point of comparison to another.

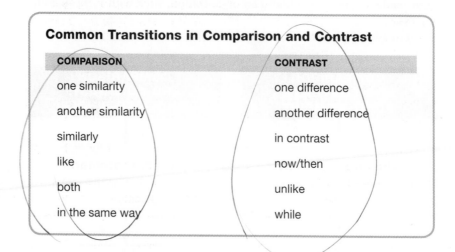

Common Transitions in Comparison and Contrast

COMPARISON	CONTRAST
one similarity	one difference
another similarity	another difference
similarly	in contrast
like	now/then
both	unlike
in the same way	while

Read and Analyze Comparison and Contrast

Read the following three examples of compare and contrast—from college, the workplace, and everyday life—and answer the questions that accompany them. For each essay, review the Four Basics of Good Comparison and Contrast (p. 151) and practice the critical reading process explained in Chapter 1.

Comparison and Contrast in College

The following is an excerpt from the textbook *Discovering Psychology*, Fifth Edition.

CRITICAL
READING
▪ Preview
▪ Read
▪ Pause
▪ Review

(See pp. 4–11.)

Don Hockenbury and Sandra Hockenbury

GUIDING QUESTION

How are anorexia nervosa and bulimia nervosa both alike and different?

1   **Anorexia nervosa** is life-threatening weight loss. Four key features define anorexia nervosa: First, the person refuses to maintain a normal body weight. With a body weight that is 15 percent or more below normal,

body mass index can drop to 12 or lower. Second, despite being danger-ously underweight, the person with anorexia is intensely afraid of gaining weight or becoming fat. Third, the anorexic has a distorted perception about the size of his or her body. Although emaciated, he or she looks in the mirror and sees someone fat or obese. And fourth, an anorexic denies the seriousness of his or her weight loss (American Psychiatric Association [APA], 2000).

2   Perfectionism and rigid thinking, poor peer relations, social isolation, and low self-esteem are common (Halmi et al., 2000). Although estimates vary, approximately 10 percent of people with anorexia nervosa die from starvation, suicide, or physical complications accompanying extreme weight loss (APA, 2000; Kaye, Klump, Frank, and Strober, 2000).

3   **Bulimia nervosa** is bingeing and purging of food. Like people with anorexia, people with bulimia nervosa fear gaining weight. Intense preoc-cupation and dissatisfaction with their bodies are also apparent. However, people with bulimia stay within a normal weight range or may even be slightly overweight. Another difference is that people with bulimia usually recognize that they have an eating disorder.

4   People with bulimia nervosa experience extreme episodes of binge eating, consuming as many as 50,000 calories in a single binge. Binges typically occur twice a week and are often triggered by negative feelings or hunger (Agras & Apple, 1997). During the binge, the person usually consumes sweet, high-calorie foods that can be swallowed quickly, such as ice cream, cake, and candy. Binges typically occur in secrecy, leaving the person feeling ashamed, guilty, and disgusted by his or her own behavior. After bingeing, the bulimic compensates by purging him- or herself of the excessive food by self-induced vomiting or by misuse of laxatives or ene-mas. After purging, he or she often feels psychologically relieved. Some people with bulimia do not purge themselves of the excess food. Rather, they use fasting and excessive exercise to keep their body weight within the normal range (APA, 2000).

PAUSE: Underline or highlight the four key features of anorexia.

PAUSE: How is bulimia similar to anorexia? How is it different?

References

Agras, W. S., & Apple, R. F. (1997). *Overcoming eating disorders: A cognitive-behavioral treatment for bulimia nervosa and binge-eating.* San Antonio, TX: Harcourt Brace.

American Psychiatric Association. (2000). Practice guidelines for the treatment of patients with eating disorders (revision). *American Journal of Psychiatry, 157* (Suppl.), 1–39.

Halmi, K. A., et al. (2000). Perfectionism in anorexia nervosa: Variation by clinical subtype, obsessionality, and pathological eating behavior. *American Journal of Psychiatry, 157,* 1799–1805.

Kaye, W. H., et al. (2000). Anorexia and bulimia nervosa. *Annual Review of Medicine, 51,* 299–313.

The documentation system used here is that of the American Psychological Association (APA) because the excerpt is from a psychology text. For English classes, use the MLA style (see Chapter 14).

1. **Summarize**. Briefly summarize the text excerpt, including the conditions being compared or contrasted, the authors' purpose, and some of the points of comparison or contrast.

CRITICAL
THINKING
■ Summarize
■ Analyze
■ Synthesize
■ Evaluate

(More on p. 12.)

2. **Analyze**. Is the excerpt organized point by point or whole to whole? Why do you think there is no formal introduction or conclusion? If there were an introduction, what information might it include? If you were writing a concluding paragraph, what would you say? What might a good title be?

3. **Synthesize**. Do you know anyone who has an eating disorder such as those described? What behaviors or characteristics have you noticed about the person or people?

4. **Evaluate**. Does the excerpt have the *Four Basics of Good Comparison and Contrast* (p. 151)? Do the authors achieve their purpose?

Comparison and Contrast at Work

The following is excerpted from an article published by a doctor on the subject of dyslexia.

Garth Vaz

Differences between Dyslexia and ADHD

GUIDING QUESTION

How are dyslexia and ADHD different?

Courtesy Garth Vaz

CRITICAL
READING
■ Preview
■ Read
■ Pause
■ Review

(See pp. 4–11.)

PAUSE:
What is Vaz's
purpose?
Who is his
audience?
Consider his
use of *we*
in the first
paragraph in
your answer.

1   For decades, dyslexics have been one of the most misunderstood groups in our society. Misconceptions and misdiagnoses abound, as when dyslexics are mislabeled stupid, retarded, or lazy and placed among the mentally deficient. Many dyslexics have been placed in special education programs along with the slow learners. Later, after appropriate remediation, these same students have gone on to become educators, lawyers, and doctors. It is therefore of great importance that we be aware of the sensitive nature of dealing with these prize products of our society. We must be diligent in our efforts to help them in their struggle for success.

2   Such misdiagnoses are due to the lack of understanding of dyslexia and conditions such as attention-deficit/hyperactivity disorder (ADHD), childhood depressive disorder (CDD), central auditory processing deficit (CAPD), and many others that share some similarities with common

symptoms of dyslexia. I will now list, in brief, some of the differences in behaviors that characterize ADHD and dyslexia in children, particularly children in the elementary school classroom.

3   A young person with ADHD cannot easily sit still, certainly a problem in the classroom. He or she often leaves his assigned seat, running around and attempting to climb on shelves, desks, and the like. When told firmly to remain in his seat, the child will try to obey but will squirm and fidget almost constantly, clearly in a state of agitation. He acts as if he is driven by a motor.

4   A child with ADHD often talks excessively and is unable to wait to be called on: instead, he blurts out answers and responses. He seems to just butt into games and conversations, not observing social norms that require a give-and-take among group members. Such behavior often alienates other children and frustrates teachers and others who try to maintain control. Other children may shun the child with ADHD. This ostracism, in turn, results in further negative effects, such as low self-esteem and greater isolation.

PAUSE: Summarize the characteristics of ADHD.

5   In contrast, a young person with dyslexia can sit still but has trouble organizing objects, belongings, and letters. She may mix up sounds, saying, for example, "plain" for "plan" or "seal" for "soul." She may have a stutter, furthering the frustration and embarrassment she already feels.

6   A dyslexic child typically reads poorly, confusing the order of letters, for example, in words such as "saw" and "was." Also, she may confuse words that have similar shapes or start and end with the same letters, as in "form" and "from" or the words cited in the last paragraph. While a dyslexic's reading is labored, his handwriting and spelling are usually worse. All of these symptoms of dyslexia, while quite different, often result in the same ostracism and loss of self-esteem. These problems then cause other behavior problems that are similar to those shown in children with ADHD and a number of other conditions. This explains why certain conditions are often confused. In addition, many children indeed have more than one condition. For example, over 40 percent of children with dyslexia have ADHD as well.

PAUSE: Summarize the characteristics of dyslexia.

7   Unfortunately, because of budgeting restrictions, dyslexics are sometimes placed among the wrong group for remediation. In order for any intervention to succeed, it must be tailored specifically for the dyslexic. There are many improved techniques now being used successfully in reading remediation that are based on the Orton-Gillingham method. Many of these can be obtained on videocassettes and CDs. Arlene Sonday and the Scottish Rite Hospital have such programs on the market, and many other good ones can be located on the internet (for example, https://dyslexiaida.org/, kidshealth.org/, and https://www.ninds.nih.gov/Disorders/All-Disorders/Dyslexia-Information-Page, among many others).

8   There are many successful dyslexics in our society, some contemporary and others in the past. Albert Einstein, Benjamin Franklin, and General George Patton are a few who have made history. Athletes Bruce [Caitlin] Jenner and Nolan Ryan and entertainers Whoopi Goldberg and Cher are among our contemporaries. Identifying with the successful dyslexic offers some hope to parents and children alike. The book *Succeeding with LD* is a collection of stories of successful dyslexics. The book was authored by Jill Lauren and published by Free Spirit Publishers. Each of these stories could make a book by itself but is short enough for the dyslexic to enjoy reading.

1.   Briefly summarize Vaz's essay, including the terms being compared or contrasted and the major similarities or differences.

2.   What organization does Vaz use? Why is it effective?

3.   Why is dyslexia so often misunderstood, according to Vaz?

4.   Why is Vaz particularly interested in dyslexia?

Comparison and Contrast in Everyday Life

The following essay appeared in *Newsweek* in 2009.

Stephanie Lindsley

CRITICAL
READING
■ Preview
■ Read
■ Pause
■ Review

(See pp. 4–11.)

Autism and Education

GUIDING QUESTION

What are some differences between the educational resources Lindsley's son and daughter receive?

PAUSE:
Who is being compared? Can you understand the writer's purpose yet?

1   My son and my daughter are happy, active, healthy children who enjoy school and are lucky to have a solid family life, but they are very different. My autistic son tests in the "severe" range in many subjects. At eight, he reads well but cannot answer basic questions about what he has read. He speaks at a three-year-old level, adores *Blue's Clues*, and is almost potty-trained.

PAUSE:
What point is Lindsley making about her daughter?

2   My daughter, meanwhile, tests in the 95th percentile nationwide on standardized tests. At twelve, she shows an amazing ability to process information, taking complex ideas apart and putting them back together to form new thoughts. She reads an entire novel most Sunday afternoons, solves the Sudoku puzzles in the paper, and memorizes the entire script—not just her own lines—for the school plays she loves to be in.

3   At school, my son spends a portion of his day in a regular classroom. But primarily he learns in a group of two to six children led by an intervention specialist, often accompanied by an aide. Even when he is in the regular classroom, he is never without an adult by his side. His intervention specialist records everything he does in daily logs that are required to ensure funding. She often presents me with new strategies to help him learn a difficult concept, which attests to the volumes of time she dedicates to addressing his unique needs.

4   My son's teachers do their absolute best for him. I know they love him. But beyond that, his government-mandated Individualized Education Plan legally ensures that he gets every opportunity to excel. In addition, his teachers spend countless hours each year filling out detailed quarterly reports and other government-required paperwork. If I decide that the school district should pay for something extra to improve my son's education, I can appeal to an independent board for mediation.

PAUSE: What point is Lindsley making about her son?

5   My daughter spends all but three hours of her school week in a regular classroom, where she often hides a book in her desk and reads while the teacher talks. She complains to me when the teacher reteaches things she learned last year, and she resents being drilled over and over on something she learned in ten minutes. For three hours a week, she is pulled from her classroom for a "gifted" program with fifteen other children, where she works either on a group project with other students or independently on her own blog or a computer-based foreign-language program.

PAUSE: How is the daughter's experience different?

6   I can only imagine how much my daughter would excel if she had a program specifically geared to her strengths, one that challenged her creativity on a daily basis. Or if she received even half the individual attention my son receives every week. What if she had a person sitting next to her to encourage her to think of new ways of doing things? What if her teacher did not have to manage a large classroom full of kids, who did not scold her for "making things confusing for everyone else"? What would happen if she spent all day in a room with two to six other gifted children, along with a couple of adults who specialized in pushing them to realize their potential?

PAUSE: What does Lindsley imagine for her daughter?

7   There is no government mandate to fund gifted education. In 2008 there was only $7.5 million in federal grants available through the **Jacob K. Javits** Gifted and Talented Students Education Program. All additional funding comes from states and private organizations. Compare that with the $24.5 billion allotted by No Child Left Behind, a federal program whose goal is to help every child, including the mentally disabled, meet minimum standards. But is that a wise investment? Wouldn't some of those billions be more wisely spent on special teachers and mandated programs for gifted children, who have the potential to make advances in science, technology, and the arts that would benefit everyone?

Jacob K. Javits: (1904–1986) U.S. senator from New York from 1957–1981.

PAUSE: What is Lindsley's main point here?

PAUSE: What
is the purpose
of Lindsley's
contrast?
How does
she justify her
position?

8   It pains me to suggest taking some of the federal money designated for my disabled son and spending it on my overperforming daughter. My son will probably meet minimum standards, but most parents of autistic children describe goals for their kids in much more modest terms: being able to bathe themselves, get a job, or live semi-independently. My daughter has the potential for much more. If she were given even a fraction of the customized education that my son receives, she could learn the skills needed to prevent the next worldwide flu pandemic, or invent a new form of nonpolluting transportation. Perhaps she could even discover a cure for autism.

1.   Briefly summarize Lindsley's essay, including what she is comparing and what major point of contrast she uses.

2.   Who is Lindsley's audience? Do the questions that she asks her readers help you identify her audience?

3.   What type of comparison/contrast organization does Lindsley use?

4.   Do you agree or disagree with Lindsley? Why or why not?

Write a Comparison and Contrast Essay

Write your own comparison and contrast essay on one of the following topics or on a topic of your own choice. Use the **COMPARISON AND CONTRAST** charts on page 155 to help you with basic organization, and follow the Writing Guide: Comparison and Contrast checklist as you write and revise (p. 163).

COLLEGE	• Compare and/or contrast two coaches, bosses, or instructors. • Compare and/or contrast two grammar practice websites.
WORK	• Compare and/or contrast two office environments. • Compare and/or contrast benefits offered by two companies.
EVERYDAY LIFE	• Compare and/or contrast good customer service and bad customer service. • Compare and/or contrast a toy that was popular in your early childhood with toys targeting similar ages today. What can we learn about our society through changes in toys?

WRITING GUIDE: Comparison and Contrast

STEPS IN COMPARISON AND CONTRAST	HOW TO DO THE STEPS
☐ Focus.	• Think about what you want to compare and contrast and your purpose for writing.
☐ Explore your topic. See Chapter 2.	• Make a side-by-side list of possible parallel points of comparison or contrast between your subjects.
☐ Write a thesis statement. Subjects + Main point = Thesis See Chapter 3.	• Include your subjects and some indication of whether you will be comparing or contrasting them.
☐ Support your thesis. See Chapter 3.	• Choose the points of comparison or contrast that your readers will understand and that will serve your purpose.
☐ Write a draft. See Chapter 4.	• Decide whether to use point-by-point or whole-to-whole organization and how to arrange your main points (by time, space, or importance). • Write topic sentences for your support paragraphs.
☐ Revise your draft. See Chapter 4.	• Reread to add any examples that will help your readers understand. • Add transitions. • Improve your introduction, thesis, and conclusion.
☐ Edit your revised draft. See Chapters 16 through 18.	• Correct errors in grammar, spelling, word use, and punctuation.
☐ Evaluate your writing.	• Does it have the Four Basics of Good Comparison and Contrast (p. 151)? • Is this the best I can do?

Reflect on the Process

Look at your writing from this chapter, from your prewriting through revision and editing, and consider these questions:

1. What was the most difficult part of the process for you? Why?

2. Did the feedback you got on your initial draft provide you with information you could use to make changes in your draft? If not, what can you do to improve the feedback you get next time? What specific questions do you need your reviewers to answer for you?

3. What will you do differently the next time you write a comparison and contrast essay?

4. Talk to someone who has taken courses in your major or who is working in your field. How is comparison and contrast used in your major or career? What kinds of comparison and contrast writing tasks can you expect in the future?

12

Cause and Effect

Writing That Explains Reasons or Results

Understand What Cause and Effect Are

A **cause** is what makes an event, or *effect*, happen. An **effect** is what happens as a result of an event, or *cause*.

Four Basics of Good Cause and Effect

1. The main idea reflects the writer's purpose — to explain causes, effects, or both (main point).

2. If the purpose is to explain causes, it presents real causes; if the purpose is to explain effects, it presents real effects (primary support).

3. It provides details and examples to illustrate and explain the causes and effects (secondary support).

4. It arranges causes and/or effects in timer order, space order, or order of importance (logical organization).

In the following paragraph, each number corresponds to one of the Four Basics of Good Cause and Effect.

1 Little doubt remains that global warming is a threat to our world, but not everyone understands why it is happening and what the effects are. 2 Many experts believe that this warming trend is largely the result of greenhouse gases, 3 including carbon dioxide emissions, mainly from cars, and pollutants from industrial processes. 2 Deforestation is another significant cause. 3 Forests absorb carbon dioxide and convert it into oxygen. Therefore, cutting trees increases the amount of greenhouse gases in the atmosphere,

4 Causes and effects arranged in order of importance.

which contributes to global warming. **2** If current warming trends continue, the entire world is at risk for negative consequences. **3** Scientists predict that sea levels will rise dangerously and flood coastal areas. There will also be more droughts and changes in precipitation patterns, such as more hurricanes and tornadoes. **2** In addition and possibly most destructive is the threat to plant and animal life and, consequently, to public health.

Analyzing causes and effects goes beyond asking "What happened?" to also ask "Why?" and "How?"

Jim Rice of Quinsigamond Community College helps his students visualize the cause-and-effect relationship by suggesting that they think of three linked rings.

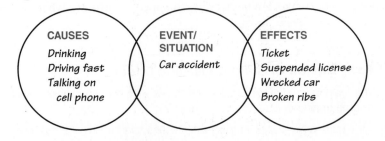

Many situations require you to determine causes or effects.

COLLEGE	In an information technology course, you must discuss the effects of a virus on a local-area computer network.
WORK	You analyze the likely effects of working five fewer hours per week.
EVERYDAY LIFE	You try to figure out what is causing your phone to need a battery charge so often.

First Basic: Main Point in Cause and Effect

The **main point** in a cause-and-effect essay should reflect your **purpose**. For example, if you are writing about why a certain event in history happened, your main point would be to explain the causes. If you are writing about what happened as a result of that event, your main point would be to explain the effects. Consider the following thesis from an essay on drunk driving.

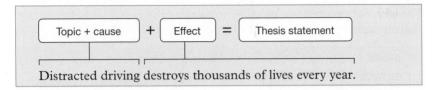

The main point of the essay is to discuss the effects of distracted driving—thousands of destroyed lives. The body of the essay will give examples.

Sometimes a thesis statement for a cause-and-effect essay will include both what caused the topic and what resulted from the topic. The topic sentence below follows this pattern.

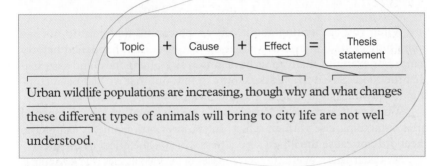

Sometimes the writer does not directly indicate causes or effects in the thesis statement, as in the following example.

> Until local police departments enforce restraining orders, women and children will continue to be the victims of violence.

Although the writer does not indicate a specific cause or effect, the main point of the essay is clear—to discuss how unenforced restraining orders have resulted in violence. The body of the essay will likely give examples of such situations.

As you begin to write cause-and-effect essays, you might find it helpful to include both the topic and an indicator of cause or effect in your thesis statement.

Second and Third Basics: Support in Cause and Effect

In a cause-and-effect essay, **support** consists of explanations of causes and effects, and it demonstrates the main point stated in your thesis. Take, for example, the following thesis statement.

> Irresponsible behavior caused my car accident.

The writer supported this thesis by presenting the causes with details that explain them.

CAUSE	Driving too fast	**CAUSE**	On my cell phone
DETAILS	Rainy and slippery	**DETAILS**	Not paying close attention
	Going too fast to control car		Hit a curve while laughing
	Could not stop		Did not react fast enough
CAUSE	Drinking	**CAUSE**	Tired
DETAILS	Not focused	**DETAILS**	Working late all week
	Slowed reaction time		Only sleeping 4–5 hours a night

When you are writing about causes, be careful that you do not say something caused an event or situation just because it happened beforehand. For example, many of us have gotten sick after a meal and assumed that the food caused the sickness, only to find out that we had been coming down with the flu even before the meal.

When writing about effects, do not confuse something that happened after something else with an effect. In the previous example, just as the meal did not cause the illness, the illness was not the effect of the meal.

Mistaken causes or effects are examples of logical fallacies (see Chapter 1, p. 9).

Fourth Basic: Organization in Cause and Effect

Cause-and-effect essays are organized in different ways depending on their purpose.

MAIN POINT	PURPOSE	ORGANIZATION
Global warming is a serious threat to life as we know it.	To explain the effects of global warming	Order of importance (saving the most serious effect for last)
Global warming will flood many coastal states.	To describe how the U.S. map eventually might look	Space order
Over the next century, the effects of global warming will be dramatic.	To describe the effects of global warming over the next 100 years	Time order

As you write your essay, add transitions to show how each cause or effect relates to your main point. Here are some common transitions that are used in cause-and-effect writing.

Common Transitions in Cause and Effect

one cause, reason, effect, result	as a result
also	because
another	thus
first, second, third, and so on	as a consequence

CAUSE AND EFFECT AT A GLANCE

Thesis Statement
Indicates causes, effects, or both

↓

Cause 1 or Effect 1
Detailed explanation or example of the first cause or effect

↓

Cause 2 or Effect 2
Detailed explanation or example of the second cause or effect

↓

Cause 3 or Effect 3
Detailed explanation or example of the third cause or effect

↓

Conclusion
Reminds your reader of your main point and makes an observation about it based on what you have written.
Note: whether you focus on causes, effects, or both, you may discuss more than three points, depending on your purpose.

Read and Analyze Cause and Effect

Read the following three examples of cause and effect—from college, the workplace, and everyday life—and answer the questions that accompany them.

For each essay, review the Four Basics of Good Cause and Effect (p. 165) and practice the critical reading process explained in Chapter 1 (pp. 4–11).

Cause and Effect in College

The following cause-and-effect essay was written for a child development course.

Jeanine Pepper

CRITICAL
READING
▪ Preview
▪ Read
▪ Pause
▪ Review

(See pp. 4–11.)

The Effects of Attachment Deprivation on Infants

GUIDING QUESTION

What are the effects of social deprivation on infants?

Harlow:
Harry Harlow, American psychologist famous for his work on social isolation

PAUSE:
Underline the two effects in this paragraph.

PAUSE:
Do any of these effects surprise you? Why or why not?

1   Infants are born with an instinct to attach themselves, to bond with, their caregivers, whether the caregiver is a parent or some other person. The instinct is so strong that experiments like **Harlow**'s have shown that infants will bond even with cloth substitutes. When infants are deprived of attachment, the effects are both immediate and long-ranging.

2   The immediate effects of attachment deprivation are obvious and sad. When babies are neglected or abused and deprived of any social stimulation, they are constantly afraid of their environment and others. Imagine being born and not being held or talked to: the world would be a pretty scary place. Another common effect is that they do not learn how to speak or communicate in any way. Because they never experience communication with others, they experience others as foreign and threatening. The infants often become totally withdrawn.

3   The effects of attachment deprivation often do not end with infancy. As the child grows older, he or she is still fearful, and that fear shows itself as anger. The child is often aggressive, defensive, and friendless. Many juvenile criminals have been shown to have been abused or neglected in infancy.

4   Individuals who are deprived of attachment in infancy are often depressed and more likely to develop drug and alcohol addictions, which in turn may lead to crime. The aggression they showed even as toddlers

is more dangerous in adults, leading to fights, lost jobs, or unhealthy or abusive relationships.

5   The saddest long-range effect of attachment deprivation is when people carry on the pattern of abuse or neglect into another generation. Studies have shown that most child abusers were abused as children. That is the childhood they knew, and they repeat it.

6   Not all children who were abused or neglected grow up with these effects. Some are able to develop normally. However, many infants who experienced attachment deprivation grow up to be very troubled human beings. The effects are serious and spread into all areas of their lives and the lives of others around them.

1. **Summarize**. Briefly summarize Pepper's essay, including her audience and purpose for writing and all the major effects.

2. **Analyze**. How does Pepper organize the effects?

3. **Synthesize**. Did you know about the effects of social deprivation on children? What other kinds of negative behaviors are often carried from one generation to another? How do you know this?

4. **Evaluate**. Does Pepper clearly present the effects? What contributes to the clarity? Would an instructor reading the essay understand what Pepper has learned about the subject? Does the essay have the Four Basics of Good Cause and Effect (see p. 165)?

> **CRITICAL THINKING**
> ■ Summarize
> ■ Analyze
> ■ Synthesize
> ■ Evaluate
>
> (More on pp. 12–18.)

Cause and Effect at Work

The following infographic was created by staff at the Centers for Disease Control and Prevention (CDC) to show the consequences (the effects) of smoking on the body. Many workplaces now use infographics to convey information and facts using a combination of photographs, graphics, and text.

Infographic

Risks from Smoking

GUIDING QUESTION

What does the CDC want the audience to understand about smoking?

Risks from Smoking

Smoking can damage every part of your body

Congenital:
present at the
time someone
is born

Cleft:
something
that is split
into two parts,
separated

Periodontitis:
gum disease

Aneurysm:
a condition
where blood
vessels swell
and can burst

**Atherosclero-
sis:** hardening
of the arteries

Ectopic:
occurring in
the wrong
place (outside
the uterus, for
pregnancies)

Cancers

Oropharynx

Larynx

Esophagus

Trachea, bronchus, and lung

Acute myeloid leukemia

Stomach

Liver

Pancreas

Kidney
and ureter

Cervix

Bladder

Colorectal

Chronic Diseases

Stroke

Blindness, cataracts, **age-related macular degeneration***

Congenital defects–maternal smoking: orofacial clefts*

Periodontitis

Aortic aneurysm, early abdominal aortic
atherosclerosis in young adults

Coronary heart disease

Pneumonia

Atherosclerotic peripheral vascular disease

Chronic obstructive pulmonary disease, **tuberculosis,***
asthma, and other respiratory effects

Diabetes*

Reproductive effects in women
(including reduced fertility)

Hip fractures

Ectopic pregnancy*

Male sexual function–erectile dysfunction*

Rheumatoid arthritis*

Immune function*

Overall diminished health

*Each condition presented in blue text and followed by an asterisk is a new disease causally linked
to smoking in the 2014 Surgeon General's Report, *The Health Consequences of Smoking—50 Years
of Progress.*

U.S. Department of Health and Human Services. *Smoking—50 Years of Progress: A Report of the Surgeon
General.* Atlanta (GA): U.S. Department of Health and Human Services, Centers for Disease Control and Prevention,
National Center for Chronic Disease Prevention and Health Promotion, Office on Smoking and Health, 2014.

1. What are the main point and purpose of this infographic?

2. How is the information in the infographic organized?

3. Why might a writer choose to present information through an infographic
   instead of a traditional essay?

4. Does the infographic show the Four Basics of Cause and Effect? Why or
   why not? What would you change about the infographic to make it more
   effective?

Cause and Effect in Everyday Life

The following example of cause-and-effect writing appeared in a *Boston Globe* article.

Christopher Shea

In Praise of Peer Pressure

GUIDING QUESTION

How can peer pressure have positive results?

CRITICAL READING
- Preview
- Read
- Pause
- Review

(See pp. 4–11.)

1　Peer pressure gets bad press, but in some cases more of it might make the world a better place. In California, psychologists recently found that they could get people to conserve electricity with a simple notice, delivered to their doorstep, telling them how their consumption compared with the neighborhood average. In the weeks that followed, homeowners who were consuming more electricity than their neighbors cut back—presumably because they were embarrassed to be out of step with the herd.

PAUSE: How is Shea defining peer pressure, based on the example in this paragraph?

2　The research, reported in *Psychological Science*, reflects growing interest in what's known as "social-norms marketing"—attempting to change behavior by telling people what their peers do. The basic concept is about two decades old, but psychologists have been intensifying efforts to find more effective ways of using it. And now, with a growing recognition of the limits of browbeating, a wide range of groups—from climate-change activists to college deans trying to keep students from drinking themselves to oblivion—have been making peer pressure their ally.

PAUSE: What is social-norms marketing?

3　"The norm is like a magnet," says Robert Cialdini, a professor at Arizona State University who is an author of the new study. "What's appropriate to do, in most people's minds, is what other people like them do."

4　The social-norms approach is part of a general movement to make productive use of insights into the quirks of the human psyche. For example, psychologists have found that presenting people with a wide range of choices (about almost anything) can frustrate and immobilize them, so that they end up making no choice at all or a bad choice. Supermarket managers and policy experts designing health plans have taken note.

PAUSE: Why would supermarket managers want to think about this?

5　Cialdini's work tends to focus on the environment. In a paper from 2003, he identified a problem with signs in the Petrified Forest National Park, in Arizona, intended to discourage the theft of ancient, irreplaceable wood. The signs sternly warned that America's "heritage" was being "vandalized" by "theft losses of petrified wood of 14 tons a year."

6　That sent the message that pocketing souvenirs was the norm for tourists, Cialdini argues. In an on-site experiment, he and his coauthors demonstrated that by making use of new signs that stressed how few

PAUSE: Is there another possible explanation for what happened at the national park?

people removed items from the park and that by symbolically isolating those who do (on the sign, thieving stick figures had red slashes through them), the park could cut vandalism substantially.

PAUSE: Can you think of an example of a positive effect of peer pressure?

7   In another experiment, Cialdini has shown that hotels will have more success encouraging their clients to reuse towels if they alter the wording of their appeals. "Join your fellow guests in helping to save the environment: a majority of our guests use their towels more than once" works better than any other approach.

8   In Minnesota, a study by the Department of Revenue found that informing taxpayers that most people don't cheat on their taxes improved tax compliance more than stressing the link between taxes and popular public programs.

9   The field is still in flux: the effects of peer pressure remain hard to measure and hard to manipulate—yet the tug of the herd mindset is everywhere. Coincidentally, I recently came across a survey that found that 80 percent of adult males in the United States have six or fewer drinks in a week. I was taken aback, assuming the average was higher. I skipped wine with dinner a few times that week.

PAUSE: What is he going to think about?

10   Later that same week, I read in an economics journal that freelance businessmen—I'm a freelancer—report only about 60 percent of their income, according to IRS estimates. Yet I'm scrupulous to the penny. Do I want to remain abnormal? Does anyone? I filed for an extension, so I've got some time to think about it.

1.   In your own words, describe the effects of peer pressure that Shea presents.

2.   Describe some effects of peer pressure that you have experienced or observed.

3.   Do you think peer pressure is a good thing? How can it be negative?

4.   Does Shea's essay have the Four Basics of Good Cause and Effect (p. 165)? Why or why not?

Write a Cause-and-Effect Essay

Write your own cause-and-effect essay on one of the following topics or on a topic of your own choice. Use CAUSE AND EFFECT AT A GLANCE as a basic organizer (p. 169), and follow the Writing Guide: Cause and Effect checklist as you write and revise (p. 175).

COLLEGE	• Explain the immediate effects of being in college or the desired long-term effects on your life of going to college. • Present the causes of a legitimate absence that resulted in your missing a test (directed to your professor).
WORK	• Discuss the causes of low employee morale. • Explain the effects of juggling work, school, and family.
EVERYDAY LIFE	• Analyze the causes of an argument with a friend or a member of your family. • Discuss the causes or effects of your current financial situation.

(handwritten notes in right margin: Stress less time money)

WRITING GUIDE: Cause and Effect

STEPS IN CAUSE AND EFFECT	HOW TO DO THE STEPS
☐ Focus.	• Think about an event or a situation that had concrete causes and/or effects.
☐ Explore your topic. See Chapter 2.	• With your purpose in mind, prewrite or use the ring diagram (p. 166) to get ideas about causes and effects.
☐ Write a thesis statement. Topic + Indication of cause or effect = Thesis See Chapter 3.	• Write a thesis statement that includes your topic and an indication of whether you will be showing causes, effects, or both.
☐ Support your thesis. See Chapter 3.	• List the major causes and/or effects. • For each cause or effect, give details that will help your readers understand how they caused or affected an event.

(handwritten diagram at bottom: Cause — Time spent w/ family, school, friends, work; Effect — Stress, less time, tired)

(Continued)

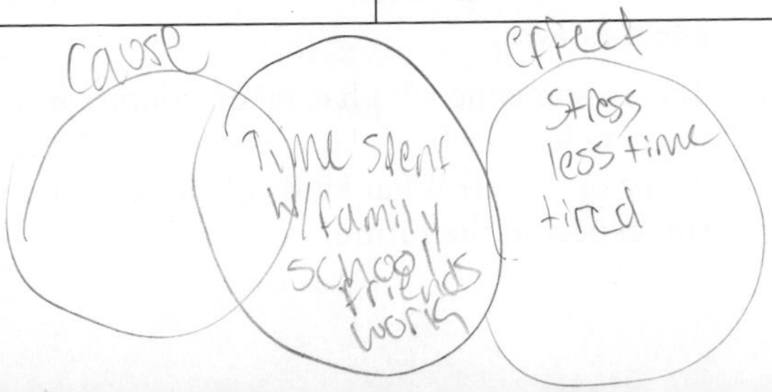

STEPS IN CAUSE AND EFFECT	HOW TO DO THE STEPS
☐ **Write a draft.** See Chapter 4.	• Arrange the causes and/or effects in a logical order (often chronological or by importance). • Write topic sentences for each major cause and/or effect and paragraphs that describe them in detail.
☐ **Revise your draft.** See Chapter 4.	• Ask another person to read and comment on your draft. • With your purpose and audience in mind, read to make sure the causes and effects are real, and if you have explained them adequately. • Add transitions. • Improve your introduction, thesis, and conclusion.
☐ **Edit your draft.** See Chapters 16 through 18.	• Correct errors in grammar, spelling, word use, and punctuation.
☐ **Evaluate your writing.**	• Does it have the Four Basics of Good Cause and Effect (p. 165)? • Is this the best I can do?

Reflect on the Process

Look at your writing from this chapter, from your prewriting through revision and editing, and consider these questions:

1. What was the most difficult part of the process for you? Why?

2. Did the feedback you got on your initial draft provide you with information you could use to make changes in your draft? If not, what can you do to improve the feedback you get next time? What specific questions do you need your reviewers to answer for you?

3. What will you do differently the next time you write a cause-and-effect essay?

4. Talk to someone who has taken courses in your major or who is working in your field. How is cause and effect analysis used in your major or career? What kinds of cause-and-effect writing tasks can you expect in the future?

13

Argument

Writing That Persuades

Understand What Argument Is

Argument is writing that takes a position on an issue and offers reasons and supporting evidence to convince someone else to accept, or at least consider, that position. Argument is also used to persuade someone to take an action (or not to take an action).

> **Four Basics of Good Argument**
>
> **1** It takes a clear position on an issue or advises a particular action (main point).
>
> **2** It provides reasons to defend the position or recommended action and considers opposing views (primary support).
>
> **3** It gives evidence to support reasons or responds to opposing views (secondary support).
>
> **4** It arranges support according to order of importance or emphasis (logical organization).

In the following paragraph, each number corresponds to one of the Four Basics of Good Argument.

1 The drinking age should be lowered from twenty-one to eighteen. **2** The government gives eighteen-year-olds the right to vote. **3** If they are adult enough to vote for the people and policies that run this country, they should be mature enough to have a drink. **2** The U.S. penal system also regards eighteen-year-olds as adults. **3** If an eighteen-year-old commits a crime and goes to trial, he or she is tried and sentenced as an adult, not as a minor. That means

4
Reasons are organized by order of importance.

177

that if the crime is murder, an eighteen-year-old could receive the death penalty. Eighteen-year-olds are not given special treatment. **2** Most important is the fact that at eighteen, individuals can enlist in the armed forces and go to war. **3** The government considers them old enough to die for their country but not old enough to have a drink? This makes no sense. **2** Opponents to lowering the drinking age justify their position by saying that if the age is lowered, teenagers will start drinking even earlier. **3** However, there is no evidence to show that legal age is a major influence on teenage drinking. Other factors involved, such as peer pressure and the availability of fake IDs, have more impact on whether teenagers drink. While the government does need to address the issue of teenage drinking, forbidding eighteen-year-olds to drink while granting them other, more important rights and responsibilities at the same age is neither consistent nor reasonable.

4
Reasons are organized by order of importance.

Argument is the method you use to persuade people to see things your way or at least to understand your position. Argument helps you to take action in problem situations rather than to stand by, silent and frustrated. Although knowing how to argue will not eliminate all such situations, it will help you to defend your position.

Many situations require good argument skills.

COLLEGE	An exit essay from a writing course contains the following instruction: "Develop a well-balanced argument on the subject of free speech on the internet."
WORK	You present reasons why you should get a promotion.
EVERYDAY LIFE	You convince a large company that it has made a mistake on your bill.

First Basic: Main Point in Argument

Your **main point** or **claim** in an argument is the position you take on the issue you are writing about. When you are free to choose an issue, choose something you care about. When you are assigned an issue, research the topic carefully so you can take a definite position.

Take a few minutes to think about the issue, talk it over with a partner, or jot down ideas related to it. Once you have decided on your position, write a thesis statement that includes the issue and your position on it.

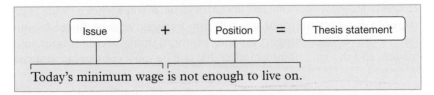

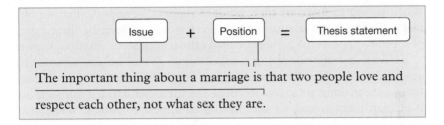

Sometimes the thesis combines the issue and the position, as in the following statement.

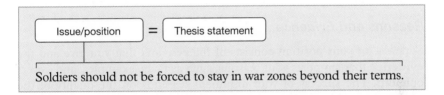

Make the thesis statement for any argument as specific as possible to help guide your writing and your readers.

VAGUE	Our health-care system is disgraceful.
MORE SPECIFIC	Two key reforms would make health care more affordable for all.
	[The paper would detail the two reforms.]

Many thesis statements for arguments use words such as the following because they clearly express a position.

could (not)	ought (not)
must (not)	requires
must have	should (not)
needs	would

Second and Third Basics: Support in Argument

However strongly you may feel about an issue, if you do not provide solid **support** for your position, you will not convince anyone to see it your way. As you develop support for your position, think carefully about your readers and the kind of information that will be most convincing to them.

Making Appeals

When we argue, there are three types of support, or appeals, that we can make. Writers often use traditional Greek words to describe these types of support: appeals to character, called **ethos**; appeals to emotion, known as **pathos**; and appeals to logic, called **logos**. When we ask someone to accept our argument based on our own credibility, expertise, or character, we are making an appeal to ethos. On the other hand, if our support is primarily emotional, we are making an appeal to pathos. While academic writing may include appeals to ethos and pathos, the most widely accepted support in academic writing involves logic and careful reasoning, or an appeal to logos. We make such an appeal by presenting reasons and evidence.

The fact that a person's opinion appears on a website does not necessarily mean that he or she has any expertise. When in doubt about a source's authority, consult your instructor or a research librarian.

For more on finding sources, using quotations, and citing sources, see Chapter 14.

Reasons and Evidence

Support for your position consists of the **reasons** that you give and the **evidence** that supports your reasons, such as facts, examples, and expert opinions. The success of your argument depends on the quality of the reasons and evidence that you present to support your position.

Facts are statements or observations that can be proved true. **Statistics**—numerical facts based on research—can be persuasive evidence to back up your position. (Although be careful in evaluating and using statistics: the same numbers can be used to say different, even contradictory, things.) **Examples** are specific experiences or pieces of information that support your position. **Expert opinion** is the opinion of someone who is considered an expert in the area you are writing about. Here are some reasons and evidence to support the position that it pays to stay in college:

POSITION	It pays to stay in college.
REASON	College graduates earn more than high school graduates.
EVIDENCE/FACT	College graduates earn 55 percent more than high school graduates.

REASON	Students learn up-to-date skills that they will need to find a job.
EVIDENCE/ EXAMPLE	Understanding how to use technology in your field may make the difference between getting a job and coming in second.
REASON	Many jobs require college degrees.
EVIDENCE/EXPERT OPINION	John Sterling, president of one of the largest recruiting agencies, said recently, "Ten years ago, a college degree was perceived as an advantage. Today, the college degree is the basic ticket of entry for the majority of jobs."

When you use expert opinion, you need to identify the source of direct quotations.

As you choose reasons and evidence to support your position, consider your readers. Are they likely to agree with you, to be uncommitted, or to be hostile? Choose the support that is most likely to convince them, drawing on outside sources (such as the library or internet) as needed.

Opposing Positions

Part of the support for your position should involve the opposing position: acknowledge this position and the reasons for it (known as **counterarguments**), and present some evidence against them. Your evidence against the counterargument is your **rebuttal**. If, for example, you are arguing in favor of lowering the drinking age to eighteen, you should not ignore the position that it should be kept at age twenty-one. If you do not say anything about the other position, you are leaving your argument unprotected. To defend your own position, show some weakness in the opposing position.

The writer of the paragraph on page 177 might consider the opposing position as follows.

POSITION	The drinking age should be lowered from twenty-one to eighteen.
OPPOSING POSITION	The drinking age should not be lowered because people begin drinking before the legal age. If the age were lowered to eighteen, more sixteen-year-olds would drink.
RECOGNIZE AND REBUT COUNTER-ARGUMENT	First, laws should not be based on the extent to which they are likely to be abused or broken. They should be based on what's right. Even so, there is no evidence to show that legal age is a major influence on teenage drinking. Other factors involved, such as peer pressure and the availability of fake IDs, have more impact on whether teenagers drink.

As you gather support for your position, keep the opposing position in mind.

Faulty Reasoning

As you write and review the support for your position, be sure that your evidence is good and your reasoning is logical. Unfortunately, we are exposed to **faulty reasoning** all the time, especially in advertising. Certain kinds of errors in logic are so common that there is a name for them — **logical fallacies**. Be aware of the common fallacies so you can avoid them. For a review of logical fallacies, see Chapter 1, pages 12–18.

Fourth Basic: Organization in Argument

Argument most often uses **order of importance** to organize reasons for the writer's position on the issue. Arrange your reasons and evidence so that they build the strongest case for your position, and save the most convincing reason for last. Do not forget to acknowledge and address the opposing position somewhere in your argument.

As you write your argument, use transitions such as those in the box below to move your readers from one reason or point to the next.

Common Transitions in Argument

FROM ONE POINT TO ANOTHER	TO ADD EMPHASIS
also	above all
another fact to consider	best of all
another reason	especially
another thing	in fact
consider that	in particular
for example	more important
in addition	most important
in the first place	remember
furthermore	the last point to consider
on the other hand	worst of all

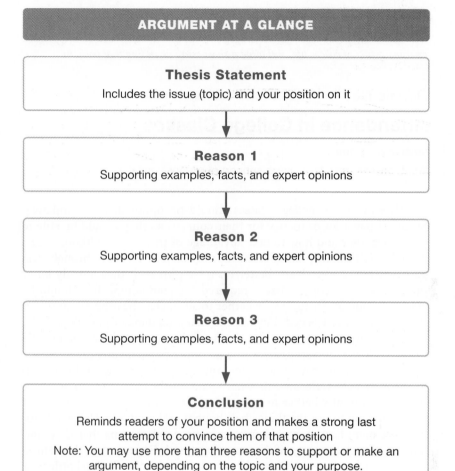

ARGUMENT AT A GLANCE

Thesis Statement
Includes the issue (topic) and your position on it

Reason 1
Supporting examples, facts, and expert opinions

Reason 2
Supporting examples, facts, and expert opinions

Reason 3
Supporting examples, facts, and expert opinions

Conclusion
Reminds readers of your position and makes a strong last attempt to convince them of that position
Note: You may use more than three reasons to support or make an argument, depending on the topic and your purpose.

Read and Analyze Argument

Read the following three examples of argument—from college, the workplace, and everyday life—and answer the questions that accompany them. As you read, notice that argument uses many of the other kinds of writing you have studied to support a position. It may tell a story, give examples, describe something, explain how something works, break a large point into categories, define a term, compare two or more things, or show cause and effect.

For each essay, review the Four Basics of Good Argument (p. 177) and practice the critical reading process explained in Chapter 1.

Argument in College

The following essay was written in response to this assignment: *Take a position on some aspect of college life, and write a short essay defending that position.*

Donnie Ney

CRITICAL
READING
■ Preview
■ Read
■ Pause
■ Review

(See pp. 4–11.)

Attendance in College Classes

GUIDING QUESTION

What reasons does Ney give in support of his position?

PAUSE:
What is Ney's claim? What reasons has Ney included in this paragraph?

1   **A**ttendance in college classes should be optional, not mandatory. Students pay a lot of money for their courses, so they should be able to decide whether and how to take advantage of them. Also, although class participation can help many students, not all students learn through class participation. If they learn better on their own or if they already know the content of a course that is required for graduation, they should be able to decide for themselves whether to sit in class hearing about things they already have learned. Finally, optional attendance would benefit the students who want to go to class because the student-to-instructor ratio would be lower, and students would get more personal attention.

PAUSE: Do you agree that paying for the course should give students the right to attend or not without a penalty?

2   First, students pay tuition, fees, and the cost of books and materials to enroll in a class. Because they have paid for the class, they should have the choice about whether to attend. Isn't it a basic right of a consumer to decide how to use the things he's bought and paid for? Also, students' lives are complicated, and there are many good reasons that they may have to miss classes, even if they want to attend. For example, this semester I have missed several classes because of my child's ongoing battle with severe asthma. I cannot jeopardize her health in order to get to a class. On the other hand, I do not want to fail because I have missed more than the allowed number of classes. Such a policy does not seem fair.

3   Also, it seems unfair to require students who already know the course content or who learn it on their own to waste their time hearing about it again. Although most students attend classes because they want to learn, there are some required courses that students have to take whether they want to or not. For example, I have had to attend basic computer classes to teach me procedures such as how to turn on a computer, what email is, and how to access the internet. I have known these things for years. Why should I sit through classes that repeat what I know when I could be spending my time doing the many things I really need to do? Why should I fail if I miss too many of these classes? Such policies do not benefit me or anyone else. In addition, although colleges do not like to admit this,

attendance does not always correspond to grades. For example, some students can read and understand the materials assigned without any help from the teacher. If the goal of a college course is to learn, and a student can learn without attending class, why should that student need to attend lectures?

4   The best reason for making attendance optional is that students who do choose to attend could benefit from smaller classes and more personal attention. Classes could include more one-on-one instruction, which might improve students' grades and their ability to understand and retain course content. Many students struggle with course content and really need more of the instructor's time. However, with large classes, instructors do not have much chance to spend lots of time with individual students.

5   For all these reasons, I believe that attendance should be optional in college courses. Students do not all learn in the same way. Some students learn best by studying a lot rather than sitting in class. With more study time and less class time, some students will achieve better results on tests. Attendance should be the students' choice. If they need to go to class to pass, they will attend; if they do not need to go to class to learn, they should not be penalized.

PAUSE: Where does Ney acknowledge the opposition?

PAUSE: Note that this benefit is an effect of Ney's position.

PAUSE: What, to you, is the most persuasive reason Ney gives?

1.   **Summarize**. Briefly summarize Ney's essay, including the topic, his position on it, and the main support he gives.

2.   **Analyze**. How does Ney use transitions in his essay? How does he connect his concluding paragraph to his thesis statement? Do you see any evidence of bias in the essay?

3.   **Synthesize**. Read the attendance policy on the syllabus for this course. How would Ney respond to it? Have you had discussions about this topic with other students?

4.   **Evaluate**. Does Ney make a good argument? Do you agree with him? Does his essay have the Four Basics of Good Argument (p. 177)? Are there any logical fallacies?

CRITICAL THINKING
■ Summarize
■ Analyze
■ Synthesize
■ Evaluate

(More on pp. 12–18.)

Argument at Work

The director of a nonprofit organization wrote this letter to support the parole request of a young man he had worked with.

Shawn Brown

Letter to a Parole Board

GUIDING QUESTION

What is Brown's purpose, and what is his overall point?

Courtesy Shawn Brown

Shawn Brown
Founder, Diamond Educators

CRITICAL READING
■ Preview
■ Read
■ Pause
■ Review

(See pp. 4–11.)

PAUSE: How does Brown introduce his topic and claim? What do you think the next paragraph will be about?

PAUSE: What conditions does Brown list as causes of bad life choices? Why does Brown write about Diamond Educators here rather than talking about Rodney?

PAUSE: Why is the last sentence here important to Brown's argument?

To Whom It May Concern:

1   It is with enthusiasm that I am writing to support parole for Rodney Strong. In his work for Diamond Educators as a mentor to young men, he has made a positive contribution to the at-risk youth in the city of Boston.

2   Diamond Educators is a nonprofit mentoring program that serves at-risk young males who attend Boston public schools or who live in the inner-city neighborhoods of Boston. The mentors of the Diamond Educators program are multicultural male educators and professionals who grew up in the city of Boston and who dealt with adverse conditions that the majority of our young minority males face every day, conditions that often result in bad life choices. The adverse conditions I refer to are living in an environment where young men cope with peer pressure to join a gang and involve themselves with drugs, crime, and violence; single-parent homes; and a lack of positive male role models. Our mentors help young men chart a course through their difficult situations. These mentors are an invaluable resource for our young, urban, minority males.

3   As a mentor, Rodney demonstrated commitment and dedication to our program and to our students. Rodney worked long hours, but he found time to meet and counsel his mentees. He showed his mentees the importance of meeting commitments, taking responsibility, and having a positive purpose in life. He was a good example of how positive peer relationships can transform lives.

4   Rodney gave these young boys hope. He showed his mentees that by applying themselves and taking advantage of the resources available to them, they could achieve success in life. Many of the boys otherwise live without hope of any kind and choose paths that jeopardize their own well-being and that of others in the community. That hope is essential to becoming a productive member of the human community. Rodney is a leader with a strong will to achieve his own success and to help others find theirs.

5   The path to success for urban minority males is extremely difficult, and, as with many difficult courses, progress is not always direct and uninterrupted. Rodney stepped off course and made a poor decision when he committed a crime. However, he has demonstrated that he has learned from his mistake and is ready to return to his community as a positive force. He is ready to contribute to society, and to keep him incarcerated deprives us of a good man, a good leader, and a good role model for young men. His release will show his mentees that there is hope of a good, lawful life after jail.

6   Rodney is dedicated to being a good father and a good community influence. Unlike many who return to the community after incarceration, Rodney will not persist in a life of crime; he will return to his path of success and contribution. Keeping him from that serves no purpose.

7   I support Rodney Strong and will continue to support him after his return to the community. I urge you to consider his good work and to allow him to continue it.

Sincerely,
Shawn Brown, Cofounder
Diamond Educators

1. Briefly summarize Brown's essay, including the topic, his position on it, and the main reasons he gives.
2. In what paragraph does Brown acknowledge and respond to an opposing view?
3. If you were an officer of the court, would Brown's letter alone persuade you to support parole for Rodney Strong? Why or why not? What else would you want or need to know?
4. How might Brown's point of view differ from a member of the criminal justice system's?
5. What, to you, is the strongest reason Brown presents? Why?

Argument in Everyday Life

After a class discussion and assignment on the unfairness of federal financial aid regulations, student John Around Him wrote the following letter to Senator John Kerry, who not only responded to the letter but also visited Around Him's college class. Because of this contact, John Around Him was hired to work as a policy intern in Kerry's Massachusetts office.

GUIDING QUESTION

Why does the author think the financial aid system is not fair to many students?

CRITICAL READING

■ Preview
■ Read
■ Pause
■ Review

(See pp. 4–11.)

Dear Senator Kerry:
1   My name is John Around Him, and I am a student at Bunker Hill Community College in Boston, Massachusetts. I am Native American and a veteran of the war in Iraq. I know that you, as a veteran of the Vietnam War, can relate to putting your life on the line in an environment of gunfire, explosions, chaos, and confusion, wondering if the next second might be your last. For most young people, being in the middle of a dangerous war—being shot at and surrounded by death and violence—is not an appealing way to earn money for college. However, for students like me who do not qualify for federal financial aid, it may be the only way to go to college, and this is why I am writing to you. The federal financial

PAUSE: How does Around Him appeal to his audience here?

PAUSE: Note that Around Him uses narration in this paragraph.

PAUSE: Summarize what Around Him says about the criteria for eligibility. What kind of evidence does he use in this paragraph?

aid system needs to be changed because it is not effective in helping students, especially low-income and minority students, pay for college.

2   I grew up on the Pine Ridge Reservation in South Dakota and graduated from Little Wound High School in 2001. I was an average student, with a grade-point average of just under 3.0. I always wanted to go to college, but I asked myself, "How would I pay for it?" I lived with a single-parent father and with two other families, and my father would often help others who needed it. My father was a language teacher, not highly paid, so for me family financial support for college was out of the question. I had to find another answer.

3   When I turned to the federal financial aid system, I found that there is money to help some students pay for college, but none for a student like me. According to the College Board's report, "Trends in College Pricing, 2006," the average tuition, room, and board costs for public universities is $12,796 (though many are much more, as is the case here in Massachusetts) — way out of line for my family's finances. Yet according to the financial aid formula, my father made too much money.

4   The formulas used to determine a student's financial need are not realistic: They do not represent the average student's situation. For example, according to the formula, to be considered independent (which largely determines eligibility) a student must meet one of the following criteria: he or she must be either twenty-four years of age or older, married, a veteran, or an orphan or ward of the court. Many students today, however, are financially independent as soon as they graduate from high school. In 2005, according to the National Center for Education Statistics, 64 percent of students at community colleges and 37 percent at public colleges and universities were financially independent. Fifty-eight percent of those students worked at least thirty-five hours per week, and 67 percent delayed entering college to earn money to help pay for it. Still, those under age twenty-four are not considered to be independent, and their family income is taken into consideration, even when the student receives no family support. As a result, many students have to try to meet one of the other eligibility requirements. For too many, the answer is joining the military, going to war.

5   I am not saying that students should not enlist in the military. Would I have signed on if I had received financial aid? I don't know. I support our troops and enjoyed my time in the service. The military's values and discipline and my experiences there have contributed to who I am today, and I am thankful for that. However, I don't believe that students should have to risk their lives to qualify for financial aid.

6   I am writing to you not only on my own behalf but for the well-being of my family and my country. The federal financial aid system ignores a majority of students in need of aid. Despite rising tuition costs, our

financial aid options are slim, and more and more students are not able to achieve a college education, our path to success. This problem is like a cancer; unless treated, it will spread and will hurt our nation's future.

PAUSE: Why is this conclusion effective?

Sincerely yours,
John Around Him

1. Briefly summarize John Around Him's argument, including his main point and reasons.
2. Where does Around Him acknowledge the opposing view?
3. Is the argument a strong one? Why?
4. Where does Around Him address possible counterarguments or misunderstandings? Is his response effective?

Write an Argument Essay

Write your own argument essay on one of the following topics or on a topic of your own choice. Use ARGUMENT AT A GLANCE as a basic organizer (p. 183), and follow the Writing Guide: Argument checklist as you write and revise (p. 190). Select an issue that you care about so that you can argue powerfully.

COLLEGE	• Present your instructor with reasons why you should be able to make up a test that you missed. • Write a letter to the Student Affairs office proposing a student service that does not currently exist.
WORK	• Argue that you should get a promotion. • Argue that employers should or should not monitor employee email or social media use.
EVERYDAY LIFE	• Argue against a rent increase. • Take a stand on a local issue or policy that you believe is unfair.

WRITING GUIDE: Argument	
STEPS IN ARGUMENT	**HOW TO DO THE STEPS**
☐ **Focus.**	• Think about your position on an issue and how you can persuade your readers of that position.
☐ **Explore your topic.** See Chapter 2.	• Think about why you have taken the position you have. • Prewrite to find good support for your argument.
☐ **Write a thesis statement.** Topic + <u>Position</u> = Thesis See Chapter 3.	• Write a thesis statement that includes your topic and your position. • Make sure it is a strong statement with a clear position.
☐ **Support your thesis.** See Chapter 3.	• Provide facts, examples, and expert opinions to support your position. • Examine your reasons to make sure they are not faulty reasoning (see p. 9). • Consider the opposing view. • Give details to strengthen each of your main points.
☐ **Write a draft.** See Chapter 4.	• Arrange your points by order of importance, leaving the one that will have the most impact until last. • Write topic sentences for each major point and paragraphs that demonstrate and prove them. • Write a conclusion that has energy and reminds your readers of your position and main support for it.
☐ **Revise your draft.** See Chapter 4.	• With your audience in mind, read to make sure your supporting points are persuasive and complete. • Add transitions. • Improve your introduction, thesis, and conclusion.

(Continued)

STEPS IN ARGUMENT	HOW TO DO THE STEPS
☐ **Edit your draft.** See Chapters 16 through 18.	• Correct errors in grammar, spelling, word use, and punctuation.
☐ **Evaluate your writing.**	• Does it have the Four Basics of Good Argument (p. 177)? • Is this the best I can do?

Reflect on the Process

Look at your writing from this chapter, from your prewriting through revision and editing, and consider these questions:

1. What was the most difficult part of the process for you? Why?

2. Did the feedback you got on your initial draft provide you with information you could use to make changes in your draft? If not, what can you do to improve the feedback you get next time? What specific questions do you need your reviewers to answer for you?

3. What will you do differently the next time you write an argument essay?

4. Talk to someone who has taken courses in your major or who is working in your field. How is argument used in your major or career? What kinds of argument-writing tasks can you expect in the future?

Research Essays

Using Outside Sources

This chapter will guide you through the process of writing a research essay. Throughout the chapter, we show how one student, Michael McQuiston, worked through key steps in the process. Michael's completed research essay appears on page 217.

Make a Schedule

After you receive your assignment, make a schedule that divides your research assignment into small, manageable tasks. There is no way that you can do every step the day (or even a few days) before the assignment is due, so give yourself a reasonable amount of time. You can use the Writing Guide: Research Essay (p. 221) as a guide for planning your schedule.

Choose a Topic

For more on finding and exploring a topic, see Chapter 2. Your instructor may assign a topic, or you might be expected to think of your own. If you are free to choose your own topic, find a subject that you are personally interested in or curious about or use one of those listed below.

POSSIBLE TOPICS FOR A RESEARCH ESSAY	
• College loans • Banning texting (in class, while driving) • Copyright and streaming audio/video online • Cosplay culture • Dieting/eating disorders • Diversity in arts and awards programs • The evolving family in America • Fake news • Gender roles in the workplace • Identity theft • Language change and slang • Legalization of marijuana • Obesity in the United States	• Outsourcing jobs to foreign countries • Patients' rights • Pets and mental health • Presidential campaigns • Rights of children of undocumented immigrants • Sexual harassment • Smart cars • Standardized testing • Uses and abuses of technology in the classroom • Veterans' issues • Wearable technology • Women's sports on college campuses

When you have chosen a general topic, you will need to narrow it using the same process you learned about in Chapter 2. Although a research essay may be longer than some of the other essays you have written, the topic still needs to be narrow enough to write about in the assigned length.

Before moving ahead with a narrowed topic, check its appropriateness with your instructor if you have any doubt. You might also check library resources to see if information is available on your planned topic. You do not need to actually look at the sources at this point, but you should assure yourself that a reasonable number of sources exist on your topic.

Before writing a working thesis statement, choose a **guiding research question** about your narrowed topic. For example, Michael McQuiston's paper on green landscaping began with the question, "What are the benefits of green landscaping?"

After choosing and narrowing a topic and developing a guiding research question, you are ready to find and evaluate sources that you will use.

Find Sources

There are a wealth of resources you can search to find information about your topic.

Library Resources

Turn first to your college's library. Before visiting the library in person, review its website to get general information. You may be able to do some initial research from the website, but you will need to visit the library in person to access books and other print materials.

Librarians

Librarians are essential resources to help you find appropriate information in both print and electronic forms. If your library allows it, make an appointment with a librarian to discuss your project and information needs. Alternatively, you and some other students might arrange to go together for a helpful orientation. Before your appointment, make a list of questions you would like to ask, either based on what you have seen on the library website or some of the following questions.

QUESTIONS FOR THE LIBRARIAN

- Can you show me how to use the library catalog? How do I use the information I find there?

- What are databases? How does database information differ from what I can find in the library catalog?

- Can I access the library catalog and article databases when I'm not on campus?

- Based on my topic, what other reference tools would you recommend that I use for my research?

- Once I identify a potentially useful source in the catalog or a database, how can I find the material?

- Can you recommend some keywords that I can use for my particular topic?

- Can you recommend an internet search engine that will help me find information on my topic? Can you recommend some useful reference sites for my topic?

- How can I tell whether an online source is reliable?

- I have already found some online articles related to my topic. Can you suggest some other places to look? How can I find good print sources on my topic?

Books

To find books on your topic, use the library catalog, which is likely to be online. By typing the keywords *green landscaping* into the library catalog, student Michael McQuiston found the following item:

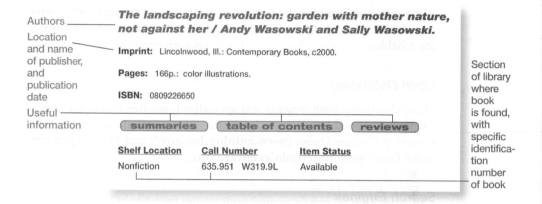

Authors

Location and name of publisher, and publication date

Useful information

The landscaping revolution: garden with mother nature, not against her / Andy Wasowski and Sally Wasowski.

Imprint: Lincolnwood, Ill.: Contemporary Books, c2000.

Pages: 166p.: color illustrations.

ISBN: 0809226650

summaries   table of contents   reviews

Shelf Location	Call Number	Item Status
Nonfiction	635.951 W319.9L	Available

Section of library where book is found, with specific identification number of book

Online Databases/Periodical Indexes

Most libraries subscribe to online **databases,** which are lists of all **periodical** (journal, newspaper, and magazine) articles on different topics. Because the library pays a subscription fee for these databases, only library members may use them. By entering your student ID or student library card number on the college library website, you can access all these helpful reference sources, which have already been checked for reliability. Some databases are general; some are more specialized with a focus on, for example, psychology or education. Some databases have the full texts of the periodicals online, which is handy.

Most college libraries subscribe to the most popular and comprehensive subscription databases: Academic Search Premier, LexisNexis Academic, ProQuest Research Library, and InfoTrac. These databases are excellent places to start looking for sources because they cover the widest range of periodicals.

NOTE Most resources referred to here can be accessed through a print reference guide as well as online. A librarian can direct you to the right area of the library and help you find good sources to start your research.

Encyclopedias

Encyclopedias give brief, basic information on a wide range of subjects. Like databases, encyclopedias can be general or specialized. The *Encyclopædia Britannica,* a reliable general encyclopedia, used to be in print (and older versions may still be available in your library) and can be found online (**www.britannica.com**). Specialized encyclopedias exist for almost any subject you can imagine; you can find them in the reference section or in the online catalog. Encyclopedias might be a good place to get an overview of your topic, but many instructors want students to use more specialized sources in their writing.

Questions for Evaluating All Sources

Before using a source for your paper, apply the following questions to all sources: print, electronic, and open access Web.

Who Is the Author?

Is the author actually an expert on the topic? Many celebrities, for example, are involved in worthwhile charitable causes that they learn a great deal about. But just because Matt Damon, George Clooney, or Angelina Jolie writes a statement or an article about a cause does not make him or her an expert.

Most sources provide some information about authors. Books have an "About the Author" section, usually at the end or on the book jacket. Periodicals have biographical headnotes or notes about the author at the end of each article. Read this information to make sure that the author has the authority and knowledge to make the source reliable.

Is the Source Well Known and Respected?

Certain sources are generally agreed to be reliable, though not always unbiased. National magazines such as *Time, Newsweek, National Geographic,* and others verify information before publishing it. Periodicals that you find on a subscription database are also usually reliable. Newspapers too usually verify information before using it, though the tabloids (like the ones sold in the supermarket checkout lines) are not reliable. Their purpose is to shock and entertain, not necessarily to tell the truth.

If you are searching online, watch out for fake news sites. Some of these have URLs that are very similar to more reliable sites. **abcnews .com.co,** for example, is not the official site of *ABC News* (**abcnews .go.com**); instead, it is a satirical site designed to be funny. Similarly, **realnewsrightnow.com** appears to be a serious news site, but if you look carefully at information provided about the site's author, you will see that the information is not reliable.

Is the Source Up-to-Date?

Look to see when a source was published. If your topic is in a rapidly changing field (e.g., science or medicine), your source should be as recent as possible to include the most current knowledge. On the other hand, if you learn about a person or a work that is considered classic (something that has been respected for a long time), the publication date is not as important. For example, Michael McQuiston's topic, green landscaping, is a relatively new practice, so he should be looking for works that have been published recently. In his reading, however, if he learns of a practice that changed the whole direction of landscaping, that would be considered classic work. Depending on his purpose, he might want to include a reference to that work, in addition to new findings. Whatever your topic is, judge each possible source for how current the information is.

Is the Source Unbiased?

Every writer reflects some personal opinion on the subject he or she writes about. However, a good source balances those opinions with reasonable evidence. But facts and numbers can be used differently by people with different biases. For example, a researcher who believes in strict gun control may cite statistics about how many children are killed each year in gun accidents. A researcher who believes in the individual right to own guns may use statistics about how many people are killed in robberies or burglaries. Both writers use accurate numbers to argue different positions.

Consider the author's background to determine if he or she is likely to be biased in a way that interferes with reliability. In the gun issue, if an author is president of an organization named CeaseFire, he has a bias in favor of gun control. If an author is president of a National Rifle Association club, he has a bias in favor of gun ownership. If you think an author is strongly advocating one side of an issue without addressing the other side, move on to another source, or include both sides in your essay.

Questions for Evaluating Websites

The Web is open to anyone with internet access, which is one of the great things about it. Anyone can develop a website to promote anything he or she wants. That very openness means, though, that you have to be even more critical in evaluating information that you find on a website, especially if you are using a general search engine such as Google or Bing.

The extension to the Uniform Resource Locator (URL) is the letters after the first period (or "dot"). Different extensions convey information about the site's sponsor.

EXTENSION	INDICATES
.com	a commercial or personal site
.edu	an educational institution's site
.gov	a government agency's site
.net	a commercial or personal site
.org	a nonprofit group's site

Create Clear, Complete Records of Source Information

For each source that you take notes on, create an individual notecard or file on your computer. It should include the source's author(s) and title, the page number(s) where you found the specific information, and what method you are using to present it: summary, paraphrase, or **direct quotation** (which is word for word what the source says). A sample card or entry might look like this.

Last name(s) of author(s): List as in works cited list.

Category of information: McQuiston is sorting information into categories, each a benefit of green landscaping.

Information: McQuiston includes a general summary of the source, an important quotation, and a paraphrase of a main point.

Information source

> Welsh, Welch, Duble
>
> Water Conservation
>
> Summary: In this article, the authors discuss how Texas is encouraging xeriscaping, which aims to save water through landscaping. The authors introduce the main principles of xeriscaping, from planning to choosing plants and grasses. In addition, the authors explain how ordinary homeowners can water and maintain lawns while still conserving water. They explain two types of irrigation systems (sprinklers and drip-systems), and they emphasize that Texans can conserve water and still enjoy a beautiful landscape.
>
> Direct Quotation: "In urban areas of Texas about 25 percent of the water supply is used for landscape and garden watering."
>
> Paraphrase: Fertilizer is an easy and cost-efficient way to maintain a lawn, but homeowners must be careful to use fertilizers appropriately. Too much of chemical fertilizers can pollute local water sources.
>
> "Landscape Water Conservation: Xeriscape." *Aggie Horticulture.* 26 Oct. 2000. www.plantanswers.com/watersaver5.htm.

Summary

As you learned in Chapter 1, a summary is your condensed version of a longer piece of writing, which should include the main point of what you are summarizing. It should also be written as much as possible in your own words, and not by using many of the same words or phrases from the longer source.

One way to include outside source material as evidence or support in your own writing is to summarize. Look back at "Attendance in College Classes" on page 184, and then read the two summaries that follow here. The first is unacceptable because it uses too many words and phrases from the original. The second is an acceptable summary.

UNACCEPTABLE SUMMARY

> In his essay "Attendance in College Classes" (184), Donnie Ney argues that attendance in college classes should be optional, not mandatory. One reason he gives is that because students have paid for the class, they should have the right to decide whether to attend or not, particularly since their lives are often complicated. He also says that many students already know the course content and should not have to waste time hearing about it again. He also argues that optional attendance would result in smaller classes with more personal attention, which would be good for students who do choose to attend class.

Direct quotation should be in quotation marks.

Phrase is a common expression, though it is from the original; here, however, it is part of a pattern of using exact phrases from the original, and so should be in quotation marks.

Exact wording of original; should be in quotation marks.

ACCEPTABLE SUMMARY

> In his essay "Attendance in College Classes" (184), Donnie Ney argues that college students should not be required to attend classes because since they have paid for the course, like a consumer purchase, it should be up to the purchaser to use or not use it. He goes on to give other reasons that expand on his basic assumption that students have the right to choose if and when they should attend a class.

The acceptable summary does not use the language of the original, other than those words that refer to the topic. It also focuses on the main point of the piece rather than including all the specific support points. This summary gives the "big picture" of the essay in a condensed form.

Paraphrase

A paraphrase restates another person's idea in your own words. Unlike a summary, a paraphrase is not necessarily a condensed version of the original; it is the idea expressed in your own words. You cannot paraphrase a whole essay or article. Again, you should not use the same wording or phrasing that is in the original.

When you are taking notes from a source and find an idea that you might want to paraphrase, try this: look away from the source, write the idea in your own words, and then look back at the original piece. If what you have written repeats a large number of words or phrases in the original, either try again or use a direct quotation.

Some students try to paraphrase by first copying a sentence word for word and then changing just a few words or substituting a few synonyms. This usually leads to an unacceptable paraphrase: the sentence structure

As you write and revise your essay, your thesis statement may change, but having a good working one helps you focus your writing and see where you might need to do additional research.

Make an Outline

For more on outlining, see Chapter 3.

To organize your notes, you need to make an outline that shows how you will support your thesis. First, write down your thesis statement. Then, review your notes to decide what your three or four major support points will be. Write these under your thesis statement and number them. Under each of your major support points, write two or three supporting details, and number them.

As you read McQuiston's outline, note that although he started with four benefits of green landscaping (*water conservation, fertilizers/safety, effect on wildlife, maintenance*), as he read and took notes, he decided to put "effect on wildlife" into the "fertilizers/safety" category. Note also that he is reviewing his organized notes and sources and trying to fit them into appropriate places in his essay (the names in parentheses that are set in boldface).

MICHAEL MCQUISTON'S OUTLINE

I. **Thesis Statement (introductory paragraph):** Landscaping with drought-tolerant native plants conserves water, reduces the use of toxic soil conditioners, and makes maintenance easier.

First support point ——— II. **Water Use**

Supporting details

    A. A limited natural resource already strained
    B. Landscaping uses lots of water **(Welsh?)**
    C. Native plants **(Tufts?)**
        1. use less water, drought-tolerant
        2. many kinds
        3. lower water bills/save money and water

Second support point ——— III. **Fertilizers/Pest Control/Safety**

Supporting details

    A. Poisonous, kids, pets **(Native Plant, Texas Wildscapes?)**
    B. Good bugs/wildlife
    C. Native plants use little or none

Third support point ——— IV. **Maintenance**

Supporting details

    A. Foreign plants, lots of water, lots of time and money
    B. Native plants, not much maintenance **(Lueck?)**

V. **Conclusion**
    A. Review benefits
    B. Observation

Write Your Essay

Using your outline, write a draft of your research essay. (For more information on writing a draft, see Chapter 4.)

Your *introduction* should include your *thesis statement* and a preview of the support you will provide in the body of the essay. If you are taking a stand on an issue, the introduction should let your readers know what your position is. The *body* of the essay will present your major support points for your thesis backed by supporting details from your research. The *conclusion* will remind readers of your main point and make a further observation based on the information you have presented.

As you write, incorporate your sources into your paper with *introductory phrases*. Most often, you will state the name of the source or author before adding the information you are using. Use a comma after the introductory phrases.

INTRODUCTORY PHRASE IDENTIFYING SOURCE

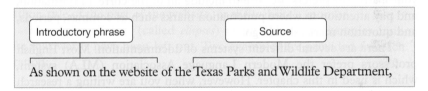

Introductory phrase	Source

As shown on the website of the Texas Parks and Wildlife Department,

INTRODUCTORY PHRASE IDENTIFYING AUTHOR AND SOURCE

In his article "Sustaining Mother Nature with Native Plants," Bill Ward states,

Common Introductory Phrases

according to [source]

as [source] claims	as [source] says
as [source] explains	as [source] shows
as [source] notes	as [source] states
as [source] points out	as [source] writes

When you have finished writing your draft essay, take a break from it. Then, definitely allow time to reread, revise, and edit it. At this point,

> According to Sen et al., . . . (659).
>
> The overuse of antibiotics can result in . . . (Sen et al. 659).

Group, Corporation, or Government Agency Use the name of the group, corporation, or government agency. The source can be abbreviated in the parentheses, as shown in the second example.

> The Texas Parks and Wildlife Department offers guidelines for landscaping . . . (26).
>
> Texas has more native plants than any other . . . (Texas Parks and Wildlife Dept. 26).

Author Not Named Use the article title in quotations, shortened if it is a long title.

> In the article "Texas Wildscapes," . . . (7).
>
> Many areas of Texas are filled with drought-tolerant native . . . ("Texas Wildscapes" 7).

Encyclopedia or Other Reference Work Use the name of the entry you are using as a source.

> In its entry on xeriscaping, the *Landscape Encyclopedia* claims that . . . ("Xeriscaping").
>
> Xeriscaping is often used in . . . ("Xeriscaping").

Work in an Anthology Use the name of the author(s) of the piece you are using as a source.

> As Rich Chiappone believes, . . . (200).
>
> Fly fishing is as much a spiritual . . . (Chiappone 200).

Interview, Email, Speech Use the name of the person interviewed or the author of an email.

> As University of Texas Vice President of Student Affairs Juan Gonzalez said in an interview, . . .
>
> Students have many resources available to . . . (Gonzalez).

Use a Works Cited List at the End of Your Essay

In the eighth edition of the *MLA Handbook*, the Modern Language Association (MLA) provides new guidelines for citing sources. Instead of suggesting they be listed in specific ways depending on their type (e.g., article, book, website, etc.), the MLA lays out a more flexible system that uses information commonly associated with most sources to create Works

Cited entries. This new format relies on the context in which a source is found. Although it provides a more flexible model for citation, it also requires you to think carefully about the most useful and accurate way to provide source information.

The two most basic elements of any citation are the author's name and the title of the work, both of which are followed by a period:

> Lutz, Iva. *The Passenger.*   (novel)
> Coles, Kimberly Anne. "The Matter of Belief in John Donne's
>   Holy Sonnets."   (periodical)
> Levy, Shawn. *Stranger Things.*   (TV series)

MLA then requires you to place these elements within the context of what it calls a "container." The container is the larger work in which you found the material you are citing. If you cite a passage from a novel, the novel *is* the container. However, for an essay or article, the container might be a newspaper, magazine, or radio show; for an online article, it could be a podcast, website, or database. Whatever the origin of the container, you should provide as many of the following elements as you can find or that apply to the source you are citing, in the order shown:

- the title of the container,
- the names of other contributors (such as editors and translators),
- the version (e.g., revised, expanded, 2nd ed., director's cut, etc.),
- the number (e.g., volume and issue numbers),
- the publisher,
- the date of publication (use day-month-year format and abbreviate names of all months longer than four letters, e.g., 6 Feb. 2018 or 17 June 2018),
- the location of the information (a page number, DOI, pemalink, or URL).

Each of these items is followed by a comma, except the last one, which ends with a period.

> Lutz, Iva. *The Passenger.* Simon and Schuster, 2016, p. 26.
> Coles, Kimberly Anne. "The Matter of Belief in John Donne's
>   Holy Sonnets." *Renaissance Quarterly*, vol. 68, no. 3, Fall 2015,
>   pp. 899–931.
> "Holly Jolly." *Stranger Things*, produced by Shawn Levy, written by
>   Matt and Ross Duffer, Netflix, 2016.

In some cases, the container you cite might itself be part of a larger container. In that case, simply add the same information listed on page 211, in the order shown, after the title of the second container:

> Coles, Kimberly Anne. "The Matter of Belief in John Donne's Holy Sonnets." *Renaissance Quarterly*, vol. 68, no. 3, Fall 2015, pp. 899–931. *JSTOR*, doi:10.1086/683855.

Books

For each set of entries, the first example shows the format; the second is an example of the format. Note that titles of books are in italics.

One Author

> Author's Last Name, First Name. *Title of Book: Subtitle.* Name of Publisher, Publication Date.

> Shipler, David K. *The Working Poor: Invisible in America.* Knopf, 2004.

Two Authors

> Author's Last Name, First Name, and Other Authors' First and Last Names. *Title of Book: Subtitle.* Name of Publisher, Publication Date.

> Picciotto, Richard, and Daniel Paisner. *Last Man Down: A New York City Fire Chief and the Collapse of the World Trade Center.* Berkeley, 2002.

Three or More Authors

> Author's Last Name, First Name, et al. *Title of Book: Subtitle.* Name of Publisher, Publication Date.

> Roark, James L., et al. *The American Promise: A History of the United States.* 7th ed. Macmillan, 2017.

Group, Corporation, or Government Agency

> Name of Group, Corporation, or Agency. *Title of Book: Subtitle.* Name of Publisher, Publication Date.

> Human Rights Watch. *World Report 2017: Events of 2016.* Seven Stories Press, 2017.

Editor

> Editor's Last Name, First Name, editor. *Title of Book: Subtitle.* Name of Publisher, Publication Date.

Canellos, Peter S., editor. *The Last Lion: The Fall and Rise of Ted Kennedy.* Simon & Schuster, 2009.

Work in an Anthology

Selection Author's Last Name, First Name. "Title of Selection in the Anthology." *Anthology Title: Subtitle*, edited by First and Last Name of Anthology Editor(s), Name of Publisher, Publication Date, Pages of Selection.

Sayrafiezadeh, Said. "Paranoia." *New American Stories*, edited by Ben Marcus, Vintage Books, 2015, pp. 3–29.

Encyclopedia

NOTE: The citation here is for an online encyclopedia and includes the container in which the encyclopedia was found and the DOI.

Entry Author's Last Name, First Name. "Title of Entry." *Title of Encyclopedia*, Edition Number [1st, 2nd, 3rd] ed., Date of publication. Name of Publisher.

Araya, Yoseph. "Ecology of Water Relations in Plants." *Encyclopedia of Life Sciences*, 8 Aug. 2014. *Wiley Online Library*, doi:10.1002/9780470015902.a0003201.pub2.

Periodicals

Note that titles of periodicals are in *italics*.

Magazine Article, Print

Author's Last Name, First Name. "Title of Article." *Title of Magazine*, Day Abbrev. Month Year of Publication, Page Numbers.

Sanneh, Kelefa. "Skin in the Game." *The New Yorker*, 24 Mar. 2014, pp. 48–55.

Newspaper Article, Print

Author's Last Name, First Name. "Title of Article." *Title of Newspaper*, Day Abbrev. Month Year of Publication, Page Numbers.

Barringer, Felicity. "Indians Join Fight for an Oklahoma Lake's Flow." *The New York Times*, 12 Apr. 2011, p. A1+.

Editorial in a Magazine or Newspaper, Author Known

Author's Last Name, First Name. "Title of Editorial." Editorial. *Title of Newspaper*, Day Abbrev. Month Year of Publication, Page Numbers.

Udall, Don. "When Someone Is Alive but Not Living." Editorial. *Newsweek*, 14 June 1999, p. 12.

Editorial in a Magazine or Newspaper, Author Unknown

"Title of Editorial." Editorial. *Title of Magazine or Newspaper*, Day Abbrev. Month Year of Publication, Page Numbers.

"What the Women's March Stands For." Editorial. *The New York Times*, 20 Jan. 2017, p. A26.

Article, Scholarly Journal with Numbered Volumes

Author's Last Name, First Name. "Title of Article." *Title of Journal*, Volume Number, Issue Number, Publication Date, Page Numbers.

Fountain, Glinda H. "Inverting the Southern Belle: Romance Writers Redefine Gender Myths." *Journal of Popular Culture*, vol. 41, issue 1, Feb. 2008, pp. 37–55.

Electronic Sources

Electronic sources include websites; databases or subscription services such as *ERIC*, *InfoTrac*, *LexisNexis*, and *ProQuest*; and electronic communications such as email. They may be a primary source of information, such as an article in an online magazine, or a secondary container, such as a database that contains a periodical you cite an article from.

To indicate the location of an online source, provide a DOI (digital object identifier), a permalink (a stable URL), or at least the current URL for a site. As websites can rapidly become obsolete, you should note the date you accessed a site at the end of your entry *if* the site provides no information about when it was produced or published.

Work from a Database (such as InfoTrac)

Author's Last Name, First Name. "Title of Article." *Title of Periodical*, Volume number, Issue number, Publication Date, Page Numbers. *Database Title*, doi.

Coles, Kimberly Anne. "The Matter of John Donne's Holy Sonnets." *Renaissance Quarterly*, vol. 68, no. 3, Fall 2015, pp. 899–931. *JSTOR*, doi:10.1086/683855.

Newspaper Article, Online

Author's Last Name, First Name. "Title of Article." *Title of Newspaper*, Day Abbrev. Month Year of Publication, URL.

Wolfers, Justin, et al. "1.5 Million Missing Black Men." *The New York Times*, 20 Apr. 2015, nyti.ms/1P5Gpa7.

Magazine Article, Online

Author's Last Name, First Name. "Title of Article." Title of Magazine, Day Abbrev. Month Year of Publication, URL.

Leonard, Andrew. "The Surveillance State High School."
Salon, 27 Nov. 2012, www.salon.com/2012/11/27/
the_surveillance_state_high_school/.

Entire Website or Blog

Note that titles of websites are in italics.

Author's Last Name, First Name. *Title of Website or Blog.* Sponsor of
website, publication date, DOI or URL. [Include date of access
if there is no publication date on the website.]

Ng, Amy. *Pikaland.* Pikaland Media, 2015, www.pikaland.com/.

Short Work from a Website

Author's Last Name, First Name. "Title of Work." *Title of Website,*
Publication Date, doi or URL. [Include date of access if there is
no publication date on the website.]

Bali, Karan. "Kishore Kumar." *Upperstall.com*, upperstall.com/pro-
file/kishore-kumar/. Accessed 2 Mar. 2017.

Email

Last Name, First Name of Author of Email Message. "Subject of
Email." Name of Person Who Received Email, Day Month Year
Email Received.

Willey, Liz. "Happy Holidays from Paraguay." Received by Miriam
Moore, 4 Jan. 2017.

Tweet

Twitter handle (Real Name of Twitter Account Holder, if known).
"Text of entire tweet." *Twitter*, Date and Time of Tweet, Twitter
URL.

@ftrain (Paul Ford). "We are finally having the long-deferred national conversation on everything." *Twitter*, 25 Jan. 2017, 2:30
p.m., twitter.com/ftrain.

Other Sources

Personal Interview

Last Name, First Name of Person Interviewed. Personal interview,
Day Month Year of Interview.

Okayo, Margaret. Personal interview, 16 Apr. 2017.

Revise and Edit Your Essay

After a break, reread your draft with fresh eyes and an open mind. Then, ask yourself these questions.

- Does my introduction state my thesis?
- Does each of the body paragraphs contain a topic sentence that directly supports my thesis? Do the supporting details in each paragraph relate to and explain the topic sentence?
- Do I provide a conclusion that reminds readers of my main point and makes a further observation?
- Have I included enough support for the thesis that readers are likely to see my topic the way I do? Is there anything else I could add to make my point?
- Do transitions help readers move from one idea to the next?
- Have I integrated source material smoothly into the essay? Do I need to smooth out anything that seems to be just dumped in?
- Have I reread the essay carefully, looking for errors in grammar, spelling, and punctuation?
- Have I cited and documented my sources?
- Are all of my citations and Works Cited entries in correct form (MLA or whatever style the instructor specifies)?
- Is this the best I can do?

For more on revising, see Chapter 4. When checking for grammar, spelling, and punctuation errors, consult Chapters 16 through 18 of this book.

After reading the annotated student essay that follows, use the Writing Guide on page 222 to write your research essay.

Sample Student Research Essay

The student essay that follows is annotated to show both typical features of research essays (such as references to sources) and elements of good writing (such as the thesis statement and topic sentences). The paper also shows formatting (such as margins, spacing between lines, and placement of the title). Your instructor may specify different or additional formatting in class or in your syllabus.

Michael McQuiston

Professor Bicknell

Composition 1

21 Apr. 2017

To Be Green or Not to Be Green

When people make landscaping decisions, many do not realize that the choices they make affect not just the immediate appearance of their yard but also the present and future environment. Lady Bird Johnson, a champion of native landscaping, once said, "My special cause, the one that alerts my interest and quickens the pace of my life, is to preserve the wildflowers and native plants that define the regions of our land—to encourage and promote their use in appropriate areas" ("The First Lady's Gallery"). Many people share her feelings and might want to know how landscaping can accomplish such preservation. When planning your landscaping, it is important to choose plants that will be not only aesthetically pleasing but low-maintenance and cost-effective as well. After owning a lawn care and landscape business in Texas for six years, I am a firm believer in green landscaping. Landscaping with drought-tolerant native plants conserves water, reduces the use of toxic soil conditioners, and requires little maintenance.

As the world's population grows, it strains our earth's limited supply of natural resources. One resource essential to both plants and animals is water. Many cities and towns already restrict watering during the hot summer months to certain days of the week or certain times of day. In an online article written for Texas A&M University, Welsh et al. state that "in urban areas of Texas about 25 percent of the water supply is used for landscape and garden watering." Some homeowners argue that water is necessary to ensure the survival of the plants in their yards.

However, part of the problem lies with the types of flowering plants, trees, and grass used in urban and suburban landscaping, many of them to achieve a certain "look." But these plants can require a great deal of water, as they often originate in areas with much higher rainfall per year or a more constant amount of rain throughout the year. In order to sustain plants native to a climate zone that gets more rain, many homeowners not only see their water bills double during the arid summer months, but also contribute to the overall potential environmental water-shortage problem.

First support point

Fortunately, there is a way to have a beautiful yard in Texas without depleting our water supply: use plants that are drought-tolerant or native to the area. The nonprofit organization Wild Ones Natural Landscapers defines *native plants* as "those that

In-text citation

were growing naturally in the area before humans introduced plants from a distant place" ("Landscaping"). Plants native to a certain area can survive with the amount of water available through local bodies of water and rainfall. Some native Texas

Body paragraphs

plants that will still look beautiful in the midsummer after two weeks of record-high temperatures and drought include flowers such as the Bluebonnet, Indian Blanket, Indian Paintbrush, Lantana, and many others, as well as many shrubs and trees. Homeowners need only ask at their local nursery or ask a landscape professional to find out what plants, grass, and trees are native and drought-tolerant. Many respected websites also provide similar advice. Green landscaping significantly reduces people's water bills and at the same time conserves water, a limited natural resource.

On a typical Saturday in suburbia, one might hear, "Don't let the kids go in the yard today. I put down fertilizer." But, wait—aren't the pets and other wildlife out there too? Although many homeowners and landscape services recognize the harmful effects of fertilizer and pesticides, they think having the "best-looking yard on the block" is worth the risk. According to the California Department of Pesticide Regulation's "Community Guide to Recognizing and Reporting Pesticide Problems," pesticides are safest if used properly, but they are still dangerous. Children and people with asthma or other chronic diseases are much more likely to get sick from pesticides than healthy adults, and "some individuals are also more sensitive to the odor or other irritant effects of certain pesticides" (29).

    Using native plants and grasses instead of turf grass in the landscape eliminates the need for fertilizers and pesticides, making the yard a safer place for both people and beneficial insects. Jane Scott, a gardener and naturalist, argues in her book *Field and Forest* that although the creation of a landscape of any kind causes some disturbance of land and soil, not all the harm landscaping and gardening does is necessary, and native plants would help reduce our environmental impact (4). Native plants do not need fertilizer to condition the soil because it is the soil they will naturally grow best in; there is no need to worry about the correct pH balance or the perfect balance of nitrogen-potash-iron in the fertilizer. The need for pesticides is also diminished because plants that grow naturally in an area have developed defenses against harmful local insects.

    Green landscaping also saves local wildlife, which can have a hard time finding food and water in the hot, dry summer months. Natural vegetation not only provides a safe haven for these creatures but also nourishes them. Planting native and drought-tolerant vegetation in the yard transforms it into an extension of these creatures' homes, and in exchange for food, water, and shelter, the creatures offer homeowners an exclusive peek into the wild world around them. The Texas Parks and Wildlife Department recognizes the importance of native plants in providing food for native species of animals, birds, and butterflies, even going so far as to offer a "habitat restoration and conservation plan for rural and urban areas" ("Texas Wildscapes"). Bill Ward's article "Sustaining Mother Nature with Native Plants" illustrates the necessity of native plants for insect life. Monarch butterfly larvae depend on the milkweed for their survival, but as can be gathered from its name, this Texas native is often eradicated because it is considered a weed. "Bugs in native plant gardens," Ward states, "are helping to sustain the ecosystem by supporting a diverse and balanced food web. The same cannot be said about yards landscaped with predominantly exotic plants."

In addition to the environmental effects of nonnative landscape plantings, the regular upkeep of a nonnative lawn can prove too much for busy homeowners. What began as the best-looking yard on the block can quickly deteriorate into the neighborhood eyesore without the necessary maintenance and regular application of extra water and pesticides. While all plants require some care, native plants require far less than the transplanted ones, and Jane Scott argues that native plants are just as attractive as common exotics: "The more we know about the native plant communities that surround us, the more we will come to appreciate their inherent beauty and diversity and the more effectively we can accommodate them in the places where we live" (4). So, native plants offer peace of mind that the yard will look good season after season without constant daily care.

In this time of growing environmental awareness, planting nonnative, high-maintenance plants is irresponsible. Native plants do not strain the environment, and they provide food and shelter for various species of wildlife. The low-maintenance nature of native plants makes them friendly to the busy homeowner concerned about the environment. With less fertilizer and pesticide on the lawn, the yard will be a healthier place for families to spend their time and enjoy the outdoors. Green landscaping makes sense for everyone, for now and for the future. Be green.

Works Cited

"Community Guide to Recognizing and Reporting Pesticide Problems." *California Department of Pesticide Regulation*, State of California, Jun. 2014, cdpr.ca.gov/docs/dept/comguide/index.htm.

"The First Lady's Gallery." *LBJ Presidential Library*, www.lbjlibrary.net/museum/permanent-collection/first-ladys-gallery.html Accessed 10 Jan. 2017.

Scott, Jane. *Field and Forest*. Walker, 1992.

"Texas Wildscapes: Gardening for Wildlife in Backyards, Schoolyards, and Corporate Parks." *Texas Parks and Wildlife*. tpwd.texas.gov/huntwild/wild/ wildlife_diversity/ wildscapes/. Accessed 2 Mar. 2017.

Ward, Bill. "Sustaining Mother Nature with Native Plants." *Native Plant Society of Texas*, 29 May 2010, npsot.org/wp/story/2010/436/.

Welsh, Douglas F., et al. "Landscape Water Conservation: Xeriscape." *Plant Answers.com*, 26 Oct. 2000, www.plantanswers.com/watersaver5.htm.

Wild Ones Landscaping with Native Plants, 4th ed. Wild Ones: Native Plants, Natural Landscapes, 2008.

Double space between and within all entries in a works cited list.

Note that in works cited entries, all lines after the first are indented.

After you have taken notes, found outside sources, and written a draft thesis statement, use the writing guide that follows to help you write your research essay.

WRITING GUIDE: Research Essay	
STEPS	**HOW TO DO THE STEPS**
☐ **Make a schedule.** See page 192.	• Include the due date and dates for doing research, finishing a draft, revising, documenting sources, and editing.
☐ **Choose a topic.** See page 192.	• Choose a topic that interests you. • Make sure the topic is narrow enough to cover in the assigned length of the paper.
☐ **Ask a guiding research question.** See page 193.	• Ask a question that will guide your research.
☐ **Find and evaluate sources.** See pages 194 and 197.	• Use library resources. • Consider the reliability of each source.
☐ **Take notes to avoid plagiarism.** See page 200.	• Note the publication information. • Make an entry for each piece of information (p. 201).
☐ **Write a thesis statement.** See Chapter 3.	• Based on what you have read, write a thesis statement that includes the main point of your essay. • Turn your research question into a statement: **Research question:** What are the benefits of green landscaping? **Thesis statement:** There are many clear benefits of green landscaping. **Revised after taking notes from sources:** Landscaping with drought-tolerant native plants conserves water, reduces the use of toxic soil conditioners, and requires little maintenance.
☐ **Support your thesis.** See Chapter 3.	• Review all notes to choose the best points. • Do further research if you do not have enough support to convince your readers of your main point.

(Continued)

STEPS	HOW TO DO THE STEPS
☐ **Write a draft essay.** See Chapter 4.	• Make an outline that organizes your support. • Write an introduction that includes your thesis statement. • Write topic sentences and paragraphs that give support and supporting details. • Work in your outside sources using introductory phrases (see p. 207). • Write a conclusion that reminds your readers of your main point and support and makes an observation. • Title your essay.
☐ **Revise your draft.** See Chapter 4.	• Is the thesis clear? • Do I have enough support? • Do I end strongly? • Have I integrated outside sources smoothly in the essay (and cited them)? • Are all sources documented correctly?
☐ **Cite and document your sources.**	• For in-text citations, see page 208. For works cited entries, see page 210.
☐ **Edit your essay.** See Chapters 16 through 18.	• Reread your essay, looking for errors in grammar, spelling, and punctuation.

Reflect on the Process

1. What was new or surprising to you about research?

2. What did you learn in your past courses about research and writing from sources? Did this chapter confirm, contradict, or complicate that information? Explain.

3. What questions or concerns do you have about research, citation rules, summary, or paraphrase?

4. Talk to a friend or an instructor in your major. What kinds of research do students and professionals in your discipline do? What citation style is used most often?

5. How can you apply the research and writing strategies you have learned in the section to your other courses? To your future courses? To your future work?

15

Basic Grammar

An Overview

This chapter will review the basic elements of the sentence. In the examples in this chapter, subjects are underlined once and verbs are underlined twice.

The Parts of Speech

There are seven basic parts of speech in English:

1. A **noun** names a person, place, or thing.

    > <u>Heroin</u> <u><u>is</u></u> a drug.

2. A **pronoun** replaces a noun in a sentence. A pronoun can be the subject of a sentence (*I, you, he, she, it, we, they*), or it can be the object of a sentence (*me, you, him, her, us, them*). A pronoun can also show possession (*mine, yours, his, her, its, our, their*).

    > <u>It</u> <u><u>causes</u></u> addiction.

3. A **verb** tells what the subject does, or it links a subject to another word that describes it.

    > <u>Heroin</u> <u><u>*causes*</u></u> addiction.   [The verb *causes* is what the subject *Heroin* does.]
    >
    > <u>It</u> <u><u>*is*</u></u> dangerous.   [The verb *is* links the subject *It* to a word that describes it: *dangerous*.]

4. An **adjective** describes a noun or pronoun.

> Heroin is *dangerous*.   [The adjective *dangerous* describes the
>   noun *Heroin*.]
>
> It is *lethal*.   [The adjective *lethal* describes the pro-
>   noun *It*.]

5. An **adverb** describes an adjective, a verb, or another adverb. Many
    adverbs end in *-ly*.

> Heroin is *very* dangerous.   [The adverb *very* describes the
>   adjective *dangerous*.]
>
> Addiction occurs *quickly*.   [The adverb *quickly* describes
>   the verb *occurs*.]
>
> Addiction occurs *very quickly*. [The adverb *very* describes the
>   adverb *quickly*.]

6. A **preposition** connects a noun, pronoun, or verb with some other
    information about it (*across, at, in, of, on, around, over,* and *to* are
    some prepositions).

> Dealers often sell drugs *around* schools.
>
> [The preposition *around* connects the noun *drugs* with the noun *schools*.]

7. A **conjunction** (*for, and, nor, but, or, yet, so*) connects words,
    phrases, or sentences to show a logical relationship.

> Heroin is very dangerous, *and* current versions of the drug can
> be fatal.

The Basic Sentence

A **sentence** is the basic unit of written communication. A complete sentence written in standard English must have three elements:

- A verb
- A subject
- A complete thought

Verbs

Every sentence has a **main verb**, the word or words that tell what the subject does or that link the subject to another word that describes it. The main verb of a sentence indicates the time of the events or descriptions in the sentence (past, present, future) and the nature of the events or descriptions (in progress or completed). In addition, the main verb can help writers find the subject of the sentence. Thus, when analyzing a sentence, writers often look for the main verb first.

There are three kinds of verbs — *action verbs*, *linking verbs*, and *helping verbs*.

Action Verbs

An **action verb** tells what action the subject performs.

To find the main action verb in a sentence, ask yourself, "What action occurs in this sentence?"

The <u>baby</u> <u>cried</u> all night.

The <u>building</u> <u>collapsed</u> around midnight.

After work, <u>we</u> often <u>go</u> to Tallie's.

My <u>aunt and uncle</u> <u>train</u> service dogs.

Linking Verbs

A **linking verb** connects (links) the subject to a word or group of words that describes the subject. Linking verbs show no action. The most common linking verb is *be*, along with all its forms (*am*, *is*, *are*, and so on). Other linking verbs, such as *seem* and *become*, can usually be replaced by the corresponding form of *be*, and the sentence will still make sense.

To find linking verbs, ask yourself: What word joins the subject and the words that describe the subject? You can also ask about time: Which word shows if the sentence was true in the past, present, or future?

The <u>dinner</u> <u>is</u> delicious.

<u>I</u> <u>felt</u> great this morning.

This <u>lasagna</u> <u>tastes</u> just like my mother's.

The <u>doctor</u> <u>looks</u> extremely tired.

Some words can be either action verbs or linking verbs, depending on how they are used in a particular sentence.

ACTION VERB	The <u>dog</u> <u>smelled</u> Jake's shoes.
LINKING VERB	The <u>dog</u> <u>smelled</u> terrible.

Common Linking Verbs

Forms of *Be*	am, are, is, was, were
Forms of *Become* and *Seem*	become/becomes/became; seems/seems/ seemed
Forms of *Sense* Verbs	appear/appears, appeared; feel/feels/felt; look/ looks/looked; smell/smells/smelled; taste/ tastes/tasted

Helping Verbs

A **helping verb** (also called an **auxiliary verb**) joins with the main verb in the sentence to form the **complete verb**. The helping verb is often a form of the verb *be*, *have*, or *do*. A sentence may have more than one helping verb along with the main verb.

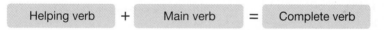

Helping verb   +   Main verb   =   Complete verb

<u>Sunil</u> <u>was talking</u> on his cell phone.

[The helping verb is *was*, and the main verb is *talking*. The complete verb is *was talking*.]

<u>Charisse</u> <u>is taking</u> three courses this semester.

<u>Tomas</u> <u>has missed</u> the last four meetings.

My <u>brother</u> <u>might have passed</u> the test.

Common Helping Verbs

Forms of *Be*	am, are, been, being, is, was were
Forms of *Have*	have, has, had
Forms of *Do*	do, does, did
Other	can, could, may, might, must, should, will, would

For a list of pronoun types, see page 224.

Subjects

The **subject** of a sentence is the person, place, or thing that does the action in the sentence or that is described in the sentence. The subject of the sentence can be a noun (a word that names the person, place, or thing) or a pronoun (a word that replaces the noun, such as *I, you, she,* or *they*).

To find the subject, first identify the verb. Then create a question, using the verb to fill in the blank: who or what _____?

PERSON AS SUBJECT Vivian works for the police department.
[*Who* works for the police department? *Vivian*]

THING AS SUBJECT The tickets cost $65 apiece.
[*What* costs $65 apiece? The *tickets*]

A **compound subject** consists of two (or more) subjects joined by *and, or,* or *nor.*

TWO SUBJECTS Nick and Chelsea have a new baby girl.

SEVERAL SUBJECTS The jacket, pants, and sweater match perfectly.

SEVERAL SUBJECTS Kim, Juan, or Melba will bring dessert.

A **prepositional phrase** is a word group that begins with a preposition and ends with a noun or pronoun. A **preposition** is a word that connects a noun, pronoun, or verb with some other information about it.

The subject of a sentence is *never* in a prepositional phrase.

        Preposition

The <u>check</u> <u>is</u> in the mail.

        Prepositional phrase

The subject of the sentence is *check*. The subject cannot be the word *mail*, which is in the prepositional phrase *in the mail*.

   Preposition

<u>One</u> of my best friends <u>is</u> a circus clown.

      Prepositional phrase

Although the word *friends* may seem to be the subject of the sentence, it is not. *One* is the subject. The word *friends* is not the subject because it is in the prepositional phrase *of my best friends*.

    When you are looking for the subject of a sentence in your writing, it may help to cross out any prepositional phrases, as in the following sentences.

The <u>rules</u> ~~about smoking~~ <u>are posted</u> everywhere.

The <u>sound</u> ~~of lightning striking a tree~~ <u>is</u> like gunfire.

<u>Many</u> ~~of the students~~ <u>work</u> part-time.

Common Prepositions

about	beneath	like	to
above	beside	near	toward
across	between	next to	under
after	by	of	until
against	down	off	up
along	during	on	upon
among	except	out	with
around	for	outside	within
at	from	over	without
before	in	past	
behind	inside	since	
below	into	through	

Complete Thoughts

A **complete thought** is an idea that is expressed in a sentence and that makes sense by itself, without other sentences. An incomplete thought leaves readers wondering what is going on.

INCOMPLETE THOUGHT	as I was leaving [*What is going on?*]
COMPLETE THOUGHT	The <u>phone</u> <u>rang</u> as I was leaving.
INCOMPLETE THOUGHT	the <u>people</u> selling the car [*What is going on?*]
COMPLETE THOUGHT	The <u>people</u> selling the car <u>placed</u> the ad.

To identify a complete thought, ask yourself, "Do I know what is going on, or do I have to ask a question to understand?"

INCOMPLETE THOUGHT	in the apartment next door
	[Do I know what is going on, or do I have to ask a question to understand? *You would have to ask a question, so this is not a complete thought.*]
COMPLETE THOUGHT	<u>Carlos</u> <u>lives</u> in the apartment next door.

Six Basic Sentence Patterns

In English, there are six basic sentence patterns, some of which you have already worked with in this chapter. Although there are other patterns, they build on these six.

1. **Subject-Verb (S-V)**

   This is the most basic pattern, as you have already seen.

   > S   V
   > <u>Airplanes</u> <u>pollute</u>.

2. **Subject-Linking Verb-Noun (S-LV-N)**

   > S   LV   N
   > <u>Fuel</u> <u>is</u> a pollutant.

3. **Subject–Linking Verb–Adjective (S–LV–ADJ)**

    > S   LV   ADJ
    >
    > <u>Travel</u> <u>seems</u> cheap.

4. **Subject–Verb–Adverb (S–V–ADV)**

    > S   V   ADV
    >
    > <u>Pollution</u> <u>costs</u> dearly.

5. **Subject–Verb–Direct Object (S–V–DO)**

    A *direct object* directly receives the action of the verb.

    > S   V   DO
    >
    > <u>It</u> <u>degrades</u> ozone.

6. **Subject–Verb–Indirect Object–Direct Object**

    An *indirect object* does not directly receive the action of the verb.

    > S   V IO DO
    >
    > <u>Biofuels</u> <u>offer</u> us hope.

16

The Four Most Serious Errors

This chapter emphasizes four major grammar errors that people most often notice.

These four errors typically cause misunderstanding within your writing, and they definitely give readers a bad impression of you. It is like going for a job interview in pajamas. People *will* notice. Learning how to correct these errors will make a big difference in your writing.

1. Fragments
2. Run-ons: fused sentences
3. Problems with subject-verb agreement
4. Problems with verb form and tense

In the examples in this chapter, <u>subjects</u> are underlined once and <u>verbs</u> are underlined twice.

Fragments

A **fragment** is a group of words that is punctuated like a sentence but is missing one of the three required elements of an independent clause: a *subject*, a *verb*, or *completeness*.

SENTENCE	<u>I</u> <u>am going</u> to a concert on Friday at Memorial Arena.
FRAGMENT	<u>I</u> <u>am going</u> to a concert on Friday. *At Memorial Arena.*
	[*At Memorial Arena* does not have a subject or a verb.]

To find fragments in your own writing, look for the five kinds of fragments discussed in this chapter. When you find a fragment, you can usually correct it in one of two ways.

WAYS TO CORRECT FRAGMENTS

▪ Add what is missing (a subject, a verb, or both).

▪ Attach the fragment to the sentence before or after it.

Fragments That Start with Prepositions

Whenever a preposition starts what you think is a sentence, check for a subject, a verb, and a complete thought. If any one of those is missing, you have a fragment.

For a list of common prepositions, see page 229.

> **FRAGMENT**   The <u>plane</u> <u>crashed</u> into the house. *With a deafening roar.*
>
> [*With a deafening roar* is a prepositional phrase that starts with the preposition *with*. The phrase has neither a subject nor a verb. It is a fragment.]

Correct the fragment by connecting it to the sentence either before or after it. If you connect the fragment to the sentence after it, put a comma after the fragment to join it to the sentence.

> **FRAGMENT**   The <u>plane</u> <u>crashed</u> into the house. *From a height of eight hundred feet.*
>
> **CORRECTED**   The <u>plane</u> <u>crashed</u> into the house, From a height of eight hundred feet.
>
> **CORRECTED**   From a height of eight hundred feet, the <u>plane</u> <u>crashed</u> into the house.

Fragments That Start with Dependent Words

A **dependent word** (also called a **subordinating conjunction**) is the first word in a dependent clause, which does not express a complete thought even though it has a subject and a verb. Whenever a dependent word starts what you think is a sentence, look for a subject, a verb, and, especially, a complete thought.

FRAGMENT	Leila is still out of work. *Even though the economy is recovering.*
	[*Even though* introduces the dependent clause *even though the economy is recovering.* The clause has a subject, *economy*, and a verb, *is recovering*, but it does not express a complete thought.]

Correct the fragment by connecting it to the sentence either before or after it. If you connect the fragment to the sentence after it, put a comma after the fragment to join it to the sentence.

FRAGMENT	I took the bus. *Because* I missed my ride.
CORRECTED	I took the bus because I missed my ride.
CORRECTED	Because I missed my ride, I took the bus.

Common Dependent Words

after	if	what(ever)
although	since	when(ever)
as	so that	where
because	that	whether
before	though	which(ever)
even though	unless	while
how	until	who/whose

Fragments That Start with *-ing* Verb Forms

An *-ing* verb form is the form of a verb that ends in -ing: *walking, writing, swimming.* Unless it has a helping verb (*was* walking, *was* writing, *was* swimming), it is not a main verb in a sentence. Sometimes an *-ing* verb form functions as a noun (called a **gerund**) and is used as a subject at the beginning of a complete sentence. Sometimes an *-ing* verb form functions as an adjective and is used to describe the subject at the beginning of a complete sentence.

-*ING* FORM USED WITH A HELPING VERB AS A MAIN VERB

I *am working* full-time this semester.

[In this sentence, *am* is the helping verb; *am working* is the complete verb.]

-*ING* FORM USED AS A SUBJECT

Swimming is a wonderful form of exercise.

[In this sentence, *swimming* is the subject and *is* is the verb.]

-*ING* FORM USED AS AN ADJECTIVE

Smiling with delight, the <u>teacher</u> <u>returned</u> the student's paper.

[In this sentence, *smiling* is an adjective describing the teacher.]

Whenever a word group begins with a word in -*ing* form, look carefully to see if the word group contains a subject and a verb and if it expresses a complete thought.

FRAGMENT	Snoring so loudly I couldn't sleep.
	[If *snoring* is the main verb, what is the subject? There isn't one. Is there a helping verb used with *snoring*? No. It is a fragment.]

Correct a fragment that starts with an -*ing* verb form either by adding whatever sentence elements are missing (usually a subject and a helping verb) or by connecting the fragment to the sentence before or after it. Usually, you will need to put a comma before or after the fragment to join it to the complete sentence.

-*ING* FRAGMENT	*Working two jobs and going to school.* I <u>am</u> tired all the time.
CORRECTED	Working two jobs and going to school<s>.</s>, I <u>am</u> tired all the time.
CORRECTED	^{I am working} <s>Working</s> two jobs and going to school. I <u>am</u> tired all the time.

Fragments That Start with *to* and a Verb

An **infinitive** is the word *to* plus a verb — *to hire, to eat, to study.* Although they contain verbs, infinitive forms function as nouns, adjectives, or adverbs.

If a word group begins with *to* and a verb, it must have another verb or it is not a complete sentence.

FRAGMENT	Last week, a <u>couple</u> in New York <u>fulfilled</u> their wedding fantasy. *To get married on the top of the Empire State Building.*
	[The first word group is a sentence, with *couple* as the subject, and *fulfilled* as the verb. In the second word group, there is no subject or verb outside of the infinitive.]

Correct a fragment that starts with *to* and a verb by connecting it to the sentence before or after it or by adding the missing sentence elements (a subject and a verb).

FRAGMENT	*To save on her monthly gas bills.* <u>Tammy</u> <u>sold</u> her SUV and <u>got</u> a hybrid car.
CORRECTED	To save on her monthly gas bills /, <u>Tammy</u> <u>sold</u> her SUV and <u>got</u> a hybrid car.
CORRECTED	^{Tammy wanted to} ~~To~~ save on her monthly gas bills. ^{She} ~~Tammy~~ <u>sold</u> her SUV and <u>got</u> a hybrid car.

Fragments That Are Examples or Explanations

As you edit your writing, pay special attention to groups of words that are examples or explanations of information you presented in the previous sentences. These word groups may be fragments.

FRAGMENT	<u>Parking</u> on this campus <u>is</u> a real nightmare. *Especially between 8:00 and 8:30 a.m.*
	[The second word group has no subject and no verb.]

Finding fragments that start with examples or explanations can be difficult, because there is no single kind of word to look for. The following are a few starting words that may signal an example or explanation, but fragments that are examples or explanations do not always start with these words:

especially   for example   like   such as

When a group of words that you think is a sentence gives an example or explanation of information in the previous sentence, stop to see if it has a subject and a verb and if it expresses a complete thought. If it is missing any of these elements, it is a fragment.

FRAGMENT	The <u>web</u> <u>has</u> many job search sites. *Such as Monster.com.*
	[Does the second word group have a subject? No. A verb? No. It is a fragment.]

To correct a fragment that starts with an example or an explanation, connect it either to the previous sentence or to the next one. Sometimes, you can add the missing sentence elements (a subject, a verb, or both) instead. When you connect the fragment to a sentence, you may need to reword or to change some punctuation. For example, fragments that are examples and fragments that are negatives are often set off by commas.

FRAGMENT	I <u>pushed</u> seven different voice-mail buttons before I spoke to a real person. *Not a helpful one, though.*
CORRECTED	I <u>pushed</u> seven different voice-mail buttons before I spoke to a real person, ~~Not a helpful one, though.~~ , though not a helpful one.
CORRECTED	I <u>pushed</u> seven different voice-mail buttons before I spoke to a real person. ~~Not a~~ He was not helpful ~~one,~~ though.

Run-Ons

A sentence is also called an **independent clause**, a group of words with a subject and a verb that expresses a complete thought. Sometimes, two independent clauses can be joined correctly in one sentence.

SENTENCES WITH TWO INDEPENDENT CLAUSES

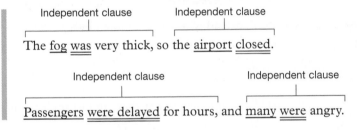

The <u>fog</u> <u>was</u> very thick, so the <u>airport</u> <u>closed</u>.

<u>Passengers</u> <u>were delayed</u> for hours, and <u>many</u> <u>were</u> angry.

A **run-on** is two complete sentences (independent clauses) that are joined incorrectly and written as one sentence. There are two kinds of run-ons—fused sentences and comma splices.

A **fused sentence** is two complete sentences joined without any punctuation.

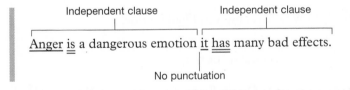

<u>Anger</u> <u>is</u> a dangerous emotion <u>it</u> <u>has</u> many bad effects.

No punctuation

A **comma splice** is two complete sentences joined by only a comma instead of a comma and one of these words: *and, but, for, nor, or, so, yet.*

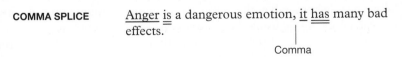

COMMA SPLICE	<u>Anger</u> <u>is</u> a dangerous emotion, <u>it</u> <u>has</u> many bad effects.

Comma

These words are known as coordinating conjunctions. They are discussed on page 238.

When you find a run-on in your writing, you can correct it in one of three ways.

WAYS TO CORRECT A RUN-ON

- Add a period or a semicolon.
- Add a comma and a coordinating conjunction.
- Add a dependent word.

Add a Period or a Semicolon

You can correct a run-on by adding a period to make two separate sentences.

> I <u>called</u> about my bill. I <u>got</u> four useless recorded messages.
>
> . M
> I finally <u>hung up/</u> my question <u>remained</u> unanswered.

A semicolon (;) can be used instead of a period to join closely related sentences.

> ;
> My <u>father</u> <u>had</u> a heart attack <u>he</u> <u>is</u> in the hospital.
>
> ;
> My <u>mother</u> <u>called</u> 911/ the <u>ambulance</u> <u>was</u> there in just under four minutes.

A semicolon is sometimes used before a transition from one independent clause to another, and the transition word is followed by a comma.

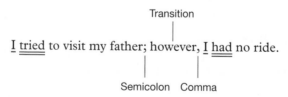

> Transition
>
> I <u>tried</u> to visit my father; however, I <u>had</u> no ride.
>
> Semicolon   Comma

Add a Comma and a Coordinating Conjunction

TIP Note that there is no comma *after* a coordinating conjunction.

Another way to correct a run-on is to add a comma and a **coordinating conjunction**: a link that joins independent clauses to form one sentence. Some people remember the seven coordinating conjunctions (*for, and, nor, but, or, yet, so*) by using the memory device of FANBOYS.

To correct a fused sentence, add both a comma and a coordinating conjunction. A comma splice already has a comma, so just add a coordinating conjunction that makes sense in the sentence.

FUSED SENTENCE **(corrected)**	, and T̲i̲m̲ h̲i̲t̲ another car ^ he w̲e̲n̲t̲ through the windshield.
COMMA SPLICE **(corrected)**	but H̲e̲ i̲s̲ d̲r̲i̲v̲i̲n̲g̲ again, ^ he always w̲e̲a̲r̲s̲ his seat belt.

Add a Dependent Word

A final way to correct a run-on is to make one of the complete sentences a dependent clause by adding a dependent word (a **subordinating conjunction** or a **relative pronoun**), such as *after, because, before, even though, if, though, unless,* or *when.* Choose the dependent word that best expresses the relationship between the two clauses.

RUN-ONS (corrected)

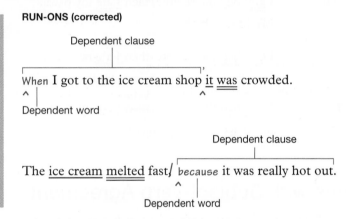

When the dependent clause starts off the sentence, you need to add a comma after it, as in the first example above. When the dependent clause is after the independent clause, there is no comma, as in the second example.

Common Dependent Words

after	if	what(ever)
although	since	when(ever)
as	so that	where
because	that	whether
before	though	which(ever)
even though	unless	while
how	until	who/whose

A Word That Can Cause Run-Ons: *Then*

Many run-ons are caused by the word *then*. You can use *then* to join two sentences, but if you add it without the correct punctuation and/or joining word, the resulting sentence will be a run-on. To correct a run-on caused by the word *then*, you can use any of the four methods presented in this chapter.

COMMA SPLICE	I grabbed the remote, then I ate my pizza.
CORRECTED	I grabbed the remote. Then I ate my pizza. [period added]
CORRECTED	I grabbed the remote; then I ate my pizza. [semicolon added]
CORRECTED	I grabbed the remote, and then I ate my pizza. [coordinating conjunction *and* added]
CORRECTED	I grabbed the remote before ~~then~~ I ate my pizza. [dependent word *before* added to make a dependent clause]

Problems with Subject-Verb Agreement

In any sentence, the subject and the verb *must match—or agree—in number*. If the subject is singular (one person, place, or thing), then the verb must also be singular. If the subject is plural (more than one), the verb must also be plural.

SINGULAR	The phone rings constantly at work. [The subject, *phone*, is singular—just one phone—so the verb must take the singular form: *rings*.]
PLURAL	The phones ring constantly at work. [The subject, *phones*, is plural—more than one phone—so the verb must take the plural form: *ring*.]

For more on regular verbs and how they differ from irregular verbs, see page 245.

Regular verbs follow standard English patterns. For regular verbs in the present tense, only third-person singular verbs take an ending, and that ending is *-s*.

Regular Verbs, Present Tense

	SINGULAR FORM	PLURAL FORM
First person	I walk.	We walk.
Second person	You walk.	You walk.
Third person	He/ she/ it walks.	They walk.
	Percy walks.	Percy and Don walk.
	The dog walks.	The dogs walk.

To find problems with subject-verb agreement in your own writing, look for the five trouble spots that follow.

The Verb Is a Form of *Be, Have,* or *Do*

The verbs *be, have,* and *do* do not follow the regular patterns for forming singular and plural forms; they are **irregular verbs**.

These verbs cause problems for people who use only one form of the verb in casual conversation: *You be the richest* (incorrect). *You are the richest* (correct). In college and at work, use the correct standard form of the verbs *be, have,* and *do* as shown in the charts that follow.

You ~~is~~ the craziest person I have ever known.
(are)

Johnson ~~have~~ the best car in the lot.
(has)

Valery ~~do~~ the bill paying on the first of every month.
(does)

Forms of the Verb *Be*

PRESENT TENSE	SINGULAR	PLURAL
First person	I am	we are
Second person	you are	you are
Third person	she/he/it is	they are
	the student/Joe is	the students are
PAST TENSE	**SINGULAR**	**PLURAL**
First person	I was	we were
Second person	you were	you were
Third person	she/he/it was	they were
	the student/Joe was	the students were

Forms of the Verb *Have*, Present Tense

	SINGULAR	PLURAL
First person	I have	we have
Second person	you have	you have
Third person	she/he/it has	they have
	the student/Joe has	the students have

Forms of the Verb *Do*, Present Tense

	SINGULAR	PLURAL
First person	I do	we do
Second person	you do	you do
Third person	she/he/it does	they do
	the student/Joe does	the students do

Words Come between the Subject and the Verb

When the subject and the verb are not right next to each other, it can be difficult to make sure that they agree. Most often, what comes between the subject and the verb is either a prepositional phrase or a dependent clause.

Prepositional Phrase between the Subject and the Verb

For a list of common prepositions, see page 229.

A **prepositional phrase** starts with a preposition and ends with a noun or pronoun: The line *for the movie* went *around the corner*.

Remember, the subject of a sentence is never in a prepositional phrase. When you are looking for the subject, you can cross out any prepositional phrases. This strategy should help you find the real subject and decide whether it agrees with the verb.

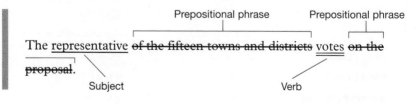

Dependent Clause between the Subject and the Verb

A **dependent clause** has a subject and a verb, but it does not express a complete thought. When a dependent clause comes between the subject and the verb, it usually starts with the word *who, whose, whom, that,* or *which*.

The subject of a sentence is never in the dependent clause. When you are looking for the subject, you can cross out any dependent clauses.

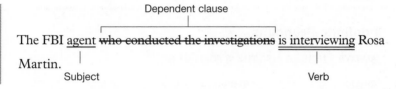

Dependent clause

The FBI <u>agent</u> ~~who conducted the investigations~~ <u>is interviewing</u> Rosa
Martin.
    Subject   Verb

The Sentence Has a Compound Subject

A **compound subject** consists of two (or more) subjects connected by *and, or,* or *nor* (as in *neither/nor* expressions). If two subjects are joined by *and,* they combine to become a plural subject, and the verb must take a plural form as well.

Subject *and*   Subject   Plural form of verb

The <u>director</u> *and* the <u>producer</u> <u>decide</u> how the film will be made.

If two subjects are connected by *or* or *nor,* they are considered separate, and the verb should agree with the subject closest to it.

Subject *or*   Singular subject   Singular form of verb

The <u>director</u> *or* the <u>producer</u> <u>decides</u> how the film will be made.

Subject *nor*   Singular subject Singular form of verb

Neither the <u>director</u> *nor* the <u>producer</u> <u>wants</u> to give up control.

Subject *or*   Plural subject   Plural form of verb

The <u>director</u> *or* his <u>assistants</u> <u>decide</u> how the film will be made.

Subject *nor*   Plural subject   Plural form of verb

Neither the <u>director</u> *nor* his <u>assistants</u> <u>want</u> to give up control.

The Subject Is an Indefinite Pronoun

Indefinite pronouns, which refer to unspecified people or objects, are often singular, although there are exceptions.

When you find an indefinite pronoun in your writing, use the following to help you determine the correct verb form, singular or plural. If the pronoun may be singular or plural, you will need to check whether the word it refers to is singular or plural to determine what verb form to use.

Indefinite Pronouns

ALWAYS SINGULAR (USE THE *IS* FORM OF *BE*)

anybody	everyone	nothing
anyone	everything	one (of)
anything	much	somebody
each (of)	neither (of)	someone
either (of)	nobody	something
everybody	no one	

ALWAYS PLURAL (USE THE *ARE* FORM OF *BE*)

both	many

MAY BE SINGULAR OR PLURAL (USE THE *IS* OR *ARE* FORM)

all	none
any	some

Everyone <u>loves</u> vacations.

[*Everyone* is always singular, so it takes the singular verb *loves*.]

<u>Some</u> of the wreckage <u>was recovered</u> after the crash.

[In this case, *some* is singular, referring to *wreckage*, so it takes the singular verb *was recovered*.]

<u>Some</u> of the workers <u>were delayed</u> by the storm.

[In this case, *some* is plural, referring to *workers*, so it takes the plural verb *were delayed*.]

The Verb Comes before the Subject

In most sentences, the subject comes before the verb. Two kinds of sentences reverse that order—questions and sentences that begin with *here* or *there*.

To find the subject and verb in these types of sentences, you can turn them around: answer the question or move *here/there* to the end.

<u>Are</u> the <u>keys</u> in the car? The <u>keys</u> <u>are</u> in the car.

Here <u>are</u> the <u>hot dog rolls</u>. The <u>hot dog rolls</u> <u>are</u> here.

Problems with Verb Tense

Verb tense tells *when* the action of a sentence occurs—in the present, in the past, or in the future. Verbs change their form and use the helping verbs *have* or *be* to indicate different tenses.

PRESENT TENSE	<u>Teresa</u> and <u>I</u> <u>talk</u> every day.
PAST TENSE	Yesterday, <u>we</u> <u>talked</u> for two hours.
FUTURE TENSE	Tomorrow, <u>we</u> <u>will talk</u> again.
PRESENT TENSE	<u>Krystal</u> <u>plays</u> varsity basketball.
PAST TENSE	<u>Alicia</u> <u>washed</u> dirty dishes all night.

Regular Verbs

To avoid mistakes with regular verbs, understand the basic patterns for forming the present, past, and future tenses.

Present Tense Endings

The **simple present tense** is used to describe facts, habits, and actions that are on-going. There are two forms for the simple present tense of regular verbs—**-*s* ending** or **no added ending**. Use the *-s* ending when the subject is *she, he,* or *it,* or the name of one person or thing. Do not add any ending for other subjects.

Regular Verbs in the Simple Present Tense

	SINGULAR	PLURAL
First person	I <u>laugh</u>.	We <u>laugh</u>.
Second person	You <u>laugh</u>.	You <u>laugh</u>.
Third person	She/he/it <u>laughs</u>.	They <u>laugh</u>.
	The <u>baby</u> <u>laughs</u>.	The <u>babies</u> <u>laugh</u>.

Past Tense Endings

The **simple past tense** is used for actions that began and ended in the past. An **-ed** or **-d ending** is needed for all regular verbs in the past tense.

	SIMPLE PRESENT	SIMPLE PAST
First person	I rush to work.	I rushed to work.
Second person	You lock the door.	You locked the door.
Third person	Rufus lives nearby.	Rufus lived nearby.

The past-tense form of regular verbs can also serve as the past participle, which can be paired with a helping verb such as *have*. (To learn about when past participles are used, see p. 250.)

PAST TENSE	My car stalled.
PAST PARTICIPLE	My car has stalled often.

Irregular Verbs

Unlike regular verbs, which have past-tense forms that end in *-ed* or *-d*, **irregular verbs** change spelling or sometimes do not change at all from the present-tense form. The most common irregular verbs are *be, have,* and *do* (see chart below).

As you write and edit, consult the following chart to make sure that you use the correct form of irregular verbs.

NOTE: What is called "Present Tense" in the chart below is sometimes called the base form of the verb.

Irregular Verb Forms

PRESENT TENSE	PAST TENSE	PAST PARTICIPLE (used with helping verb)
be (am/are/is)	**was/were**	**been**
become	became	become
begin	began	begun
bite	bit	bitten
blow	blew	blown
break	broke	broken
bring	brought	brought
build	built	built
buy	bought	bought

(Continued)

PRESENT TENSE	PAST TENSE	PAST PARTICIPLE (used with helping verb)
catch	caught	caught
choose	chose	chosen
come	came	come
cost	cost	cost
dive	dived, dove	dived
do	**did**	**done**
draw	drew	drawn
drink	drank	drunk
drive	drove	driven
eat	ate	eaten
fall	fell	fallen
feed	fed	fed
feel	felt	felt
fight	fought	fought
find	found	found
fly	flew	flown
forget	forgot	forgotten
freeze	froze	frozen
get	got	gotten
give	gave	given
go	went	gone
grow	grew	grown
have/has	**had**	**had**
hear	heard	heard
hide	hid	hidden
hit	hit	hit
hold	held	held
hurt	hurt	hurt

(Continued)

PRESENT TENSE	PAST TENSE	PAST PARTICIPLE (used with helping verb)
keep	kept	kept
know	knew	known
lay	laid	laid
leave	left	left
let	let	let
lie	lay	lain
light	lit	lit
lose	lost	lost
make	made	made
mean	meant	meant
meet	met	met
pay	paid	paid
put	put	put
quit	quit	quit
read	read	read
ride	rode	ridden
ring	rang	rung
rise	rose	risen
run	ran	run
say	said	said
see	saw	seen
sell	sold	sold
send	sent	sent
set (to place)	set	set

(Continued)

PRESENT TENSE	PAST TENSE	PAST PARTICIPLE (used with helping verb)
shake	shook	shaken
show	showed	shown
shrink	shrank	shrunk
shut	shut	shut
sing	sang	sung
sink	sank	sunk
sit (to be seated)	sat	sat
sleep	slept	slept
speak	spoke	spoken
spend	spent	spent
stand	stood	stood
steal	stole	stolen
stick	stuck	stuck
sting	stung	stung
strike	struck	struck, stricken
swim	swam	swum
take	took	taken
teach	taught	taught
tear	tore	torn
tell	told	told
think	thought	thought
throw	threw	thrown
understand	understood	understood
wake	woke	woken
wear	wore	worn
win	won	won
write	wrote	written

Past Participles

A **past participle,** by itself, cannot be the main verb of a sentence. When a past participle is combined with a **helping verb,** however, it can be used to make the present perfect tense and the past perfect tense.

The **present perfect** tense is used for an action that began in the past and either continues into the present or was completed at some unknown time in the past.

> My <u>car</u> <u>has stalled</u> several times recently.

The **past perfect tense** is used for an action that began and ended in the past before some other past action took place. It is formed as follows.

> My <u>head</u> <u>had ached</u> for a week before <u>I</u> <u>called</u> a doctor.
> [Both of the actions (*head ached* and *I called*) happened in the past, but the ache happened before the calling.]

Be careful not to confuse the simple past tense with the past perfect tense.

SIMPLE PAST TENSE	My <u>daughter</u> <u>left</u>.
	[One action (the daughter leaving) occurred in the past.]
PAST PERFECT TENSE	By the time Jill arrived, my <u>daughter</u> <u>had left</u>.
	[Two actions (Jill's arrival and the daughter leaving) occurred in the past, but the daughter left before Jill's arrival.]

Passive Voice

A sentence that is written in the **passive voice** has a subject that performs no action. Instead, the subject is acted upon. To create the passive voice, combine a form of the verb *be* with a past participle.

PASSIVE	The <u>memo</u> <u>was written</u> by an employee.
	[The subject, *memo*, did not write itself. An employee wrote the memo, but the subject in the sentence, *memo*, performs no action.]

In sentences that use the **active voice**, the subject performs the action.

ACTIVE	An <u>employee</u> <u>wrote</u> the memo.

Use the passive voice when no one person performed the action, when you don't know who performed the action, or when you want to emphasize the receiver of the action. Use the active voice whenever possible, and use passive voice sparingly.

PASSIVE	The <u>dog</u> <u>was hit</u> by a passing car. [If the writer wants to focus on the dog as the receiver of the action, the passive voice is acceptable.]
ACTIVE	A passing <u>car</u> <u>hit</u> the dog.

17

Other Grammar
and Style Concerns

In addition to checking your writing for the four most serious errors covered in Chapter 16, you will want to be aware of common trouble spots in other areas of grammar and style: pronouns, adjectives and adverbs, modifiers, coordination and subordination, parallelism, sentence variety, and word choice. Matters of punctuation and capitalization are covered in Chapter 18.

Pronouns

Pronouns replace nouns (or other pronouns) in a sentence so that you do not have to repeat the nouns.

> *her*
> Tessa let me borrow ~~Tessa's~~ jacket.
>   ^

> *He*
> You have met Carl. ~~Carl~~ is my cousin.
>   ^

The noun (or pronoun) that a pronoun replaces is called the **antecedent**. The word *antecedent* means "something that comes before." In most cases, a pronoun refers to a specific antecedent nearby. In the second example above, "Carl" is the antecedent and "He" is the pronoun that replaces "Carl."

There are three basic types of pronouns—**subject** pronouns, **object** pronouns, and **possessive** pronouns. Note the pronouns in the following sentences.

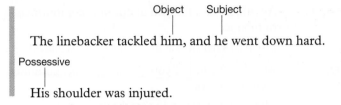

Object   Subject

The linebacker tackled him, and he went down hard.

Possessive

His shoulder was injured.

Pronoun Types

	SUBJECT	OBJECT	POSSESSIVE
First person (singular/plural)	I/we	me/us	my, mine/our, ours
Second person (singular/plural)	you/you	you/you	your, yours/your, yours
Third person (singular)	he, she, it who	him, her, it whom	his, her, hers, its whose
Third person (plural)	they	them	their, theirs

Check for Pronoun Agreement

A pronoun must agree with (match) the noun or pronoun it refers to in number: it must be singular (one) or plural (more than one). If it is singular, it must also match its noun or pronoun in gender (*he*, *she*, or *it*).

CONSISTENT   Sherry talked to *her* aunt.

[*Her* agrees with *Sherry* because both are singular and feminine.]

CONSISTENT   The Romanos sold *their* restaurant.

[*Their* agrees with *Romanos* because both are plural.]

Watch out for singular nouns that are not specific. If a noun is singular, the pronoun must be singular as well.

> **INCONSISTENT**   An athlete can tell you about *their* commitment to practice.
>
> [*Athlete* is singular, but the pronoun *their* is plural.]
>
> **CONSISTENT**   An athlete can tell you about *his* or *her* commitment to practice.
>
> [*Athlete* is singular, and so are the pronouns *his* and *her*.]

As an alternative to using the phrase *his or her*, make the subject plural if you can.

> **CONSISTENT**   All athletes can tell you about *their* commitment to practice.

Two types of words often cause errors in pronoun agreement—indefinite pronouns and collective nouns.

Indefinite Pronouns

TIP Focus on the "significant seven" indefinite pronouns: *any, each, either, neither,* and words ending in *-one, -thing,* or *-body.*

An **indefinite pronoun** does not refer to a specific person, place, or thing; it is general. Indefinite pronouns often take singular verbs. Whenever a pronoun refers to an indefinite person, place, or thing, check for agreement.

> his
> Someone forgot ~~their~~ coat.
> ^
>
> his or her
> Everybody practiced ~~their~~ lines.
> ^

NOTE: Although it is grammatically correct, using a masculine pronoun (*he, his,* or *him*) alone to refer to a singular indefinite pronoun such as *everyone* is now considered sexist. Here are two ways to avoid this problem:

1. Use *his or her.*

   Someone forgot his or her coat.

2. Change the sentence so that the pronoun refers to a plural noun or pronoun.

   The children forgot their coats.

Indefinite Pronouns

ALWAYS SINGULAR (USE THE *IS* FORM OF *BE*)

anybody	everyone	nothing
anyone	everything	one (of)
anything	much	somebody
each (of)	neither (of)	someone
either (of)	nobody	something
everybody	no one	

ALWAYS PLURAL (USE THE *ARE* FORM OF *BE*)

both	many

MAY BE SINGULAR OR PLURAL (USE THE *IS* OR *ARE* FORM OF *BE*)

all	none
any	some

Collective Nouns

A **collective noun** names a group that acts as a single unit. Some common collective nouns are *audience, class, company, crowd, family, government, group*, and *society*. Collective nouns are usually singular, so when you use a pronoun to refer to a collective noun, it too must usually be singular.

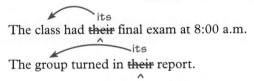

The class had ~~their~~ final exam at 8:00 a.m.
          its

The group turned in ~~their~~ report.
          its

If the people in a group are acting as individuals, however, the noun is plural and should be used with a plural pronoun.

The audience took *their* seats.

The drenched crowd huddled under *their* umbrellas.

Make Pronoun Reference Clear

If the reader isn't sure what a pronoun refers to, the sentence may be confusing.

Avoid Ambiguous or Vague Pronoun References

In an **ambiguous pronoun reference**, the pronoun could refer to more than one noun.

> AMBIGUOUS   Michelle told Carla that she needed new shoes.
>
> [Did Michelle tell Carla that Michelle herself needed new shoes? Or did Michelle tell Carla that Carla needed new shoes?]
>
> EDITED   Michelle needed new shoes. She told her friend Carla.

In a **vague pronoun reference**, the pronoun does not refer clearly to any particular person or thing. To correct a vague pronoun reference, substitute a more specific noun for the pronoun.

> VAGUE   After an accident at the intersection, they installed a traffic light.
>
> [Who installed the traffic light?]
>
> EDITED   After an accident at the intersection, the highway department installed a traffic light.

Avoid Repetitious Pronoun References

In a **repetitious pronoun reference**, the pronoun repeats a reference to a noun rather than replacing the noun. Remove the repetitious pronoun.

> The police officer ~~he~~ told me I had not stopped at the sign.
>
> The sign~~, it~~ was hidden by a tree.

Three Types of Pronouns

As you can see on the chart on page 255, there are several types of pronouns—*subject* pronouns, *object* pronouns, and *possessive* pronouns, each of which has a different function.

Subject Pronouns

Subject pronouns serve as the subject of a verb.

For more on subjects, see Chapter 15.

She took my parking space.

I honked my horn.

Object Pronouns

Object pronouns either receive the action of a verb (the object of the verb) or are part of a prepositional phrase (the object of the preposition).

OBJECT OF THE VERB	Carolyn asked *me* to drive. Carolyn gave *me* the keys.
OBJECT OF THE PREPOSITION	Carolyn gave the keys to *me*.

Possessive Pronouns

Possessive pronouns show ownership. Note that you never need an apostrophe with a possessive pronoun.

Giselle is *my* best friend.

That jacket is *hers*.

Use the Right Pronoun

Certain kinds of sentences can make choosing the right type of pronoun a little more difficult—those that have compound subjects or objects, those that make a comparison, and those where you have to choose between *who* or *whom*.

Pronouns Used with Compound Subjects and Objects

A **compound subject** has more than one subject joined by a conjunction such as *and* or *or*. A **compound object** has more than one object joined by a conjunction.

COMPOUND SUBJECT	Tim and *I* work together.
COMPOUND OBJECT	Kayla baked the cookies for Jim and *me*.

To decide what type of pronoun to use in a compound construction, try leaving out the other part of the compound and the conjunction. Then, say the sentence aloud to yourself.

> ~~Jerome and~~ (me /⟨I⟩) like chili dogs.
>
> [Think: *I* like chili dogs.]
>
> The package was for ~~Karen and~~ (she /⟨her⟩).
>
> [Think: The package was for *her.*]

When you are writing about yourself and others, always put the others first, choosing the correct type of pronoun.

> **INCORRECT**   Gene bought the tickets for *me* and my friends.
>
> **CORRECT**   Gene bought the tickets for my friends and *me.*
>
> [Sentence puts others first and uses the object pronoun, *me.*]

If a pronoun is part of a compound object in a prepositional phrase, use an object pronoun.

> Please keep that information just between you and *me.*
>
> [*Between you and me* is a prepositional phrase, so it uses the object pronoun, *me.*]

Many people make the mistake of writing *between you and I.* The correct pronoun is the object pronoun, *me.*

Pronouns Used in Comparisons

Using the wrong type of pronoun in comparisons can give a sentence an unintended meaning. Editing sentences that contain comparisons can be tricky because comparisons often imply words that are not actually included in the sentence.

To find comparisons, look for the words *than* or *as.* To decide whether to use a subject or object pronoun in a comparison, try adding the implied words and saying the sentence aloud.

> Bill likes Chinese food more than *me.*
>
> [This sentence means Bill likes Chinese food more than he likes me. The implied words after *than* are *he likes.*]
>
> Bill likes Chinese food more than *I.*
>
> [This sentence means Bill likes Chinese food more than I like it. The implied word after *I* is *do.*]

The professor knows more than (us /we).

[Think: The professor knows more than *we know*.]

Jen likes other professors more than (he /him).

[Think: Jen likes other professors more than *she likes him*.]

Choosing between Who and Whom

Who is always a subject; use it if the pronoun performs an action. *Whom* is always an object; use it if the pronoun does not perform any action.

WHO = SUBJECT Janis is the friend *who* introduced me to Billy.

WHOM = OBJECT Billy is the man *whom* I met last night.

In most cases, for sentences where the pronoun is followed by a verb, use *who*. When the pronoun is followed by a noun or pronoun, use *whom*.

The person (who / whom) spoke was boring.

[The pronoun is followed by the verb *spoke*. Use *who*.]

The person (who / whom) I met was boring.

[The pronoun is followed by another pronoun: *I*. Use *whom*.]

Whoever is a subject pronoun; *whomever* is an object pronoun.

Make Pronouns Consistent

Pronouns have to be consistent in **person**, which is the point of view a writer uses. Pronouns may be in first person (*I, we*); second person (*you*); or third person (*he, she, it,* or *they*). (See the chart on p. 253.)

INCONSISTENT PERSON After *a caller* presses 1, *you* get a recording.

[The sentence starts with the third person (*a caller*) but shifts to the second person (*you*).]

CONSISTENT PERSON After *a caller* presses 1, *he or she* gets a recording.

CONSISTENT PERSON, PLURAL After *callers* press 1, *they* get a recording.

Adjectives and Adverbs

Adjectives describe nouns (words that name people, places, or things) and pronouns (words that replace nouns). They add information about what kind, which one, or how many.

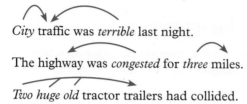

City traffic was *terrible* last night.

The highway was *congested* for *three* miles.

Two huge old tractor trailers had collided.

Adverbs describe verbs (words that tell what happens in a sentence), adjectives, or other adverbs. They add information about how, how much, when, where, why, or to what degree. Adverbs often end with *-ly*.

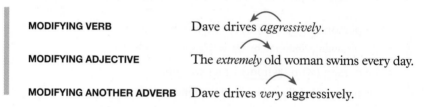

MODIFYING VERB	Dave drives *aggressively*.
MODIFYING ADJECTIVE	The *extremely* old woman swims every day.
MODIFYING ANOTHER ADVERB	Dave drives *very* aggressively.

Adjectives usually come *before* the words they modify; adverbs come either before or after. You can also use more than one adjective or adverb to modify a word.

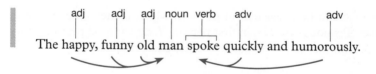

adj   adj   adj   noun   verb   adv   adv

The happy, funny old man spoke quickly and humorously.

Choosing between Adjective and Adverb Forms

Many adverbs are formed by adding *-ly* to the end of an adjective. To decide whether to use an adjective form or an adverb form, find the word you want to describe. If that word is a noun or a pronoun, use the adjective form. If it is a verb, an adjective, or another adverb, use the adverb form.

ADJECTIVE	ADVERB
The *new* student introduced himself.	The couple is *newly* married.
That is an *honest* answer.	Please answer *honestly*.

Adjectives and Adverbs in Comparisons

To compare two persons, places, or things, use the **comparative** form of adjectives or adverbs.

Sheehan drives *faster* than I do.

Francis is *more talkative* than Destina is.

To compare three or more persons, places, or things, use the **super-lative** form of adjectives or adverbs.

Sheehan drives the *fastest* of all our friends.

Francis is the *most talkative* of the children.

Comparative and Superlative Forms

ADJECTIVE OR ADVERB	COMPARATIVE	SUPERLATIVE
ADVERBS AND ADJECTIVES OF ONE SYLLABLE		
tall	taller	tallest
fast	faster	fastest
ADJECTIVES ENDING IN Y		
happy	happier	happiest
silly	sillier	silliest
ADVERBS AND ADJECTIVES OF MORE THAN ONE SYLLABLE		
graceful	more graceful	most graceful
gracefully	more gracefully	most gracefully
intelligent	more intelligent	most intelligent
intelligently	more intelligently	most intelligently

NOTE: Use either an ending (*-er* or *-est*) or an extra word (*more* or *most*) to form a comparative or superlative—not both at once.

One of the ~~most~~ easiest ways to beat stress is to exercise regularly.

It is ~~more~~ harder to study late at night than during the day.

Good, Well, Bad, and Badly

Four common adjectives and adverbs have irregular forms—*good*, *well*, *bad*, and *badly*.

People often are confused about whether to use *good* or *well*. *Good* is an adjective, so use it to describe a noun or pronoun. *Well* is an adverb, so use it to describe a verb or an adjective.

Forms of Good, Well, Bad, and Badly

	COMPARATIVE	SUPERLATIVE
ADJECTIVE		
good	better	best
bad	worse	worst
ADVERB		
well	better	best
badly	worse	worst

ADJECTIVE   She is a *good* friend.

ADVERB   He works *well* with his colleagues.

Well can also be an adjective to describe someone's health:

I am not *well* today.

Misplaced and Dangling Modifiers

Modifiers are words or word groups that describe other words in a sentence. If a modifier is not near the words it modifies, the sentence can be misleading or unintentionally funny.

Misplaced Modifiers

A **misplaced modifier**, because it is not correctly placed in the sentence, describes the wrong word or words. To correct a misplaced modifier, move the modifier as close as possible to the word or words it modifies. The safest choice is often to put the modifier directly before the sentence element it modifies.

MISPLACED   Rudy saw my dog *driving on the highway.*

[Was my dog driving a car? No, Rudy was, so the modifier must come right before or right after his name.]

CORRECT   *Driving on the highway,* Rudy saw my dog.

Four sentence constructions in particular often lead to misplaced modifiers:

1. **Modifiers such as *only, almost, hardly, nearly*, and *just***

   almost
   Molly ~~almost~~ slept for ten hours.

   [Was Molly awake, *almost* sleeping for ten hours? No, she slept for just under ten hours.]

2. **Modifiers that start with *-ing* verbs**

   Using cash,
   Timothy bought the car. ~~using cash.~~

   [Note that when you move the phrase beginning with an *-ing* verb to the beginning of the sentence, you need to follow it with a comma.]

3. **Modifiers that are prepositional phrases**

   With binoculars, we
   ~~We~~ saw the rare bird. ~~with binoculars.~~

4. **Modifiers that are clauses starting with *who, whose, that,* or *which***

   who call people during dinner
   Telemarketers are sure to be annoying. ~~who call people during dinner.~~

Dangling Modifiers

A **dangling modifier** "dangles" because the word or words it is supposed to modify are not in the sentence. Dangling modifiers usually appear at the beginning of a sentence and may seem to modify the noun or pronoun that immediately follows—but they do not.

Correct dangling modifiers either by adding the word being modified right after the opening modifier or by adding the word being modified to the opening modifier. Note that to correct a dangling modifier, you might have to reword the sentence.

DANGLING	*Talking on the telephone*, the dinner burned.
	[Was the dinner talking on the telephone? No.]
CORRECT	*While Sharon was talking on the telephone*, the dinner burned.
	The dinner burned *while Sharon was talking on the telephone*.
DANGLING	*While waiting in line*, the alarms went off.
	[Were the alarms waiting in line? No.]
CORRECT	*While waiting in line*, I heard the alarms go off.
	While I was waiting in line, the alarms went off.

Coordination and Subordination

When you join two sentences, you can use either coordination or subordination.

Joining two sentences with related ideas can make your writing less choppy.

Coordination

In **coordination**, two complete sentences (independent clauses) are joined with a comma and a coordinating conjunction, a semicolon alone, or a semicolon and a conjunctive adverb.

TWO SENTENCES	This internship is prestigious. Many interns have gone on to get good jobs.

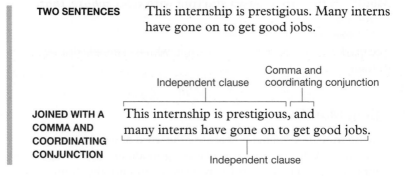

JOINED WITH A COMMA AND COORDINATING CONJUNCTION	This internship is prestigious, and many interns have gone on to get good jobs.

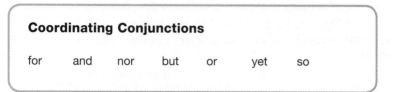

Coordinating Conjunctions

for   and   nor   but   or   yet   so

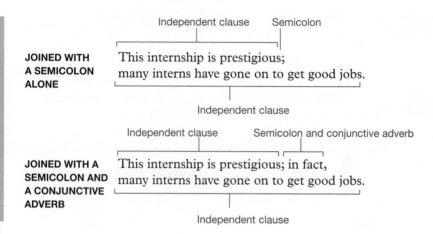

JOINED WITH A SEMICOLON ALONE

Independent clause   Semicolon

This internship is prestigious;
many interns have gone on to get good jobs.

Independent clause

JOINED WITH A SEMICOLON AND A CONJUNCTIVE ADVERB

Independent clause   Semicolon and conjunctive adverb

This internship is prestigious; in fact,
many interns have gone on to get good jobs.

Independent clause

Common Conjunctive Adverbs

afterward	frequently	instead
also	however	still
as a result	in addition	then
besides	in fact	therefore
consequently		

Subordination

In **subordination,** you put a dependent word **(subordinating conjunction)** in front of one of the two sentences, which then becomes a dependent clause and is no longer a complete sentence.

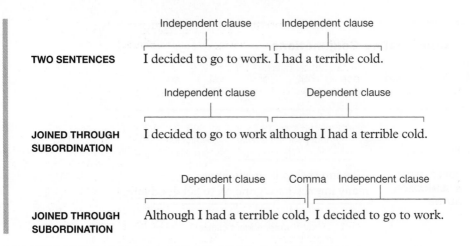

TWO SENTENCES	Independent clause · Independent clause I decided to go to work. I had a terrible cold.
JOINED THROUGH SUBORDINATION	Independent clause · Dependent clause I decided to go to work although I had a terrible cold.
JOINED THROUGH SUBORDINATION	Dependent clause · Comma · Independent clause Although I had a terrible cold, I decided to go to work.

Common Dependent Words (subordinating conjunctions)

after	if	unless
although	if only	until
as	now that	when
as if	once	whenever
because	since	where
before	so that	while
even though		

Parallelism

Parallelism in writing means that similar parts in a sentence are balanced by having the same grammatical structure. When making comparisons or listing items in a series, put nouns with nouns, verbs with verbs, and phrases with phrases.

NOT PARALLEL	I like <u>math</u> more than <u>studying English</u>.
	[*Math* is a noun, but *studying English* is a phrase.]
PARALLEL	I like <u>math</u> more than <u>English</u>.
NOT PARALLEL	In class, we <u>read</u>, <u>worked</u> in groups, and <u>were writing</u> an essay.
	[Verbs must be in the same tense to be parallel.]
PARALLEL	In class, we <u>read</u>, <u>worked</u> in groups, and <u>wrote</u> an essay.
NOT PARALLEL	Last night we went <u>to a movie</u> and <u>dancing at a club</u>.
	[*To a movie* and *dancing at a club* are both phrases, but they have different forms. *To a movie* should be paired with another prepositional phrase: *to a dance club*.]
PARALLEL	Last night we went <u>to a movie</u> and <u>to a dance club</u>.

When a sentence uses certain paired words called **correlative conjunctions**, the items joined by these paired words must be parallel. Correlative conjunctions, shown below, link two equal elements and show the relationship between them.

both . . . and	neither . . . nor	rather . . . than
either . . . or	not only . . . but also	

NOT PARALLEL	Brianna dislikes *both* <u>fruit</u> *and* <u>eating vegetables</u>.
PARALLEL	Brianna dislikes *both* <u>fruit</u> *and* <u>vegetables</u>.
NOT PARALLEL	She would *rather* <u>eat</u> popcorn every night *than* <u>to cook</u>.
PARALLEL	She would *rather* <u>eat</u> popcorn every night *than* <u>cook</u>.

Sentence Variety

Having **sentence variety** in your writing means using assorted sentence patterns, lengths, and rhythms. Here are some strategies for achieving more sentence variety in your writing.

Start Some Sentences with Adverbs

Adverbs are words that describe verbs, adjectives, or other adverbs; they often end with *-ly*. As long as the meaning is clear, you can place an adverb at the beginning of a sentence or near the word it describes. An adverb at the beginning is usually followed by a comma.

ADVERB AT BEGINNING	*Frequently*, stories about haunted houses surface at Halloween.
ADVERB NEAR A VERB	Stories about haunted houses *frequently* surface at Halloween.

Join Ideas Using an *-ing* Verb Form

One way to combine sentences is to turn one of them into a phrase using an ***-ing* verb form** (such as *walking* or *racing*). The *-ing* verb form indicates that the two parts of the sentence are happening at the same time. The more important idea (the one you want to emphasize) should be in the main clause, not in the phrase you make by adding the *-ing* verb form. In the examples that follow, the idea the writer wanted to emphasize is underlined.

TWO SENTENCES	Jonah did well in the high jump. He came in second.
JOINED WITH *-ING* **VERB FORM**	Jonah did well in the high jump, coming in second.
	Doing well in the high jump, Jonah came in second.

Join Ideas Using an *-ed* Verb Form

Another way to combine sentences is to turn one of them into a phrase using an ***-ed* verb form** (such as *waited* or *walked*). You can join sentences this way if one of them has a form of *be* as a helping verb along with the *-ed* verb form.

TWO SENTENCES	Leonardo da Vinci was a man of many talents. He was noted most often for his painting.
JOINED WITH –*ED* VERB FORM	Noted most often for his painting, Leonardo da Vinci was a man of many talents.

Join Ideas Using an Appositive

An **appositive** is a phrase that renames a noun. Appositives, which are nouns or noun phrases, can be used to combine two sentences into one.

TWO SENTENCES	Elvis Presley continues to be popular many years after his death. He is "the King."
JOINED WITH AN APPOSITIVE	Elvis Presley, "the King," continues to be popular many years after his death.
	[The phrase *"the King"* renames the noun *Elvis Presley*.]

Join Ideas Using an Adjective Clause

An **adjective clause** is a group of words with a subject and a verb that describes a noun. Adjective clauses often begin with the word *who, which,* or *that* and can be used to combine two sentences into one.

TWO SENTENCES	Lorene owns an art and framing store. She is a good friend of mine.
JOINED WITH AN ADJECTIVE CLAUSE	Lorene, who is a good friend of mine, owns an art and framing store.

NOTE: If an adjective clause can be taken out of a sentence without completely changing the meaning of the sentence, put commas around the clause.

Lorene, who is a good friend of mine, owns an art and framing store.

[The phrase *who is a good friend of mine* adds information about Lorene, but it is not essential; the sentence *Lorene owns an art and framing store* means almost the same thing as the sentence in the example.]

Word Choice

Four common problems with word choice can make it difficult for readers to understand your point. You can avoid them by using specific words that fit your meaning and make your writing clearer.

Vague and Abstract Words

Your words need to create a clear picture for your readers. **Vague and abstract words** are too general to make an impression. Here are some common vague and abstract words.

Vague and Abstract Words			
a lot	car	job	school
awesome	dumb	nice	small
awful	good	OK (okay)	stuff
bad	great	old	thing
beautiful	happy	person	very
big	house	pretty	whatever
business	huge	sad	young

When you see one of these words or another general word in your writing, try to replace it with a concrete or more specific word. A **concrete word** names something that can be seen, heard, felt, tasted, or smelled. A **specific word** names a particular individual or quality. Compare these two sentences:

VAGUE AND ABSTRACT	It was a beautiful day.
CONCRETE AND SPECIFIC	The sky was a bright, cloudless blue; the air shimmered in the sun; and the temperature was a perfect 78 degrees.

The first version is too general to be interesting. The second version creates a clear, strong image.

Some words are so vague that it is best to avoid them altogether.

| VAGUE AND ABSTRACT | It's like *whatever.* |
| | [This sentence is neither concrete nor specific.] |

Slang

Slang, the informal and casual language shared by a particular group, should be used only in informal and casual situations. Avoid it when you write, especially for college classes or at work. Use language that is appropriate for your audience and purpose.

SLANG	EDITED
I'm going to *chill* at home.	I'm going to relax at home.
I *dumped* Destina.	I ended my relationship with Destina.

Wordy Language

Using too many words in a piece of writing can obscure or weaken the point. Wordy language includes phrases that contain too many words, unnecessarily modify a statement, or use slightly different words without adding any new ideas. It also includes overblown language—unnecessarily complicated words and phrases that are often used to make the writer or writing sound important.

WORDY	We have no openings *at this point in time.*
EDITED	We have no openings now.
	[The phrase *at this point in time* uses five words to express what could be said in one word—*now.*]
WORDY	*In the opinion of this writer,* tuition is too high.
EDITED	Tuition is too high.
	[The qualifying phrase *in the opinion of this writer* is not necessary and weakens the statement.]

Common Wordy Expressions

WORDY	EDITED
A great number of	many
A large number of	many
As a result of	because
At that time	then
At the conclusion of	at the end
At this point in time	now
Due to the fact that	because
In order to	to
In spite of the fact that	although
In the event that	if
In this day and age	now
In this paper I will show that	(Just make the point; don't announce it.)
It is my opinion that	I think (or just make the point)
The fact of the matter is that	(Just state the point.)

Clichés

Clichés are phrases used so often that people no longer pay attention to them. To get your point across and to get your readers' attention, replace clichés with fresh language that precisely expresses your meaning.

CLICHÉS	EDITED
Passing the state police exam is no *walk in the park*.	Passing the state police exam requires careful preparation.
I was *sweating bullets* until the grades were posted.	I was anxious until the grades were posted.

COMMON CLICHÉS	
as big as a house	last but not least
as hard as a rock	more trouble than it's worth
as light as a feather	no way on earth
best/worst of times	110 percent
better late than never	playing with fire
break the ice	spoiled brat
climb the corporate ladder	spoiled rotten
crystal clear	starting from scratch
drop in the bucket	sweating blood/bullets
easier said than done	24/7
hell on earth	work like a dog

There are hundreds of clichés. To check if you have used a cliché, go to **clichesite.com**.

18

Punctuation and Capitalization

Commas [,]

Commas (,) are punctuation marks that help readers understand a sentence by introducing a pause at key points. Be sure you understand how to use commas in the following situations.

Commas between Items in a Series

Use commas to separate three or more items in a series. This includes the last item in the series, which usually has *and* before it.

> Last semester I took *math, reading,* and *composition.*

> Students may take the course as a *regular classroom course,* as an *online course,* or as a *distance learning course.*

Commas between Coordinate Adjectives

Coordinate adjectives are two or more adjectives that independently modify the same noun and are separated by commas. Coordinate adjectives can be separated by the word *and.*

> It was a *long, hard, complicated* test.

Do *not* use a comma between the final adjective and the noun it modifies.

> It was a *long, hard, complicated* test.

> **Cumulative adjectives** modify the same noun but form a unit and are not separated by commas. Cumulative adjectives cannot be joined by the word *and.*

▌ Our team wants to win the *big regional sales* trophy.

All of the words in italics are adjectives, but they build on each other. Moving left from *trophy*, each adjective becomes part of a larger unit.

Commas in Compound Sentences

A **compound sentence** contains two independent clauses (sentences) joined by one of these words—*for, and, nor, but, or, yet, so*. Use a comma before the joining word to separate the two clauses.

▌ Tom missed class yesterday, *and* he texted me to ask what he missed.

▌ I would have been happy to help him, *but* I was absent too.

▌ I told him I wasn't there, *so* he said he would email the professor.

A comma by itself cannot separate two sentences: doing so creates a run-on (see pages pp. 237).

A comma is not needed if the word *and, but, for, nor, or, so,* or *yet* joins two sentence elements that are not independent clauses.

Commas after Introductory Word Groups

Use a comma after an introductory word or word group. An introductory word group can be a word, a phrase, or a clause. The comma lets your readers know when the main part of the sentence is starting.

▌ **INTRODUCTORY WORD**   *Finally,* I finished the job.

INTRODUCTORY PHRASE   *According to the paper,* the crime rate went down.

INTRODUCTORY CLAUSE   *As you know,* the store is going out of business.

Commas around Appositives and Interrupters

An **appositive**, a phrase that renames a noun, comes directly before or after the noun.

For more on appositives, see page 269.

▌ Dick, *my neighbor,* has a new job.

▌ Apartment prices are high at Riverview, *the new complex.*

An **interrupter** is an aside or transition that interrupts the flow of a sentence and does not affect its meaning.

▌ Campus parking fees, *you should know,* are going up by 30 percent.

▌ A six-month sticker will now be $75, *if you can believe it.*

Commas around Adjective Clauses

An **adjective clause** is a group of words that often begins with *who,* *which,* or *that;* has a subject and verb; and describes the noun that comes before it in a sentence. An adjective clause may or may not be set off from the rest of the sentence by commas depending on its meaning in the sentence.

If an adjective clause can be taken out of a sentence without completely changing the meaning, put commas around the clause.

> SuperShop *, which is the largest supermarket in town ,* was recently bought by Big Boy Markets.
>
> I have an appointment with Dr. Kling *, who is the specialist.*

If an adjective clause is essential to the meaning of a sentence, or if it is needed to identify the specific noun, do not put commas around it. You can tell whether a clause is essential by taking it out and seeing if the meaning of the sentence changes significantly, as it would if you took the clauses out of the following examples:

> The hair salon *that I liked* recently closed.
>
> [Which salon closed? The one that I liked. The adjective clause identifies the specific noun].
>
> Salesclerks *who sell liquor to minors* are breaking the law.
>
> [Which salesclerks are breaking the law? The ones who sell liquor to minors. The adjective clause identifies the specific noun].

Commas with Quotation Marks

Quotation marks are used to show that you are using a direct quotation, repeating exactly what someone said or wrote. Generally, use commas to set off the words inside quotation marks from the rest of the sentence.

> "Excuse me ," said the old woman in back of me. "Did you know ," she asked , "that you just cut in front of me?"
>
> I exclaimed , "Oh, no. I'm so sorry!"

Notice that a comma never comes directly *after* a quotation mark.

Commas in Addresses

Use commas to separate the elements of an address included in a sentence. However, do not use a comma before a zip code.

> My address is 4498 Main Street , Bolton , Massachusetts 01740.

If a sentence continues after the address, put a comma after the address. Also, use a comma after individual elements used to name a geographical location such as a city and state.

> The house was moved from Cripple Creek, Colorado, to the lot on Forest Street.

Commas in Dates

Separate the day from the year with a comma. If you give only the month and year, do not separate them with a comma.

> She wrote the letter on April 1, 2009.

> The next session is in January 2011.

If a sentence continues after a date that includes the day, put a comma after the date.

> He waited until April 15, 2010, to file his 2008 tax return.

Commas with Names

Put commas around the name of someone you are addressing by name.

> Don, I want you to come look at this.

> Unfortunately, Marie, you need to finish the report by next week.

Commas with *Yes* or *No*

Put a comma after the word *yes* or *no* in response to a question.

> No, that isn't what I meant.
>
> [To express a strong emotion, an exclamation mark is sometimes used instead of a comma: *No! That is not what I meant.* A word or phrase that expresses emotion and stands alone (like *No!*) is called an interjection.]

Apostrophes [']

An **apostrophe** is a punctuation mark that either shows ownership (*Susan's*) or indicates that a letter has been intentionally left out to form a contraction (*I'm, that's, they're*).

Apostrophes to Show Ownership

- Add '*s* to a singular noun to show ownership even if the noun already ends in *s*.

  > Darcy's car is being repaired.
  >
  > Joan got all the information she needed from the hotel's Web site.
  >
  > The cactus's spines were dropping like fall leaves due to overwatering.

- If a noun is plural and ends in *s*, just add an apostrophe to show ownership. If it is plural but does not end in *s*, add '*s*.

  > Seven boys' coats were left at the school.
  >
  > The children's toys were all broken.

- The placement of an apostrophe makes a difference in meaning.

  > My neighbor's twelve cats are howling.
  >
  > [One neighbor who has twelve cats]
  >
  > My neighbors' twelve cats are howling.
  >
  > [Two or more neighbors who together have twelve cats]

- Do not use an apostrophe to form the plural of a noun.

  > Use the stair's or the elevator.

- Do not use an apostrophe with a possessive pronoun. These pronouns already show ownership (possession).

  > That basket is our's.

Possessive Pronouns

my	his	its	their
mine	her	our	theirs
your	hers	ours	whose
yours			

The single most common error with apostrophes and pronouns is confusing *its* (a possessive pronoun) with *it's* (a contraction meaning "it is"). Whenever you write *it's*, test to see if it's correct by reading it aloud as *it is*.

Apostrophes in Contractions

A **contraction** is formed by joining two words and leaving out one or more of the letters. When writing a contraction, put an apostrophe where the letter or letters have been left out, not between the two words.

> I'll go when you come back. = *I will* go when you come back.

Be sure to put the apostrophe in the right place.

> Don does/n't work here anymore.

Common Contractions

aren't = are not	it's = it is, it has
can't = cannot	let's = let us
couldn't = could not	she'd = she would, she had
didn't = did not	she'll = she will
doesn't = does not	she's = she is, she has
don't = do not	there's = there is, there has
he'd = he would, he had	they're = they are
he'll = he will	they've = they have
he's = he is, he has	who's = who is, who has
I'd = I would, I had	won't = will not
I'll = I will	wouldn't = would not
I'm = I am	you'll = you will
I've = I have	you're = you are
isn't = is not	you've = you have

Do not use contractions in papers or reports for college or work.

Apostrophes with Letters, Numbers, and Time

- Use *'s* to make letters and numbers plural. The apostrophe prevents confusion or misreading.

  > *Mississippi* has four i*'s.*
  > In women's shoes, size 8*'s* are more common than size 10*'s.*

- Use an apostrophe or *'s* in certain expressions in which time nouns are treated as if they possess something.

  > I get two weeks' vacation next year.
  > Last year*'s* prices were very good.

Quotation Marks [" "]

Quotation marks are punctuation marks with two common uses in college writing: they are used with direct quotations, and they are used to set off titles. They always appear in pairs.

Quotation Marks for Direct Quotations

When you write a direct quotation, you need to use quotation marks around the quoted words. These marks tell readers that the words used are exactly what was said or written.

Quoted words are usually combined with words that identify who is speaking. The identifying words can come after the quoted words, before them, or in the middle. Here are some guidelines for capitalization and punctuation.

- Capitalize the first letter in a complete sentence that's being quoted, even if it comes after some identifying words.

  > Quotation mark   Quotation mark
  >
  > The teacher said, "This assignment is due next Monday."
  >
  > Capital letter for complete sentence

- Do not capitalize the first letter in a quotation if it is not the first word in the complete sentence.

  > Quotation marks
  >
  > "If anyone needs help with it," she said, "see me during office hours."
  >
  > Not the first word in the complete sentence, no capital letter

- If it is a complete sentence and its source is clear, you can let a quotation stand on its own, without any identifying words.

  > Speaker (teacher) known
  >
  > "My office hours are on the first page of your syllabus."

- Attach identifying words to a quotation with a comma; these identifying words cannot be a sentence on their own.

  > Identifying words attached with comma
  >
  > A student asked, "May we email questions?"

- Always put quotation marks *after* commas and periods. Put quotation marks after question marks and exclamation points if they are part of the quoted sentence.

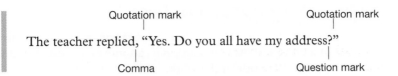

Quotation mark   Quotation mark

The teacher replied, "Yes. Do you all have my address?"

Comma   Question mark

- If a question mark or exclamation point is part of your own sentence, put it after the quotation mark.

Quotation mark   Quotation mark

What famous athlete joked, "I didn't really say everything I said"?

Comma   Question mark

For information about how to use quotations in research papers, see Chapter 14.

When you quote the exact words of an outside source in a paper, use quotation marks. You also need to cite, or give credit to, the source.

> The government needs to ensure that when a company fails, employees' pensions are protected. An article in the *Boston Globe* reported, "When Polaroid collapsed, pension funds and employee stock programs were suddenly worthless. At the same time, however, the chief financial officer walked away with a package worth more than $2 million" (Richardson B3).

For more on citing and documenting sources, see page 208.

Setting Off a Quotation within Another Quotation

Sometimes you may directly quote someone who quotes what someone else said or wrote. Put **single quotation marks** (' ') around the quotation within a quotation so that readers understand who said what.

> Terry told his instructor, "I'm sorry I missed the exam, but I would like to take a makeup exam. According to our student handbook, 'Students must be given the opportunity to make up work missed for excused absences,' and I have a good reason."

Terry's entire quotation

Here, Terry is quoting from the student handbook.

No Quotation Marks for Indirect Speech

When you report what someone said, you are writing indirect speech. Do not use quotation marks for indirect speech. Indirect speech often begin with the word *that*.

INDIRECT SPEECH	Sophie said *that* the exam was postponed.
DIRECT QUOTATION	Sophie said, "The exam was postponed."

Quotation Marks for Certain Titles

When referring to a short work such as a magazine or newspaper article, a chapter in a book, a short story, an essay, a song, or a poem, put quotation marks around the title of the work.

NEWSPAPER ARTICLE	"Mayor Warns of Budget Cuts"
SHORT STORY	"Everyday Use"
ESSAY	"Mother Tongue"

Usually, titles of longer works—such as novels, books, magazines, newspapers, movies, television programs, and CDs—are italicized. The titles of sacred books such as the Bible or the Koran are neither italicized nor surrounded by quotation marks.

BOOK	*The Chocolate War*
NEWSPAPER	*The Washington Post*
	[In MLA style you capitalize *The* when it is the first word in titles of books, movies, newspapers, and other sources.]

If you are writing a paper with many outside sources, your instructor will probably refer you to a particular system of citing sources. Follow that system's guidelines when you use titles in your paper.

NOTE: Do not put quotation marks around the title of a paper you write.

Semicolon [;]

A semicolon (;) is used to join independent clauses and to separate items in series that contain commas.

Semicolons to Join Independent Clauses (Sentences)

Use a semicolon to join very closely related sentences and make them into one sentence.

In an interview, hold your head up and don't slouch; it is important to look alert.

Make good eye contact; looking down is not appropriate in an interview.

Semicolons When Items in a Series Contain Commas

Use a semicolon to separate list items that themselves contain commas. Otherwise, it is difficult for readers to tell where one item ends and another begins.

For more on using semicolons to join sentences, see page 264.

> I have a cousin who lives in Devon, England; another cousin who lives in Derry, New Hampshire; and a third cousin who lives in Freeport, Maine.

Colon [:]

A colon is used to introduce lists, examples, and explanations and is also used in business correspondence.

Colons before Lists

Use a colon to introduce a list after an independent clause.

> In the United States, there are five significant factors causing poverty: a poor economy, lack of affordable housing, drug use, inadequate educational opportunities, and medical expenses.

Colons before Explanations or Examples

Use a colon after an independent clause to let readers know that you are about to provide an explanation or example of what you just wrote.

> The American economy has remained weak since the recession: some businesses have cut jobs or closed down and others have shipped jobs abroad.

> There is one thing I would really like to change: health care.

NOTE: A colon in a sentence must follow an independent clause. A common misuse is to place a colon after a phrase instead of an independent clause. Watch out especially for colons following the phrases *such as* or *for example*.

> **INCORRECT**   The resort offers many activities, such as: snorkeling, golf, and windsurfing.
>
> **CORRECT**   The resort offers many activities: snorkeling, golf, and windsurfing.
>
> **CORRECT**   The resort offers many activities, such as snorkeling, golf, and windsurfing.

Colons in Business Correspondence

Use a colon after a greeting (called a *salutation*) in a business letter and after the standard heading lines at the beginning of a memorandum.

> Dear Mr. Latimer:
>
> To: Craig Kleinman
>
> From: Miriam Moore

Parentheses [( )]

Use parentheses to set off information that is not essential to the meaning of a sentence. Parentheses are always used in pairs and should be used sparingly.

> My grandfather's most successful invention (his first) was the electric blanket.
>
> My worst habit (and also the hardest to break) is interrupting.

Dash [—]

Use dashes as you use parentheses: to set off additional information, particularly information that you want to emphasize.

> The essay question—worth 50 percent of the whole exam—will be open book.

A dash can also indicate a pause, much as a comma does.

> My son wants to buy a car—if he can find an affordable one.

Unlike a hyphen, a dash has a space on either side of it. In Word, people often create a dash using two hyphens, but it is better to hold down the Alt key as you type 0151 on the numeric keypad.

Hyphen [-]

A hyphen (-) is used to join words and divide them at the end of a line.

If you are unsure about whether or how to hyphenate a word or phrase, consult a dictionary or your instructor.

Hyphens to Join Words That Form a Single Description

Use a hyphen to join words that together form a single description of a person, place, or thing.

> The eighty-year-old smoker was considered a high-risk patient.

Hyphens to Divide a Word at the End of a Line

Use a hyphen to divide a word when part of the word must continue on the next line. Most word-processing programs do this automatically, but if you are writing by hand, you need to insert hyphens yourself.

> If you give me the receipt for your purchase, I will imme-
> diately issue a refund.

If you are not sure where to break a word, look it up in a dictionary. The word's main entry will show you where you can break the word: *dic • tion • ar • y.*

Capitalization

There are three basic rules of capitalization: capitalize the first letter of

- every new sentence.
- names of specific people, places, dates, and things.
- important words in titles.

Capitalization of Sentences

Capitalize the first letter in each new sentence, including the first word in a direct quotation.

> Mary was surprised when she saw all the people.
>
> She asked, "What's going on here?"

Capitalization of Names of Specific People, Places, Dates, and Things

Capitalize the first letter in names of specific people, places, dates, and things. Do not capitalize general words such as *college* as opposed to the specific name: *Lincoln College.* Look at the examples for each group.

People

Capitalize the first letter in names of specific people and in titles used with names of specific people.

The word *president* is not capitalized unless it comes directly before a name as part of that person's title: President Donald J. Trump.

SPECIFIC	NOT SPECIFIC
Carol Schopfer	my friend
Dr. D'Ambrosio	the physician
Professor Shute	your professor

The name of a family member is capitalized when the family member is being addressed directly or when the family title is standing in for a first name.

▌ Good to see you, **Dad**.   I see that **Mom** is taking classes.

In other instances, do not capitalize.

▌ It is my father's birthday.   My mom is taking classes.

Places

Capitalize the first letter in names of specific buildings, streets, cities, states, regions, and countries.

SPECIFIC	NOT SPECIFIC
Bolton Police Department	the police department
Washington Street	our street
Boston, Massachusetts	my hometown
Texas	this state
the West	the western part of the country
Italy	that country

Do not capitalize directions in a sentence: *Drive south for five blocks.*

Dates

Capitalize the first letter in the names of days, months, and holidays. Do not capitalize the names of the seasons (winter, spring, summer, fall).

SPECIFIC	NOT SPECIFIC
Monday	today
January 4	winter
Presidents' Day	my birthday

Organizations, Companies, and Groups

SPECIFIC	NOT SPECIFIC
Santa Monica College	my college
Toys"R"Us	the toy store
Merrimack Players	the theater group

Languages, Nationalities, and Religions

SPECIFIC	NOT SPECIFIC
English, Greek, Spanish	my first language
Christianity, Buddhism	your religion

The names of languages should be capitalized even if you are not referring to a specific course: *I am taking nutrition and Spanish.*

Courses

SPECIFIC	NOT SPECIFIC
Nutrition 100	the basic nutrition course

Commercial Products

SPECIFIC	NOT SPECIFIC
Diet Coke	a diet cola

Capitalization of Titles

For more on
punctuating
titles, see page
282. For a list
of common
prepositions,
see page 229.
Capitalize the first word and all other important words in titles of books, movies, television programs, magazines, newspapers, articles, stories, songs, papers, poems, legislation, and so on. Words that do not need to be capitalized (unless they are the first word) include articles (*the, a, an*), coordinating conjunctions (*and, but, for, nor, or, so, yet*), and prepositions.

American Idol is a popular television program.

Newsweek and *Time* often have similar cover stories.

"Once More to the Lake" is one of Chuck's favorite essays.

Acknowledgments *(continued from page vi)*

Josef Ameur, "Video Game Genres." Reprinted by permission.

Shawn Brown, "Letter to a Parole Board." Reprinted by permission of Shawn Brown.

"Chapter 1" from *Stillwater Saints: A Novel* by Alex Espinoza, copyright © 2007 by Alex Espinoza. Used by permission of Random House Trade Paperbacks, an imprint of Random House, a division of Penguin Random House LLC. All rights reserved.

Daniel Flanagan, "The Choice to Do It Over Again." Copyright © 2008 by Daniel Flanagan. From the book *This I Believe: On Fatherhood*, edited by Dan Gediman. Copyright © 2011 by This I Believe, Inc. Reprinted with permission of John Wiley & Sons, Inc.

"On the Front Lines—Ready or Not" from *How Starbucks Saved My Life: A Son of Privilege Learns to Live Like Everyone Else* by Michael Gill Gates, copyright © 2007 by Michael Gill Gates. Used by permission of Gotham Books, an imprint of Penguin Publishing Group, a division of Penguin Random House LLC. All rights reserved.

Juan Gonzalez, "Complete Learning." Reprinted by permission of Juan Gonzalez.

Don and Sandra Hockenbury, "Daily Hassles, That's Not What I Ordered!" from *Discovering Psychology*, 6e, p. 503. Copyright © 2014 by Worth Publishers. Used with permission of Macmillan Learning.

Don and Sandra Hockenbury, "When the Regulation of Eating Behavior Fails: Anorexia and Bulimia," from *Discovering Psychology*, 3e. Copyright © 2003 by Worth Publishers. Used with permission of Macmillan Learning.

Baxter Holmes, "My Date with Fifteen Women," *The Boston Globe*, January 11, 2009. Reprinted by permission of the author.

Gary Knoblock, "Customer Orientation." Reprinted by permission of Gary Knoblock.

Stephanie Lindsley, "Autism and Education: Who Should We Focus On—My Disabled Son or My Gifted Girl?," *Newsweek*, February 28, 2009. Copyright © 2009 by Newsweek. All rights reserved. Used by permission and protected by the Copyright Laws of the United States. The printing, copying, redistribution, or retransmission of the Content without express written permission is prohibited.

Patty Maloney, "Patient Report." Reprinted by permission.

Rebeka Mazzone, "Serving on a Nonprofit Board Need Not Be Onerous." Reprinted by permission of Rebeka Mazzone.

Jennifer Orlando, "Rattlesnake Canyon: A Place of Peace and Beauty." Reprinted by permission.

"Literacy and Health," *Parade*, January, 18, 2004. Reprinted by permission.

Jeanine Pepper, "The Effects of Attachment Deprivation on Infants." Reprinted by permission.

Monique Rizer, "When Students Are Parents," *The Chronicle of Higher Education*, December 16, 2005. Reprinted by permission of Monique Rizer.

Excerpt, adapted, from Deborah Tannen, *You Just Don't Understand: Men and Women in Conversation*. Copyright © 1990 by Deborah Tannen.

Christopher Shea "In Praise of Peer Pressure" Originally published in *The Boston Globe*, April 29, 2007. Reprinted by permission of Christopher Shea.

Index

Real Take-Away Points

Four Basics of Good Writing

1 It reflects the writer's purpose and the needs, knowledge, and expectations of its intended audience.

2 It results from a thoughtful process.

3 It includes a clear, definite point.

4 It provides support that explains or proves the main point.

2PR   The Critical Reading Process

Preview the reading.

Read the piece actively. Identify the main idea (stated or implied), and consider the quality of the support. Then paraphrase the main idea and major supporting details.

Pause to think during the reading. Identify the author's tone, and be alert for logical fallacies.

Review the reading, your marginal notes, and your questions.

Writing Critically

Summarize

- What is important about the text?
- What is the purpose, the big picture?
- Who is the intended audience?
- What are the main points and key support?

Analyze

- What elements have been used to convey the main point?
- Do any elements raise questions? Do any key points seem missing or undeveloped?

Synthesize

- What do other sources say about the topic of the text?
- How does your own (or others') experience affect how you see the topic?
- What new point(s) might you make by bringing together all the different sources and experiences?

Evaluate

- Based on your application of summary, analysis, and synthesis, what do you think about the material you have read?
- Is the work successful? Does it achieve its purpose?
- Does the author show any biases? Are there any hidden assumptions? If so, do they make the piece more or less effective?